OUR POLITICS

OUR POLITICS

REFLECTIONS

on

POLITICAL

LIFE

DOUGLAS KANE

With a Foreword by Mike Lawrence

Southern Illinois University Press
Carbondale

Southern Illinois University Press
www.siupress.com

Copyright © 2019 by Douglas Kane
All rights reserved
Printed in the United States of America

22 21 20 19   4 3 2 1

Library of Congress Cataloging-in-Publication Data
Names: Kane, Douglas, 1940– author.
Title: Our politics : reflections on political life / Douglas Kane ; with a
   foreword by Mike Lawrence.
Description: Carbondale : Southern Illinois University Press, [2019] |
   Includes bibliographical references and index.
Identifiers: LCCN 2018032494 | ISBN 9780809337095 (pbk. : alk. paper) |
   ISBN 9780809337101 (e-book)
Subjects: LCSH: Kane, Douglas, 1940– | Illinois—Politics and
   government—1951– | Politicians—Illinois—Biography. | Legislators—
   Illinois—Biography.
Classification: LCC F546.4.K36 A3 2019 | DDC 328.773092 [B]—dc23 LC
   record available at https://lccn.loc.gov/2018032494

Printed on recycled paper. ♻

The government of the world I live in was not framed . . .
in after-dinner conversations over the wine.

—Henry David Thoreau, *Walden*

The states are as the men are; they grow
out of human characters.

—Plato, *Republic*

CONTENTS

FOREWORD

AS I WAS OUTGROWING MIDDLE AGE AND FACING YET ANOTHER EXTRACTION, my dentist put it all in perspective: "Getting old ain't for sissies." Neither is getting engaged politically. That was true when Teddy Roosevelt exalted "the man who is actually in the arena, whose face is marred by dust and sweat and blood . . . but who does actually strive to do the deeds." However, the arena has become far more polarized and far less civilized since Teddy's time, and his redeeming "triumph of great achievement" has become starkly elusive—especially in Washington and increasingly in state capitals.

Billionaires and multimillionaires bankroll campaigns, including their own, with once unimaginable and often masked dollar deluges. Media consultants, who build their reputations and bank accounts on wins and losses regardless of the public policy consequences, coax candidates to overpromise, shamelessly pander, and savage opponents in TV spots—thereby fueling distrust, cynicism, and apathy. Interest groups, as did the party organizations they have essentially eclipsed, demand obedience from public officials they helped select and elect as they carry their clashing agendas and ideologies into Congress and statehouses with a disdain for the compromise crucial to the founding and functioning of our representative democracy. In the elegant building where the author of *Our Politics* operated as a top aide in the legislative and executive branches before serving eight years as a state representative, many of his frustrated successors and others in the galaxy of Illinois state government lament the suffocating pollution wrought by rigidity and rancor. Alienation among significant numbers of Illinoisans and fellow Americans is pronounced, fed by the disappointment and disillusionment fostered by unreasonable expectations. So, why commit to sustained engagement as citizen, activist, candidate, and appointed or elected official in this environment? Because the alternative means surrendering to the forces that brought us to this precarious point in our politics.

Doug Kane refuses to yield. As a pragmatic idealist, he has written a book that should educate and motivate those willing to suppress their understandable yet unrealistic urge for instant and sweeping change in favor of incremental yet more fundamental reform. He envisions energized, intense, long-term citizen engagement focused at least initially at the local level, rooted in community needs and values, resistant to the dictates of interest groups and party bosses—engagement that requires the stamina, discipline, grit, and resilience of a marathoner, engagement that is passionate but patient, engagement that is principled but practical enough to recognize that compromise often serves as the conduit for progress. Although it lacks the allure of term limits, campaign funding clamps, and other touted elixirs, Kane's remedy resists quackery and contains the medicine for reinvigorating democracy.

He has witnessed and experienced the enactment of heralded reforms that produced unintended consequences. During his first term as a state representative, Kane and his colleagues discovered in 1975 that reforms in the rules of the House designed to minimize chaos and chicanery at the end of a legislative session created mayhem and mischief throughout; indeed, good-government folks spread the rumor that a distraught lawmaker had scrawled "Stop Us Before We Reform Again" on a bathroom mirror. Five years earlier, framers of a new Illinois constitution developed what they believed would be a fail-safe resolution to resolving stalemates and one-party domination over redistricting only to have their remedy become an abettor to gerrymandering. In 1980, a politically ambitious populist rallied vengeful voters by convincing them to reduce the size of the Illinois House as payback for a smelly legislative razzle-dazzle to raise the pay of lawmakers and statewide officials. He falsely advertised that it would save millions of tax dollars. Moreover, his cutback initiative junked a unique, bipartisanship-inducing system for electing House members. So, the glittery reform proved hardly golden—particularly to those who decry enhanced partisanship and leadership muscle in the House and yearn for the collegiality of yesteryear.

At the national level, limits on individual campaign contributions spawned Political Action Committees, and then restraints on PACs begat independent groups lacking donor transparency requirements imposed on individuals, political party organizations, and PACs. "Every campaign finance reform law passed in the last thirty years has been followed in the next election cycles with more political dollars," Kane writes. "Mostly what has changed is that the dollars now flow through murkier and less accountable chambers. Just as the old political boss system came to an end when it was challenged by an alternate source of political power, so the existing power structure will be diminished only when confronted by alternative power. The question is not how do we reform our politics, but how do we create a new source of political power that is more to our liking and will challenge what now exists?"

His "new source" would come from a reinvented resource—grassroots mobilization. As Kane notes, the "All Politics Is Local" credo coined by the late U.S. House Speaker Tip O'Neill rings hollow today in a centralized political environment where mega donors, legislative leaders, interest groups, and other power brokers recruit and support congressional and statehouse candidates and hire campaign operatives who insist the candidates spew poll-tested bromides and trash opponents while they deliver honed electronic messages based on voter profiles gleaned from mining the internet. But Kane believes politics could become local anew through a revolutionary renaissance in which local political parties recruit candidates and fund them; doctors, lawyers, and others would make their own judgments on candidates based on local needs rather than bowing to less relevant agendas of state and national organizations; candidates would lead meaningful, forthright discussions on how to address community challenges; and the media would provide in-depth, balanced information to voters.

Doug Kane has seen and lived the good, the bad, and the ugly of political engagement. As an Illinois lawmaker, he balked at supporting an infrastructure package backed by the governor and Chicago mayor. As he tells it, a local banker called him and opened the conversation by saying, "There are two things I want to talk to you about, your note and your vote." The next day, Kane recalls, a state revenue auditor asked for the financial records of a restaurant in which he was a general partner. These attempts to change Kane's legislative vote by exerting pressure on his personal finances were ugly indeed. But he also watched his wife win a seat in the Wisconsin senate after rejecting a consultant's advice not to broach healthcare issues in any depth.

Kane is no Pollyanna. He's been there, done that. He remains in the arena with all of its "dust and sweat and blood." He knows the revolution he conceptualizes will come in steps, not leaps. It will require fervent, prolonged, unbowed citizen involvement and candidate candor. Those now in power will battle to retain it. "Nothing in politics happens automatically. Rebuilding local political structures capable of taking power back from the center will take time and effort. An agenda has to be agreed to, differences compromised.

Credible candidates have to be recruited. Checks actually have to be written. Campaigns have to be planned and carried out. A majority of voters have to be persuaded," Kane writes.

Not for sissies indeed. But a plausible path for those who believe we can and must do much better.

Mike Lawrence
former director of the Paul Simon Public Policy Institute,
Southern Illinois University Carbondale (2004–8)
Press secretary and senior policy adviser to Governor Jim Edgar

OUR POLITICS

INTRODUCTION
PERSONAL AND PUBLIC
PERCEPTIONS

I AM A POLITICIAN—HAVE BEEN MOST OF MY ADULT LIFE. POLITICS IS NOT usually looked on as a noble profession, so I don't tell people that is what I do when I am introduced. I would rather they get to know me first, discover something else about me that might go on the plus side to offset all the negative assumptions about politicians. I have relied on the belief that even though politics has an unsavory reputation and politicians are not highly regarded, most seem to like and respect the politicians they know personally. This has been true in my own experience. With few exceptions, the more I worked with others in the profession, the more appreciation I had for them and their efforts, even though we might not have always agreed.

Despite its reputation, politics is attractive and tends to be addictive. Once people are persuaded to become active participants, they get hooked. They find politics invigorating and fulfilling. Still, there are some who, after their first try, become disillusioned and drop out because they think that participating in the game entitles them to win, but they are not in the majority. It has not been my experience that familiarity with politics breeds contempt. Rather, familiarity brings some degree of appreciation and respect, even though one knows more about the less savory parts of the game. Contempt for politics seems strongest among those who choose to be spectators and not get involved. So I tell you without apology that I am a politician. I want to bring you into that experience so you can see for yourself what the game looks and feels like to a participant.

I was introduced to politics the year I finished a master's program in journalism and became a staff intern for the Illinois legislature. I was part of a Ford Foundation program to encourage state legislatures to develop their own sources of information and become less dependent on executive agencies and lobbyists in making decisions. That was fifty years ago.

I lived in Springfield, the state capital, for twenty-five years. For eight of those years I represented the city and surrounding area in the Illinois House of Representatives. The city lived and breathed politics. The leading families had made their fortunes doing business with the state. Who you knew was important. Loyalty mattered. Being reliable brought rewards. Politics was influence, and jobs and contracts.

It is fitting that the architecture of that prairie city is dominated by the dome of the State Capitol, legacy of Abraham Lincoln, the city's favorite son. It was Lincoln who, when dividing the spoils as a member of the Long Nine in the statehouse, saw the economic potential of politics and worked to make Springfield the state capital, letting members from other cities have the Illinois Central Railroad and the state's new land grant university.

I experienced politics from a variety of vantage points during my years in Springfield: Democratic precinct captain, candidate, township official, staff to the legislative leaders, state representative, assistant to the governor, deputy state auditor general, campaign manager, and policy consultant. I also went back to the university for a graduate degree in economics, a discipline intertwined with politics in many ways. Shortly before leaving Illinois I ran for the state senate, a race I lost badly.

Twenty-four years ago, Kathleen Vinehout and I bought a farm in rural western Wisconsin and we moved our family north. There she ran a fifty-cow dairy operation for ten years before being elected to the Wisconsin State Senate, defeating the incumbent in a close race. Since then, she has been reelected twice. From the vantage point of political spouse, I experienced politics up close and personal in a second state, one with a very different reputation from Illinois. Since 1950, Illinois handily leads Wisconsin in the number of officeholders sent to jail, but it also produced five leaders of their respective parties in Congress and one U.S. president. Both results, I think, have their origins in the fact that in Illinois, many more political families go back several generations. The young are schooled early in the game, and everyone plays for keeps. The underlying processes in the two states, however, are very similar. Political forces and incentives are not limited by state boundaries or to any particular party. The ideological differences between the Republican and Democratic Parties are great, but both play the political game the same way.

I began writing *Our Politics* as a way to make sense of the political game both for myself and for others. Why is it played the way it is? What are the forces that have shaped and changed it? What are the all too human motivations that animate the players and impact the outcomes? After one of Kathleen's campaigns, a university professor sent her a questionnaire asking about her personal reactions, because, he said, researchers don't know very much about how politics is experienced by the politician.

Lots of eyes watch politicians and record what is seen from the outside. Numerous memoirs are written by politicians that focus mostly on personalities and relationships, what happened to who and when. This book is not the personal story of an individual player in the political arena. It is not a memoir. Rather it seeks to describe, from the point of view of a player on the field, what the arena looks like, how the league is structured and the teams put together, how the rules that influence strategies and determine winners are made, and the impact those structures and forces have on the political experience of being a candidate and an elected public official.

Even those who have closely observed the process from the outside are surprised when they move to the inside. George Thiem, a Pulitzer Prize–winning political reporter for the old *Chicago Daily News*, who won his prize covering Illinois state government and was later elected to the General Assembly as part of a "blue-ribbon ticket," wrote at the end of his first and only term:

> It is only three feet from the press box in the Illinois House of Representatives to one of the big red leather chairs on the House floor. But when you make the transition from newspaper correspondent to member of the General Assembly as I did last January, you enter a new world. I never quite realized how different it would be. Now, after six months, I can say in all candor it isn't as easy as it looks. The pressures, the frustrations, the constant necessity for making decisions, the close contact with hundreds of human problems add up to a bewildering yet challenging experience.

Our Politics attempts to bridge that three-foot gap.

I HAVE THOROUGHLY ENJOYED POLITICS AND BEING A POLITICIAN. THERE IS exhilaration in the struggle of the campaign and the cheers of the crowd. Watching the votes come in on election night and being in the lead is a great high. There is a lifelong and instant camaraderie with those who have shared the political experience. Making decisions for the community and enacting laws gives a sense of meaning, importance, and direction. Being recognized on the street massages the ego, although at times I would have preferred to be anonymous. Politics has been a good life.

The endlessly fascinating part of politics has been the people I met. During the few times in my life I had a regular job, I found that I would get into a rut driving the same streets from home to work every day, running into the same people, having the same conversations. Not so with politics. I became familiar with every neighborhood and street in the city. I went to cocktail parties at mansions on the west side. I was taught to dance to the blues in small basement recreation rooms on the east side. I spent many Sunday afternoons in union halls drinking beer and eating hot dogs while listening to polka bands.

Politics provided an extended course in human nature. Because I was able to do things for people, fix a problem, or offer a job, and because I could change the law and with it people's fortunes, everybody had something they wanted to talk to me about. The publisher of the newspaper, the head of the local mafia, the president of the chamber of commerce, the factory worker, the waitress, the farmer, the chief executive officer of the bank, the kid without a job, the driver with a DUI trying to get his license back—everyone had something to tell me, something to ask. The conversations were not small talk. If you listen, you hear the motivations that move people, their hopes, their fears, the trades they are willing to make, and the price that they put on themselves.

THE PUBLIC SEES POLITICS IN A MUCH HARSHER LIGHT. THE PUBLIC DOESN'T see the personal—they see only a process driven by money and special interests, characterized by disinformation, harsh rhetoric, ideological polarization, and gridlock.

The Greek philosopher Plato, in his *Republic,* described democracy as a "charming form of government, full of variety and disorder." For many the charm has worn off. Disorder has descended to dysfunction.

General skepticism directed at politicians has long been part of human history and is embedded in popular culture. Among the ancients, Aesop noted, "We hang the petty thieves and appoint the great ones to public office." Robin Hood is the medieval precursor of all the heroes we love for coming to the aid of those "despoiled by a great baron or a rich abbot or a powerful esquire." For Dashiell Hammett, Raymond Chandler, Sara Paretsky, and a host of other authors of private detective stories, the corrupt official is a staple character. Even Father Mapple's sermon in *Moby Dick* strayed far enough from its main theme to mention the sin plucked from under the robes of senators and judges. Offhand, throwaway references to politicians by late-night comedians are almost always negative. It is true. Power does corrupt. Webster's second definition of "politician," "A person primarily interested in political offices from selfish or other narrow interests," resonates far more than the first: "A person experienced in the art or science of government."

For those of us past a certain age there is always the temptation to look with nostalgia on our more youthful adventures and assert to any who will listen that "it was better back then." The stories of an earlier paradise from which humans have fallen are reinvented by every generation, and the young listen with skepticism and amusement. It seems to me, however, that not so long ago, our political institutions were not held in such low regard. There was some level of recognition that while politics by its nature was a messy business, someone had to do the dirty work. There were compromises that had to be made and interests that had to be accommodated. As long as things didn't get too far out of hand, people were more or less content to let politicians be politicians. The mayor and the local senator were respected citizens. And even the "bad" guys—the ones who ran political machines and wielded autocratic power—were mostly local heroes.

It has taken time for the public to become alienated, to reach the point where a large majority believes that elected officials are not doing a good job, that legislators mostly do what lobbyists tell them, and that all incumbents should be voted out of office. Opinions about the institutions of government are the lowest ever in the history of polling.

Recent decades have served up good reasons to distrust politicians. In the 1960s, President Lyndon Johnson, who campaigned on a promise not to send American boys to fight an Asian war, landed the first American marines in Vietnam two months after his inauguration. By the end of his term four years later, 540,000 American troops were stationed in that country. In the 1970s, the unauthorized publication of the *Pentagon Papers* showed that successive administrations had systematically lied to both Congress and the public about the conduct and progress of the war. Later, President Richard Nixon's involvement in the burglary of the Democratic Party's offices at the Watergate Hotel forced his resignation. In the 1980s, top White House officials went to jail for directing the illegal sales of arms to the Contras in Nicaragua. In the 1990s, President Bill Clinton dallied with Monica Lewinsky, and the House voted for articles of impeachment. In the 2000s, President George W. Bush took the country into the Iraq War on false assumptions, and Vice

President Dick Cheney's chief of staff Scooter Libby went to jail for outing a CIA operative in an act of political retribution.

The public has also reacted with skepticism to the practice of "messaging"—the new "word" for propaganda—at all levels of politics. Messaging at its best is the art of conveying ideas effectively, but it quickly slides into giving words new meanings with the intent to deceive and persuade falsely. The result of widespread propaganda has always been widespread skepticism rather than widespread belief. Messages that don't match the experiences of the hearers are eventually disregarded. The propagandist may initially manipulate public opinion but in the long run loses credibility. Some of the reasons voters gave to reporters for liking Donald Trump in his run for the presidency were that "he doesn't sound like a politician," "he speaks the truth," "he is not just pandering to people," "no one else is that direct"—all of which says much about the public's view of the way politicians generally talk.

The ascendency of money and the resulting centralization of political power have also contributed to the disillusionment of voters and their feeling of powerlessness. Politics left the neighborhood when the local party precinct worker was displaced by the professionally crafted messages carried by commercial media. Since then the dollars flowing into politics have become astronomical.

With the chance to remake the states and the nation to their liking, individuals with extreme wealth and strong beliefs are increasingly willing to give millions to elect candidates who share those beliefs and will turn those beliefs into law. Their motivation, whatever it is, is intense. They wouldn't be giving millions if it were otherwise.

The centralization of political power has been ongoing, and it continues to increase. Money is the driving force. It can be gathered anywhere, sent anywhere, spent anywhere, and transformed easily into messages that can be crafted anywhere and delivered anywhere to any audience. The local, unable to match the resources from the outside, has been displaced.

Other results have followed. Partisanship and deadlock have increased. Not being affected by what happens in the lives of average residents in a community, large donors follow a no-compromise, winner-take-all strategy. Issues are pushed to the extreme. The rhetoric becomes harsher, more inflammatory, and more personal. With more contributions coming from a smaller number of sources and an accelerating need to raise more dollars, the incentive for candidates to reflect the interests of their donors is large, pushing them to take positions they otherwise might not take, loosening the ties to their own constituents, and keeping them from solving problems in ways that are not approved by the donors.

Candidates from both political parties face the same situation. Both parties are being pushed to become more ideological, to reflect more completely the beliefs of their donors and organized supporters. It is becoming more common for incumbents to be challenged in their own party's primaries because they are not pure enough and haven't voted 100 percent the "right" way. It is a toxic mix we are stirring. Today, across the political spectrum, disillusionment is more widespread, alienation more profound.

ONE YOUNG PERSON LIVING IN A SMALL COMMUNITY AND CONTEMPLATING the possibility of getting actively involved in local politics saw more minuses than pluses. The reasons she gives are personal and concrete, but the themes are familiar, and they reflect what the polls tell us.

"I would guess that I am more interested in politics than the average twentysomething-year-old in my community, and the thought has crossed my mind to run for my township board. However, I have never seriously entertained the thought. Why?

"Time is one reason. I was passionate enough that I made time to work on the 'Vote Yes' campaign to create a countywide recycling program, but I am not passionate enough about public office to dedicate the time it would take to run a campaign. Alex and I are starting a business, and all of my time outside of my day job is dedicated to that, much like many people my age dedicate their nonwork time to their marriage or kids.

"Unlikeliness of success is another. I especially am not interested in dedicating time to a campaign that it is extremely unlikely I would win. A few years ago I observed a well-run campaign by the sitting county prosecutor. He had been appointed when the last one left the office mid-term. So although he had not won the position, he was the incumbent with yard signs everywhere. Although his name seemed to be everywhere and I heard a lot of positive talk about him, he lost (I think because so many people vote straight party Republican, and he was running as a Democrat). I chatted with him later, and he was actually optimistic because he had received more of the vote than people thought he would. He is now the chair of the county's Democratic Party and told me that although he lost, it will take more and more Democrats running (even if they lose) before one wins. I see the logic in this, but I don't want to dedicate the time to lose, even if it is a step forward.

"Lack of knowledge is a third. I know I am smart, and given enough time to research the issues properly I could take an educated position on any issue. I could even talk intelligently about them if I did enough research. However, I question my current knowledge base on such varied and complicated issues, and I question if I have the time required to become educated. I think that a lack of time and knowledge in addition to the larger systemic reasons for voter disengagement have resulted in a disparity of young people involved in politics. I have had discussions with the county chairs of both parties, and both are scratching their heads as to how to get more young people involved.

"I see the merit in talking to your neighbor. This seems to be the cornerstone of how to bring politics back to the local level; however, I've seen so many people get worked up about politics/issues. They never seem to listen to the other person, they just get angrier and angrier, repeating all the talking points they've heard their candidates parrot. Frankly, I see nothing constructive in this and want nothing to do with it. Unfortunately, you can't really tell how someone will react to a political question/issue, so I just avoid talking politics to people altogether. My guess is that I would get one constructive conversation out of every ten, and my temperament just can't handle that amount of destructiveness. I would guess that many people feel the same, so no one wants to talk politics in order to avoid conflict. And when no one talks about it, it retreats in importance, thus leading to more disengagement."

––––––––––

I WAS PLAYING TENNIS RECENTLY; DOUBLES, WITH THREE OTHERS ABOUT my age, none of whom knew my life away from the courts. Between games, my partners began talking about politicians in the pejorative way I had heard often. "Easy," I said. "Be careful what you say. I'm a politician."

One looked at me and asked, "What do you do?"

"I'm on the Buffalo County Board of Supervisors," I replied.

"Hell," he said without a pause, "you're not a politician, you're a public servant."

I accepted what I think was a compliment and didn't ask where the dividing line was.

In part, *Our Politics* is about the connection between "politician" and "public servant" and the forces that pull in one direction or the other. It also describes how those forces shape the experiences of those who offer themselves as candidates, as holders of public office, as volunteers who work for political candidates, parties, or causes, and as voters who make the final decisions.

The slogan for John Dean's presidential campaign in 2004 was, "Take back our government." The question is: how? Without understanding what makes politics what it is, we can't hope to transform it into something more to our liking. We have not lacked political reform movements in our history. It is sobering to consider that all of yesterday's reforms have brought us to today's practices. Perhaps we should have been more careful when slaying yesterday's dragons not to have cleared the way for today's larger and fiercer ones.

This is a book of reflections, of looking back at events and experiences and reflecting on them in the light of understandings and conclusions I came to later. In the process, I have seen connections I hadn't made earlier. I know more now about what I experienced then than I did at the time.

I am a Democrat. As a result, many of the stories I tell to illustrate a point describe that party's practices, but the practices and the forces that promote them are the same for both parties.

There is a progression to the chapters.

"The No and Yes of Politics" explores some of the fundamental contradictions that underlie the idea of democracy and how they surface and have to be dealt with by every politician.

The next several chapters describe the essential nature of politics and how and why the political power structure has changed over recent years. That change made everything about politics different, from the recruitment of candidates, their training, campaign strategy, and where campaign support comes from to what voters experience, the choices we have, the messages we are bombarded with, and the effect on our communities. That change also impacted the legislative process and how our government functions.

The personal experience of being a legislator follows. What are the pressures, and how does one decide how to vote? What is the relationship to party leaders, fellow legislators, the governor, the voters back home, the voters who have organized themselves into an interest group and hired a lobbyist? What are the results?

The concluding chapters examine the possibility of change. How might change happen? What are some of the steps that candidates, political parties, and activists might take to make our politics better and the results more to our liking? What are the barriers?

Throughout I have tried to make the connections between underlying economic, social, technological, and political forces and what happens in the day-to-day practice of politics. The day-to-day can't be understood without knowing the underlying structures; neither can it be changed.

This book is not about *Those Politicians* but about *Our Politics*—the politics that together we have created and together we deal with. It is offered for consideration to those who appreciate the human condition, who ask why the world works the way it does, and who think about ways in which it might work differently.

1. THE NO AND YES OF POLITICS

I CAN REMEMBER AS A NEWLY ELECTED STATE REPRESENTATIVE BEING IN-vited to talk to a second grade class. Thinking I would break the ice and es-tablish some rapport, I asked those seven- and eight-year-olds if any wanted to be politicians when they grew up. Silence. Not a hand stirred. That was a bad start. So I asked who did *not* want to be politicians when they grew up. There was instant enthusiasm, a bubbling response. Every hand shot up. They were certain they did not want to be politicians.

It was the strength of their response, their emotion, the already fixed knowledge in those children that surprised me, even though I had become used to adult expressions of negativity. Almost as an experiment after that, whenever I spoke to an elementary or high school class I opened with the same question. The response was always similar. Over the years, no more than two or three lone children indicated a desire to become a politician, and those few became quite tentative when they looked around and realized not many other hands were raised.

What was always fascinating, however, was how readily those same chil-dren took to politics when I turned the classroom into a legislature. I asked them to debate and then vote on whether the driving age should be reduced to fourteen, whether school attendance should be mandatory, and whether the drinking age should be lowered from twenty-one to eighteen. Their ar-guments, reasoning, and vote-trading were not much different from what went on in the General Assembly. At the end of each hour there were always some who started to think that making decisions about the way the world is run might actually be kind of fun.

The relationship between voters and politicians is conflicted. Like other celebrities, politicians are mobbed and cheered by their supporters. They are lauded, feted, and deferred to. Their statements are given attention. In death they lie in state. Yet if you walk into any coffee shop or bar, you can hear patrons trashing all politicians as double-talking liars and agents of whoever gave them the most money.

I remember during my first race for public office, standing at the door of a supermarket shaking hands and handing out leaflets. Most people were polite even when they didn't take my handout. But one man refused to shake hands, remarking quite angrily, "You are all a bunch of crooks." I let it pass; I never did work out a good response to that charge.

When my older daughter was in high school and we were having dinner one night in a local restaurant, she turned to me and asked, "Why do you lie to everyone?" That got my attention. I asked, "Where did you get that idea from?" It turned out that the social studies text her teacher was using had a title that essentially accused all politicians of lying. A couple of weeks later, my daughter mentioned that there was a teacher's pension bill being considered in the legislature and that this same teacher had asked her to ask me to vote for it. Sensing the possibility of a "teachable moment," I suggested that the teacher might want to come and talk to me personally about improving his pension—but he never did.

Although they do not openly discuss it except among themselves, politicians have the same love/hate feelings about their constituents. Constituents can be great, but they can also be a real pain. There is a story about the venerable Everett Dirksen, onetime Republican leader in the U.S. Senate, walking down Main Street one weekend in his hometown of Pekin, Illinois, when he was challenged by one of his constituents, "You don't remember who I am, do you?" Dirksen, so the story goes, slowly looked the constituent up and down and replied, "I can't think of any reason why I should." Whenever I have told that story to any office holder, it has never failed to get an appreciative laugh, usually followed by another story of how an uppity or abusive constituent was put in his or her proper place, like the one about the senator who would respond to nasty letters with, "Just thought you ought to know, somebody is writing me stupid letters and signing your name to them."

My first memory of being aware of politics goes back to 1952, when I was twelve. There was a scandal that involved a high-ranking White House staffer who received an expensive vicuna coat as a gift. Harry Truman was defeated in the New Hampshire Democratic primary. The radio broadcast of the Republican National Convention vote in which Eisenhower defeated Taft for the presidential nomination was gripping drama. I listened to Nixon's speech in which he artfully used Pat's cloth coat and his dog, Checkers, to defend his honor and his political finances. From the other side of the world there were stories about the French fighting a war to hold onto a colonial possession called Vietnam.

I was born into an evangelical Protestant family. My parents spent fifteen years as missionaries in China, mostly during the Second World War and the years following, when the Communists fought and defeated the Nationalists. I have strayed far from those theological roots. They still tug, but over the years I have come to the conclusion that making any value absolute is dangerous. Values, more often than not, conflict with each other, and choices have to be made. We are always on the knife-edge between yes and no. Finding and keeping one's balance is not easy.

I have come to believe that the most appropriate answers to the questions of how one should practice politics are "maybe," "sometimes," and "it all depends." Should I be an idealist? A realist? Do the ends justify the means? Do I accept a flawed outcome in order to achieve part of a goal? Do I vote for what I think is right? Do I vote as my constituents want? Do I vote with my party? Do I give my supporters and contributors what they want? Am I elected to follow? Or to lead? Do I accept what I consider to be an evil in order to achieve what I think is a greater good? It seems to me that an unequivocal, universal, principled yes or no answer to any of these questions leads to bad outcomes. When the answers are "maybe," "sometimes," and "it all depends," one must continually make decisions in the moment, in response to evolving circumstances and changing tradeoffs. That is more difficult than always following principle, but the chances of getting a better result are improved.

My father often wondered out loud whether I could be an effective politician without becoming corrupted in the process. He was never very specific about the nature of the corruption, and we never talked concretely about the choices and compromises I made, but his question still intrigues me because, for me, there is not an answer that isn't ambiguous.

I grew up immersed in the Bible. Looking back, I see how it influenced my early understanding of politics, leadership, and government. The Old Testament recounts the story of the people of Israel, mostly about their leaders and what happened to the corporate entity—the state. The fortunes of the people ebbed and flowed depending on whether their leaders obeyed or disobeyed the commands of Yahweh. When the Israelites worshiped Yahweh and followed his precepts, military victories and economic prosperity followed. But Yahweh was a jealous god, and when the people and their leaders strayed to follow other gods, their cities were destroyed and they were taken into exile.

The New Testament centers not on a chosen people, but one man, Jesus, and his twelve disciples. Jesus was a carpenter, a common person looking at life from the lower levels of a community that has long been dominated by a foreign power. He told stories of the Good Samaritan, the widow's small coin, and the final judgment. In all of them he emphasized the responsibility of individuals to tend to the sick and wounded, feed the hungry, clothe the naked, give to the poor, and protect the weak. He has harsh words for the religious leaders who enforce rules and have no compassion, but he has little to say about the state, except that it should be respected, "Render to Caesar the things that are Caesar's." Whenever there is a conflict between the personal requirements of the gospel and the laws of the state, however, the gospel is obeyed—even though the right of the state to punish is recognized.

This was the religious foundation I brought to politics, not one conducive to compromising. Even on issues that didn't impact any particular principle, the question I was programmed to ask was, "Is this the right thing to do?" Being independent followed naturally, as did the inclination to question political authority. These were not characteristics likely to be appreciated as I started a career in Democratic Party politics in Illinois where Richard J. Daley was mayor of Chicago, chairman of the Cook County Democratic Party, boss of the Machine, and at the pinnacle of his political power, having just been instrumental in electing John F. Kennedy as president of the United States. I would have been better served if I had been trained in the art of making a deal and if my goal was to be reliable rather than right.

There was another strong influence on my thinking, which, for lack of a better description, can be called the Democratic Ideal—the revolutionary idea that no one has a right to rule. Leadership is conferred by the consent of equals. Decisions are arrived at through a process of open discussion and debate. Votes are not coerced, bought, or traded.

This is basic high school civics, the embedded message in the stories we tell ourselves of how we created American democracy that is an example to the world; how we fought King George and the redcoats at Lexington and Valley Forge; how the founding fathers debated and compromised in Philadelphia and produced the Constitution; and how we fought a bloody civil war to preserve the union and free the slaves and make good our declaration that "all men are created equal."

In college I was introduced to the great democratic philosophers: John Milton who believed that truth would always be recognized and chosen if the debate was free and open; John Stuart Mill who argued persuasively that the expression of every idea should be permitted; Henry David Thoreau who made the case for civil disobedience when political leaders make wrong decisions; and Mahatma Gandhi who with his march to the ocean to make salt brought the British Empire to a peaceful end, finishing what the Sons of Liberty had started with the Boston Tea Party.

The overall feeling I came away with, after what was probably a fairly typical educational experience, is that politics is basically an intellectual exercise, a matter of rational individuals debating the important issues and reaching agreement. Sure, there was the Revolutionary War and the taking up of arms to accomplish a political goal, but the goal was to be able to determine our own destiny, among ourselves, after rational discourse. To achieve the union the question of how power was going to be allocated between large and small states, and between slave and free states, required compromising the grand principle of the Declaration of Independence: "All men are created equal and endowed by their Creator with certain inalienable rights." But the compromises were presented largely as an intellectual exercise, without much attention being drawn to the conflicting economic, military, religious, racial, and power interests of the various factions—the conflicts that plague all efforts at nation-building.

Within this philosophical tradition, as it is within the religious tradition I grew up in, there is a right and a wrong. The power to determine what is right and wrong lies with the individual. And right prevails because in the "free marketplace of ideas" truth is stronger than falsehood.

John Stuart Mill acknowledges freely in *On Liberty* that it is idle sentiment to think that truth has more power than error when the dungeon and the stake are on the side of error. Sufficient application of legal or even of social penalties will generally succeed in stopping the propagation of unwelcome ideas, even when they are true. Rather, the power of a true idea lies in the fact that it will continually be resurrected until a more favorable time arrives and it becomes generally accepted. He argues strongly that good decisions will generally be reached only when all ideas can be discussed freely.

It is up to the individual to stand firm against what is wrong, and one thing that is always wrong is the coercion of the individual. When a government puts policies in place that are destructive of people's lives, liberties, and their pursuit of happiness, the Declaration of Independence declares that "it is their [the people's] right, it is their duty to throw off such government." Thoreau, in *Civil Disobedience*, explains his refusal to pay taxes to a government that recognized slavery and started an unjust war against Mexico, arguing that there are cases "in which a people, as well as an individual, must do justice, cost what it may. . . . Action from principle, the perception and performance of right, changes things and relations; it is essentially revolutionary."

This is the politics of the civic person. It is what I grew up with and believed. Individuals are assumed to be rational and altruistic. Unlike the collective theories of fascism and communism that developed later, classical liberal democracy vested ultimate authority in the individual, not the collective. The power of the rulers is limited. Authority rests in the informed consent of the governed. There is faith that when the community of individuals comes together the competition of ideas will result in decisions that are good for the community. Everyone has equal power and equal influence—an equality symbolized by the one vote that each person is entitled to cast in elections.

In due course I was introduced to a very different political philosophy; a philosophy summed up succinctly by the Chinese revolutionary and dictator Mao Tse-tung in two statements: "Ideals are important, but reality is even more important"; and, "Political power grows out of the barrel of a gun."

The "reality" that many have seen and described is that people in general are not rational. With Freud we discovered our subconscious. With Dostoevsky we began to understand the irresistibility of the irrational act. Marx demonstrated that our economic roles determine who we are and what we think. Skinner put us in a box and taught us that with the proper stimuli we can be trained to do anything. In the light of what we have learned from these and others, it is hard to argue that reason prevails over custom, emotions, feelings, beliefs, prejudices, tradition, and self-interest. We can be frightened, manipulated, and coerced. We can be easily led into making wrong decisions. Not only is the debate not rational, there is no reason to think that our decisions will be right. Because the people cannot be trusted to decide what is good, a strong leader, not democracy, is the better system. Because people can be manipulated, they should be manipulated.

Machiavelli, the medieval philosopher/politician, in *The Prince* laid out the strategy: "The experience of our times shows those princes [who] have done great things . . . have been able by astuteness to confuse men's brains. . . . Men are so simple and so ready to obey present necessities, that one who deceives will always find those who allow themselves to be deceived."

That advice from five hundred years ago has been embraced by today's political campaign managers. They have no interest in securing the informed consent of the citizens for a particular policy; their only interest is in securing the citizen's vote. To that end, everything is fair. All of the voter's human weaknesses are used against him. The voter exists to be entertained, manipulated, fooled, tricked, cajoled, have his prejudices reinforced, and all of his hot buttons pushed. He can be easily led. He is busy with other things. He wants to be left alone. He doesn't know all the facts, and his ignorance can be used against him. His actions are based on perceptions, and those perceptions can be controlled. The belief that politics is a mixture of control and manipulation has been with us a long time, but over the last half century the methods have been refined with government-sponsored propaganda, commercial advertising, and sophisticated neuroscience and motivational research.

The irrational view of how we as humans function and make decisions is reflected in much of our art and popular culture. Advertising and public relations are built on its precepts. It fits with much of what we have come to learn in recent years about human behavior from research and experiments in the social and physical sciences. We readily accept the fact that we are not rational, yet we want our politicians to treat us as though we are rational. We criticize them for appealing to our self-interests, our emotions, and our prejudices, and we forget them quickly when they appeal to our minds and then don't get enough votes to win.

Democracy, as a way of making political decisions and governing ourselves, contains within itself a paradox. Its underlying assumption is that we are rational beings and can find our way to making right decisions for our communities; yet experience shows us that we are not rational but guided by emotion, prejudice, and self-interest. When things don't turn out well, the reforms we promote are generally designed to reinforce the rational, suspend human nature, and save us from our self-interests and prejudices. Not surprisingly, reforms seldom produce the desired effects for very long. Human nature keeps getting in the way.

We have to find a way of holding onto the ideal as well as the real, together and at the same time, recognizing and accepting the tension and the conflict that exists and will continue to exist. Both must be embraced. One is what we would like to see when we look in the mirror. The other is what we do see.

One year I kept two books in my desk on the floor of the House of Representatives: Robert's *Rules of Order* and the *Little Red Book* containing the sayings of Chairman Mao. I found both useful. One sets out the rules for a group to follow when it wants to make democratic decisions in an orderly manner. The other describes how one acts when there are no rules. It seemed to me that while, on the surface, the daily legislative process followed a version

of Robert's *Rules*, underneath the political process of rounding up the necessary votes followed the *Little Red Book*.

Politics is what we are with all of our warts. Because it is not just a game
that we can walk away from and because it has real effects for real people in
a real world, it has the potential of bringing out the worst in all of us. I am
reminded of my son when he was younger and we would play games together:
he was the congenial Dr. Jekyll when he was winning, but he regularly turned
into Mr. Hyde when he was losing and time was getting short. In politics,
when the game is on the line, we are all Mr. Hyde.

Perhaps our most human trait is the desire to have our cake and eat it
too. Few of us see the contradictions in our own actions. We want services
but not taxes. We want our representatives to think for themselves, but we
want decisions made without delay and without controversy. We want our
politicians to stand up to pressure and do what is right; we also want them
to listen to us and do what we want. We all appreciate the chutzpah of Jesse
Unruh, once the Speaker of the California Assembly and the "Big Daddy" of
California politics, who famously said, "If you can't take their money, drink
their booze, use their women, and look them in the eye and vote 'no' you don't
belong in this business." That is, until it is our eye that is being stared into.

Politics is not rocket science. It's a deal. I vote for you because you are
going to do what I want. Or, to put it more genteelly, I vote for you because
we agree on the issues. It gets more complicated when one remembers that
everything is in play, everyone is playing, and multiple transactions are going
down all the time. It is not just the officeholder and the voter who are involved,
but also all the other officeholders, all the various groups and interests, all
the political activists of every persuasion, plus the reporters, bloggers, and
commentators. All, along with the ideas and prejudices of popular culture,
are part of the mix, part of the pressure, part of everything that goes into the
activity we call politics. The stakes are high. Power is up for grabs: power to
make policy, power to spend money, power to set the rules for society, power
to give economic advantage in the market. There are only a few rules for grab-
bing power. The rules for holding power are made by those who have power.

Understanding the political game requires a sympathetic appreciation
of ordinary human reaction to being taken by the devil to the top of the
mountain and tempted by the prospect of enjoying all the kingdoms of the
world and the glory of them. There is a price, however: the devil has to have
his due. In politics, one finds there are many devils—and friends—who want
only their due.

2. IT'S A DEAL

IT WAS NEAR THE END OF MY FIRST CAMPAIGN FOR REELECTION, AND I WAS on a downtown sidewalk shaking hands, passing out campaign literature, and asking for votes. A young man in his early twenties walked toward me. I reached out my hand and asked, "Will you give me your vote?" He paused, and without hesitating he replied, "What are you going to do for me?"

In thinking later about that exchange—"Will you give me your vote?" "What are you going to do for me?"—I concluded that those fourteen words captured all the essentials of democratic politics. Politics is a transaction, a trade, at times a purchase or an auction. The deal is power for reward, election for favor. The vote is central to the deal because it makes the deal possible. The vote gives power to the officeholder, making it possible in turn for the officeholder to fulfill promises made. If sufficient votes are not delivered, the candidate doesn't take office and has no power to reward. The candidate and the voter *both* have an interest in *both* winning. It is a deal they *both* make.

As my then-seven-year-old son told me one day as I was driving him home from school, "Dad, you should be president." "Why?" I asked, thinking naively that he was impressed with my abilities. But his motives were more personal. "Because I could tell you what I want, and you could pass a law," he said.

We all play the game. We all want a deal. We all want a person in office who will pass a law to give us what we want. Union members don't vote for candidates who will cut back benefits to injured and unemployed workers. Coal miners don't vote for those who would relax mine safety laws. Trial lawyers don't vote for those who would place a cap on jury awards. Seniors don't vote for those who would repeal property tax breaks for the elderly. Business owners don't vote for those who would increase the minimum wage and tighten workplace safety and environmental standards. Teachers don't vote for those who would cut funding for schools.

Students want scholarships. Industry and farmers want to use the air, water, and land to dispose of their waste products. The unemployed want jobs. Truckers want highways. ATV owners want to run their vehicles across wilderness areas. Companies want contracts. Farmers want subsidies. Businesses want tax credits. Bankrupt companies want bailouts. The wealthy want tax shelters. Everyone wants some break, some help, somewhere. "Where do you stand on the issues?" is only a variation of "What are you going to do for me?" What the voter really wants to know from the candidate is this: "If I vote for you, will my life be better?"

And so the question comes to the politician in the back room, or campaigning on Main Street, or through the mail in a questionnaire, "What are you going to do for me?" A vote, the essential element of every political deal, hangs in the balance.

In 1970, when I first ran for state representative, getting enough votes to win depended on being endorsed and actively supported by the county political party. An endorsement brought with it the support of all the party's allies. Political strength came from mobilizing and energizing the precinct captains. Campaigns were labor intensive, and most of the workers were party people who enjoyed campaigns and had knocked on doors in their own neighborhoods for many years. Campaign funds came largely from activists, friends, and organizations long identified with the local party. Endorsement by the party brought with it access to the resources necessary to run and win a campaign, and gave the candidate the broad outline of a message that reflected the coalition of philosophies and interests that made up the party. From the day I first thought about running, my attention was focused on securing the endorsement of the county party leaders, prominent local party members, and precinct captains. The votes I needed to be elected would come through their active support.

Endorsement by the county party included a straightforward deal. The party wanted a clear commitment that, if elected, I would run patronage through the party organization. In return for helping me win office, the party wanted its own strength enhanced. It wanted unity and loyalty in what mattered most to it: the maintenance and growth of the organization. The party did not want me hiring people and putting together my own organization with people loyal to me rather than to the party and the party leaders. With an organization and workers loyal to them, the leaders could deliver votes to candidates of their choice for offices ranging from township clerk and county sheriff to governor and president.

As long as whatever patronage I influenced was run through the organization, I was pretty much left alone after I was elected to follow my own judgment in whatever actions I took. In the eight years I was a state representative, I can remember only once that the county chairman talked to me about a particular vote.

By the final time I ran for the legislature, some twenty-plus years later, political power had shifted and elections had changed. The county party could no longer deliver the votes necessary to get elected. I had been recruited to run by the statewide Senate Democratic Campaign Committee that controlled the distribution of all the large donations from statewide interest groups. I was focused in that campaign on getting the senate committee to make mine one of their "targeted" races, sending a signal to donors that my race was winnable and they should contribute.

It was also no longer sufficient to talk about what I wanted to accomplish and about my general approach to government and solving problems. Within a couple of days of filing for office, I was inundated by questionnaires from political action committees representing a wide range of interests. The PACs wanted to know my position on detailed, specific issues that usually had to do in some way with protecting or expanding the group's access to income or limiting competition. If I hadn't served in the legislature previously, I wouldn't have known anything about most of the issues raised in the questionnaires. They weren't topics usually discussed around kitchen tables.

Among its fifty-five questions, the state AFL-CIO wanted to know my position on repealing the Scaffolding Act, on establishing a state-operated workers' compensation insurance fund, and on removing exemptions in the Prevailing Wage Act.

The nurses association wanted to know my position on allowing nurses to practice independently and receive direct payments from health insurance companies. The medical society asked if I opposed giving nurses that added authority.

The dentists wanted to know who I thought should be allowed to treat the temporomandibular joint. The bankers wanted to know if I would vote to allow banks to sell insurance, sell securities, and provide travel services.

The rest of the more than forty questionnaires were equally specific and related to gaining or maintaining (by law) competitive advantage in the "free" market. The cover letters made it clear that to be considered for endorsement I had to fill out, sign, and return the questionnaires. A "yes" or "no" commitment for a specific future vote was required. Although most groups were discrete in their choice of words, it was clear that help in my campaign was contingent on my commitment to vote for their interests. The dentists were direct in making the connection. "This [questionnaire] will be used as a tool to assist us in determining whether a candidate's views on issues affecting the dental profession are consistent with ours. Please return this promptly as we will be completing our analysis of the candidates by late September to determine the level of support." The bankers were even more direct, "We support only those legislators who support branch banking."

At the very beginning of the race I had to commit myself one way or the other to the agendas of all these interests. It was clear that I would never raise the money necessary to put my own message across to the voters if I made too many mistakes in choosing sides. Was I with the big banks or the little banks? The banks in general or the insurance agents? The medical society or the trial lawyers? The medical society or the nurses association? The dentists or the denturists? The manufacturers association or the unions? The optometrists or the ophthalmologists? Did I even know what side I was on? Could I have asked the right questions to find out?

In my first race in 1970, it had not been necessary to run the gauntlet of economic interests while just a candidate. I was a Democrat and generally sided with labor and consumers rather than corporate interests, but I didn't have to commit in advance to detailed positions in parochial fights. The county party's endorsement brought with it the support of all the party's allies and access to the resources necessary to run.

In a relatively short time, campaigns had changed. The patronage deal with the party was ending and being replaced by a policy deal with interest groups.

The patronage deal with the party ended primarily because the party couldn't hold up its end of the deal and deliver the necessary votes to elect the candidates it endorsed. The change happened as candidates who relied on television and direct mail to send their messages and on polling to shape those messages began to defeat candidates who relied on party organizations.

In Illinois the watershed election was 1972, when the maverick Democratic candidate for governor Dan Walker defeated Paul Simon, who had been endorsed by Mayor Daley's Chicago machine in the Democratic Party primary. Later, the party organization stopped endorsing in primaries for the simple reason that it couldn't deliver on the endorsement. Civil service laws and court decisions had cut into the ability to reward campaign workers with jobs, and television was proving to be a more reliable means of influencing votes.

The new campaign is based on a new deal. Where previously votes were delivered by precinct workers who wanted jobs, votes are now delivered by television and other media that require money. As media supplanted patronage workers, capital replaced labor as the source of energy and power. Where precinct workers used to be the essential ingredient to campaigns, money has taken their place. The new deal is with contributors rather than with party workers.

Under the new deal, the local political party organization has become almost irrelevant. There is no need for an organization of individuals held together by patronage or a core set of political beliefs when the deal is directly between the individual or interest group with money and the candidate or officeholder. The money also allows candidates to bypass whatever party organizations still exist and take their messages directly to the voters through the media. This can be considered a positive step if the instrumental role that money plays in the new order of things is ignored. After the 2004 U.S. Senate primary, the *Chicago Tribune* noted favorably that both major party nominees had "appealed directly to voters" and "owed almost nothing to this state's professional pols." The editorial writers did not recognize that the old deal was already dead and that under the new deal much was owed to the funders of those direct appeals.

Where do political dollars come from? From people who have the dollars, whose economic interests will be affected by the decisions made by the winner, and who neither need nor want patronage jobs. The people who send questionnaires to candidates are not interested in a job. Rather, they want their economic interests promoted. In a political system run on capital, the deal is money for policy decisions favorable to increasing profits. The deal that used to be limited largely to office patronage now focuses on the policy decisions of the office. For legislators, this means votes on proposals to change the law. In the governor's office, this means executive orders, rules, and the appointment of sympathetic people to decision-making positions.

The new deal, a product of the change in communication technology and the advent of television, has changed all of politics from the way campaigns are run to the political power structure itself. Not only has it brought the demise of the political parties, it has fueled the incredible increase of dollars flowing into elections and contributed to the harsher rhetoric and polarization of attitudes.

THE NEW POLITICAL STRUCTURE DIDN'T ARRIVE ALL AT ONCE BUT EVOLVED over time in response to perceived needs, new laws, court decisions, and ongoing changes in technology. PACs were created to facilitate the new deal: raise the money, screen candidates, secure commitments, and make contributions. Over time they assumed many of the functions previously performed by local political party organizations.

Political action committees increased and centralized the flow of cash into campaigns and concentrated the pressure to deliver on policy. Where a candidate might have previously solicited local doctors, now the medical society's PAC raises dollars from doctors all over the state and decides which candidates get how much. There are several advantages for the medical society. More dollars are raised, providing more clout. The decision on how much to give to which candidates is centralized and organized. The contribution is conveyed at a single time so the amount is large enough to get attention. Candidates have to meet established criteria (i.e., make the right commitments) in order to get the money. The money is delivered by those who, when the time for voting on legislation comes, will be there to remind the officeholder of commitments made. Both the raising and distributing of money are controlled by the organization's leaders. Individual doctors are discouraged from contributing directly to their own local candidates.

Other PACs might not have as many dollars as the medical society, but they all follow the same operating principles. The collection of dollars and the decisions on which candidates to support are centralized. Commitments on issues are sought as soon as a candidate announces for office. Support is contingent on a commitment. Members are instructed not to contribute to their own local candidates.

PACs were organized quite naturally at the state and national levels. Many economic and ideological groups already had state and national associations, and the policy decisions that affected their interests were made at the state and federal levels. Some had already been actively lobbying in the legislature for many years.

With money becoming the principal political ingredient and increased profits the motive for donating money, it was also natural that PACs organized around specific productive activities. Those who made their money in the same way and who had the same economic interests joined together to change policy in ways that benefited those economic interests. Plumbers, road builders, doctors, teachers, small banks, large banks, savings-and-loan associations, credit unions, tavern owners, oil companies, service-station operators, and a host of others all formed their own PACs with the intent of maximizing the influence of their group over policies that specifically and narrowly affected their interests. Because they are organized around producer interests, PACs avoid broad policy issues. To wander beyond their own interests would jeopardize the cohesion of the group.

The number of PACs has naturally snowballed. Groups that were slow to organize found their interests being undermined by their competitors. In self-defense, they formed their own PACs. Others, like the bankers, split into two or more groups (e.g., big banks and small banks) when members found that not all of their economic interests were the same.

As the number of PACs has increased, their focus has become narrower and more specialized. Just how narrow and specialized is seen in the list of separate professional health associations with registered lobbyists in Madison: anesthesiologists, anesthesiologist assistants, nurse anesthesiologists, nurse midwives, school nurses, nurses, private-duty nurses, family physicians, physician assistants, physicians, pediatricians, emergency physicians, podiatrists, ophthalmologists, optometrists, dentists, dentist hygienists, chiropractors, physical therapists, occupational therapists, massage therapists, nutritionists, acupuncturists, audiologists, hearing professionals, marriage and family counselors, psychiatrists, psychologists, local health departments, hospitals, medical group managers, healthcare providers, primary healthcare providers, women's health providers, public health providers, blood centers, hospice providers, mental health providers, ambulance companies, and specialized medical vehicle providers. Patients are notably missing.

It shouldn't be surprising that most politically active groups represent production activities rather than consumer activities. There is a monetary benefit for those who make their incomes in the same occupation to join together to make sure the law protects their livelihoods and increases their profits. It pays each of them to contribute to supporting their common interest. There is a direct connection between the payment and the payback. For consumers, on the other hand, who would benefit from lower interest rates, fewer toxins in the environment, better schools, and more affordable healthcare, none of these goals is the focus of their lives. They are busy making a living. The potential payback to a single individual from supporting a consumer group is not great enough to make the support worthwhile. Consumer groups have to rely on small voluntary contributions from a lot of individuals. For producers, political activity is part of doing business, and their PACs are well funded.

The counterpart to PACs in the new deal are the Senate and House leadership campaign committees created to accept contributions and funnel dollars to targeted races. Much of the money from PACs now flows through these centralized leadership campaign committees, which recruit, train, and run the campaigns of candidates for their respective legislative bodies. Making contributions through the legislative leaders serves the interests of both the PACs and the leaders. The PACs gain support for their policy goals from the leaders who control the law-making process. By controlling campaign resources, the leaders increase their influence over how their members vote. They are also able to increase their chances of holding majority power by concentrating spending on "targeted" races where the strength of the two parties is relatively even and the outcome is uncertain.

Even though some political money is still philosophical and party oriented, and some interest money has gravitated to one party or the other, incumbency (not party affiliation) is often the distinguishing factor between who gets money and who doesn't. This is the result one would expect when the deal is cash for a policy decision. An incumbent can deliver on the deal today. Not only is a challenger a long shot, but a challenger—even if victorious—can't deliver until after the election, and there is always time then to make a deal.

In my losing campaign for the Illinois Senate, I made a fund-raising call to a lobbyist who was an old acquaintance. His tone was friendly but distant. No, his group could not contribute, he said. They gave only to incumbents, never to challengers. But if I won, he added quickly, he would be happy to help retire whatever campaign debt I might incur.

In recent years, in addition to political action committees formed by provider groups to further their economic interests, PACs have also been created by wealthy individuals with ideological goals. Although the purposes diverge, the underlying deal is the same: money for a future policy decision. The ideological PACs are much more likely to deal with individual candidates directly and bypass the leadership committees. They are also more likely to recruit their own candidates who reflect their particular ideological views on policy and government.

THE SAME EXCHANGE UNDERLIES BOTH THE OLD DEAL AND THE NEW DEAL. There is no way to escape the conversation that begins with, "Will you give me your vote?" and continues with, "What are you going to do for me?"

And so everybody thinking about running for office is faced from the very first day with the question: what are the deals—explicit or implicit—that I am willing to make? Even without thinking about it in those terms, the question starts being answered as soon as the candidate begins planning where to look for support first. Who thinks like I do? Who shares my goals? The campaign develops much differently depending on whether those first conversations are with chamber of commerce leaders or union officials, business owners or environmentalists, farmers or teachers, bankers or consumers, liberals or conservatives. You define yourself by the allies you seek out. If elected, you dance with those who brought you. But you go to the dance in the first place with those you want to dance with.

The relationships between politicians and contributors in our new politics are infinitely nuanced and changeable, even though from the outside they may all appear as straightforward quid pro quo transactions: my donation for your vote; my vote for your donation. The connection between campaign donations and policy votes has long been noted. There is a clear correlation between money and votes, but the correlation by itself does not tell us whether it results from (1) allies supporting each other in pursuit of a common goal, (2) votes cast in return for or in expectation of a donation, or (3) donations given in return for or in expectation of a vote. In all three cases the external facts are the same: a vote is made, a donation is given. The motivations and intent among the three are, however, entirely different, changing the character of the transaction, even though the external facts are the same.

I had a conversation about donations and votes with my father one evening after dinner. It was his opinion that if I accepted a donation, I incurred an obligation. I argued otherwise that a donation came because the donor was motivated to give it. That act by the donor created no obligation on my part, just as my vote on policy creates no obligation on the part of those who benefit to donate. There is no question, however, that expectation accompanies a contribution. In most cases contributions occur because both donor and candidate genuinely think alike. They are on the same team and are helping each other, one by running, the other by contributing. That covers most issues and most contributions.

The transaction creeps very close to the near occasion of sin, however, when a person or group with a specific interest makes contributing and helping contingent on the answers a candidate gives to their questions. This is not necessarily a quid pro quo arrangement. Voters are entitled to know what candidates think about a wide range of issues as part of making up their minds about whom to support and vote for, but there is an uncomfortableness about answering detailed questionnaires from an economic interest group, an uncomfortableness that is not present at neighborhood gatherings where those present also ask you about what you think about issues and decide whether to vote for you or not based on how you answer. The neighborhood gathering provides an opportunity for discussion and interaction that the questionnaire does not. Those present want to know how you think and what your reasons are. Their concerns are not exclusively economic. The single-interest provider groups, on the other hand, just want a commitment on their specific goals. You sign their questionnaires saying how you intend to vote. They decide if they are going to support you. Even though there might not be an explicit quid pro quo transaction, the feeling of it is there. Your answers may only reflect your best thinking at the time, but they are considered by the questioners to be commitments for future votes, and any change of mind based on additional information, or anything else, is considered a "betrayal."

Faced with the question, "What are you going to do for me?," the candidate instinctively begins to calculate, "How far do I have to go to get this vote?" As the issues become more important, the groups involved more influential, and the donations larger, the temptation to do the appropriate calculation increases. Interest groups are not shy about forcing you to make the calculation. They want you to take their potential support or opposition into account when you make decisions. The effectiveness of the Illinois Medical Society rests on a combination of campaign contributions, the economic and social position of physicians in (particularly rural) communities, its organizational strength, and its willingness to use its political power in campaigns. In an interview with me about an article I was writing after I left office, the chief lobbyist for the doctors explained the society's influence this way: "We're willing to try to beat people. When Ann Willer was defeated, she came back [to the capitol] and told everyone how the docs had gotten her. Thank you, Ann! The message gets around. We're willing to organize and contribute and not lie down when someone bangs us on the head. At the same time we will help those who have been with us. We stay with our friends." When one incumbent is defeated, every other incumbent gets the message. There is a price to pay for being on the wrong side.

On the other hand, when legislators, particularly leaders, hold a fundraiser, it is impossible for contributors, as they contemplate writing a check, to avoid thinking about the potential impact on the next bill they want passed. Even when there is no quid pro quo transaction, things happen because of the twin motivations that are almost always present to some degree in all players of the political game: the desire to ingratiate and the fear of retribution.

There is no escaping the fact that the fundamental transaction underlying politics in a democracy—"Will you give me your vote?" "What will you do for me?"—is inherently corrupting. There is no cure for it, but that doesn't mean all politics is corrupt. Too often we consider politicians principled or corrupt based on whether we agree with their actions. Democrats think Republicans have sold out to big business and insurance companies; Republicans think Democrats are wholly owned by the unions and environmentalists. The most common explanation by progressives in her district of why Kathleen voted against a statewide smoking ban was that she had "sold out" to the "powerful" Tavern League. Too often we are reluctant to acknowledge that principled differences of opinion exist and that we all support the candidates we agree with.

We come back to the questions every officeholder has to answer, questions that are more difficult to answer under the new deal. How shall I decide? Should I vote my conscience for what I believe is best? Should I vote as my constituents want? Should I vote as my contributors want? Should I vote for what is in my political interest? The philosophical and practical questions of knowing what is "best" and knowing what my many constituents think are difficult to answer. My contributors' desires, on the other hand, are clear.

The answer is a combination. You do what you think is best. You do what your constituents want you to do. You do what is in your best interest. You do all three because that is what people expect. They want you to listen to them. They also want you to be independent. They understand that you have alliances. They expect you to dance with those who brought you. They just don't want you to be wholly owned by anyone. They don't want you to outsource your vote. They want you to be able to say "no" to your friends when the occasion demands.

The eighteenth-century English politician and philosopher Edmund Burke had a lot to say about the relationship between politicians and constituents. He mostly came down on the side that officeholders should vote for what they think is right. In his essay "Bristol, Ireland and Commercial Freedom" he writes, "Your representative owes you, not his industry only, but his judgment; and he betrays, instead of serving you, if he sacrifices it to your opinion." He reached that conclusion based on his belief that the elite (among whom he included himself) should rule because they had more knowledge than their constituents. "We are the expert artists, we are the skillful workmen, to shape their [the people's] desires into perfect form. . . . They are the sufferers, they tell the symptoms of the complaint . . . but we know how to apply the remedy."

But Burke was not consistent. He also wrote that the "country will sink to nothing" if the common person doesn't take an active interest in public affairs. It is the people's duty to judge their representatives and decide whether they "look most to their own interests," whether their "counsels . . . be wise or foolish," and whether "things go well or ill in their hands," and then to take action on the basis of that judgment.

In his own colorful way, Jesse Unruh described what is probably the most appropriate political response to the creative tension between doing what *you* think is best and doing what *they* want. "I have sold myself many times. In fact, I have probably sold 160 percent of myself, but I never gave anyone controlling interest." There is always that tension between "yes" and "no." You may sell 160 percent of yourself, but you don't give anyone else controlling interest.

The dance of an incumbent with a supporting group can change over time. As they work together and become more familiar with each other, the level of trust can increase, resulting in more compromise and accommodation of each other's goals. The relative balance of power may also shift along with the recognition of who leads the dance. A new candidate who needs a supporting group to deliver enough votes to win will be more dependent than an incumbent who is increasingly able to personally garner the votes necessary for reelection. Whoever has more influence over delivering votes in the next election leads the dance. Who is likely to win is part of every group's calculation when deciding whom to support.

Even though the choreography may change, there is always a deal, there is always the invitation to dance. "Will you give me your vote?" "What are you going to do for me?"

3. THE POWER STRUCTURE HAS CHANGED

ALL POLITICS IS (NOT)
LOCAL (ANYMORE)

IT WAS NOT THAT LONG AGO THAT TIP O'NEILL, THE RUMPLED WARD POLI-
tician from Boston who rose to the pinnacle of power as Speaker of the U.S.
House of Representatives, titled his primer for aspiring politicians *All Politics
Is Local*. In it he tells stories to illustrate the "rules of the game." What comes
through most clearly is that the game he knew and played so well was rooted
in friendship, shared trust, personal connection, and neighborhood.

O'Neill's world is far different from the one we encounter today. Politics
has left the neighborhood. It is no longer something we do, but something
that is done *to us* by those with power and money. *They* influence what we
think by shaping the messages we hear, and *they* control the decisions that
rule our lives with campaign contributions and armies of lobbyists.

Few of us feel in charge of our own governing. In a recent Wisconsin poll,
only 12 percent of respondents said they thought that voters determine how
tax dollars are spent, while 82 percent believe that lobbyists make those decisions. Only 10 percent think that elected officials represent the voters, and
only 2 percent think they "almost always" do what is right.

At the most fundamental level, our unhappiness with politics is a question of
power. How can we get enough of it to feel that we can influence our own destinies?

The basic unit of power in a democracy is the one vote that every citizen
over the age of eighteen is entitled to. This power is spread evenly across the
electorate; each one of us has our part of it. Organized political power, however, is based on the ability to influence and deliver those votes as a package.
Communication is the foundation of organized political power because it
is through communication that votes are influenced and delivered. What
political power looks like, who wields it, and how it functions are all shaped
by the demands of whatever communication technology is most effective in
influencing and delivering votes.

As the dominant communication technology for influencing votes changes over time, so does the political power structure. What that structure looks like at any particular moment depends on the skills needed to mobilize the resources required by the dominant communication technology. When word of mouth dominated, political power rested on the ability to mobilize labor to knock on doors, and the power structure took the form of political patronage machines that were very effective at sending your neighbor to your front door asking for your vote. Since television became dominant, political power has rested on the ability to mobilize capital to pay for advertising. Political party bosses with their armies of door-knockers have been replaced in the power structure by the money donors and media consultants who pay for and create the persuasive messages delivered on small screens of all kinds.

The new power structure looks and acts differently because the skills and resources needed to produce media messages are not the same as those needed to put neighbors on your front porch. The power, however, rests on the same foundation: the ability to influence and deliver votes. The changeover began when candidates who used media to carry their messages began to beat candidates who relied on party organization.

At first, television was the instrument of "reform." It allowed candidates to bypass the political bosses and their ward organizations and present themselves directly to the voters. But over time, media-based politics has institutionalized itself into a new power structure more centralized and in many ways less accountable than the old. Everything in politics has been affected: who makes the decisions, how and by whom candidates are selected, how campaigns are run, which offices are important, how the relationship is maintained between elected officials and their constituents, what level of partisanship exists, and how problems are solved through political compromise. They are all connected.

The old power structure was local. It was hierarchical, built on personal relationships, favors, and loyalty. There was always somebody close by to talk to. The conversation went both ways. You talked with your neighborhood precinct captain when your sidewalk needed repair, when you couldn't get car insurance coverage for your teenager, when your daughter back from college needed a summer job, or when storm-felled branches in your yard needed to be removed. At election time, the captain stopped by your house to talk to you about voting for the candidates he or she was supporting. The captain knew who to talk to about getting your problems solved because the people who held those jobs were all part of the same party organization. The candidates supported by the captain ran the offices where those people worked. The "machine" was an efficient mechanism that connected government services, contracts, and jobs with neighborhood votes. A "boss" with personal charisma and the ability to motivate and organize people made the decisions and got the notoriety, but the effectiveness of the organization depended on the exchanges that took place on the front porches in the neighborhoods. The local organization selected its own local candidates as well as those who represented the area in the state capital and Washington. Gubernatorial and presidential candidates came to the local organization hat in hand looking for support. Power was local. It was connected to a particular place. It was an integral part of the community.

Since money and electronic messages are not tied to a particular place and both can be instantly moved, the new power structure based on collecting money and creating carefully crafted and targeted messages is increasingly centralized. At the top, the people who make the important political decisions are those with the ability and connections to raise money. The money hires the pollsters and communications experts who craft the messages that get sent back to the neighborhoods in a whole variety of ways to influence votes. Voting and the political office itself are still tied to place. You vote at your local polling place for people to run your school district, your township, your city, your county, your state senate district, your congressional district and your state. The voter and the candidate still have to live within the same geographical boundaries, but the political power that used to be located within those same boundaries has now moved outside them, and we find we have less influence over our own destinies. Our candidates are selected by outsiders, and the messages that elect them are crafted and paid for by outsiders.

The pools of money gathered at the center can be enormous, far larger than what can be raised locally to support local interests. The wealthy individuals who contribute those dollars have national agendas and very specific goals. They also tend to cloak their activities by funneling their dollars through multiple front groups with friendly names. What might otherwise be low-key local contests become occasions for centralized interests to extend their influence.

The centralization of political power has been going on for some time and continues to increase. Although made possible by the revolution in communication technology and the accompanying transformation of politics into a capital-intensive activity, that centralization has been furthered by changes in campaign finance laws, court decisions, and the creation of PACs, super PACs, and other campaign organizations. The driving centralizing force,

THE POWER STRUCTURE HAS CHANGED

however, is the money that can be gathered anywhere, sent anywhere, spent anywhere, and transformed easily into messages that can be crafted anywhere and delivered anywhere to any audience. The local has been displaced.

SO-CALLED CAMPAIGN FINANCE "REFORM" HAS CONTRIBUTED TO THE change. Over the years reforms have placed limits primarily on the more local and more public political players—individual candidate campaign committees and political parties. The result has been what could have been expected: political money increasingly flows through centralized "independent expenditure groups" that are not limited in what they can collect and spend.

In Wisconsin, the campaign committee of a candidate for the state senate can accept up to $2,000 from any one individual and up to $2,000 from any political action committee. There are no limits, however, on what independent groups can raise and spend. In each of Kathleen's first two campaigns, her campaign committee "Voters for Vinehout" raised and spent about $200,000. The independent groups probably spent twice that much on her behalf. The same approximate numbers applied to her opponents and the independent groups that supported them.

Voters find that their choice of who is going to represent them in Madison or Washington can be heavily influenced by outside groups with narrow interests and lots of money who may care little or nothing about the quality of life in the local community. Whether or not that happens may be little more than a matter of chance. Sometime in the three weeks prior to Kathleen's first election, a coalition of statewide groups met to decide whether to continue to prioritize her race and spend money for her on television advertising and direct mail. Kathleen didn't learn of that meeting until almost a year later, and she still doesn't know all the organizations involved or how they voted, just that the decision to keep supporting her was decided by a one-vote margin. The outcome of the election may not have been determined by that private vote, but it is possible, since the group did make a major television buy. Similar decisions allocating large resources to specific races are increasingly being made by faraway and faceless individuals with profound effects on the democratic electoral process.

One result is that candidates lose control of their own races. Since there can be no coordination between independent groups and the candidate, the messages crafted in Madison (or Washington) may not support or reinforce the candidate's own messages and may not resonate with local voters. In several western Wisconsin races, a direct-mail piece on jobs that did not take into account local business closings backfired. In one of Kathleen's races, a piece lauding her work on behalf of rural schools was directed to voters in Eau Claire. Eau Claire may be rural from Madison's perspective, but nobody in Eau Claire considers themselves as rural, and there was already a perception that Kathleen paid more attention to the more rural parts of her district than to Eau Claire.

Regardless of the messages sent by outside independent groups and whether or not the candidate agrees with those messages, it is impossible for candidates to disassociate themselves from them. As a professor of government at UW-Milwaukee commented to the *Chicago Tribune* about a Wisconsin Supreme Court race, "The campaigns have been kidnapped by these larger issues and larger forces. Whether they like it or not, the two candidates are left in the passive role of watching the campaign that they are barely participants in."

When "independent groups" first became active in Wisconsin, they tended to be spin-offs of organizations that had long been active in state politics: the unions on the Democratic side and corporations on the Republican side. As centralization has progressed over time, however, independent groups formed and funded by large donors at the national level are getting more involved and playing major roles in local races. Most of the negative direct-mail pieces against Kathleen in her second race came from a national committee headquartered in Virginia.

In the 2011 Wisconsin Supreme Court race, outside groups spent an acknowledged $4.5 million, six times the amount that the candidates themselves were able to raise and spend. Most of the money supporting the Democratic candidate came from labor unions acting through the Greater Wisconsin Committee. The money supporting the Republican candidate came from Wisconsin Manufacturing and Commerce, Wisconsin Club for Growth, Citizens for a Strong America, and Wisconsin Family Action. According to the Center for Media and Democracy's PR Watch, much of the money flowing to those groups came in turn from the Wellspring Committee and the Center to Protect Patient Rights (which got most of its funding from Freedom Partners), all three of which have connections with Americans for Prosperity and the political operation run by the Koch brothers, billionaires whose widespread corporate activities are headquartered in Oklahoma.

A municipal referendum in Albuquerque, New Mexico, to ban abortions after twenty weeks attracted roughly $1 million from national sources, paying for advertising and ground operations of "unprecedented scope and size" for that city (according to the *New York Times*). Independence USA, a super PAC funded and run by billionaire Michael Bloomberg, former mayor of New York City, spent $1.3 million in the Democratic primary for an Illinois congressional seat, "far more than any of the contenders" (*Chicago Tribune*). In two Republican primaries in Wisconsin to fill Assembly vacancies, the American Federation for Children Action Fund (largely supported by the DeVos family of Michigan, heirs to the Amway fortune) spent substantially more than the candidates themselves to win the nomination for the two who favored increased state funding of private schools.

In the 2013 Los Angeles school board race, outside groups contributed almost $5 million, with Bloomberg contributing $1 million (*New York Times*). The president of the teacher's union was quoted as saying, "This is a race for Los Angeles, not the school board race of America. It would be really tragic if the voices are drowned out by folks who have no sense of what is going on here to begin with."

Even city council races in Coralville, Iowa, were not too small for Americans for Prosperity to get involved in, paying for newspaper ads, direct-mail pieces, and a door-to-door campaign.

The goals of the individuals and groups that lavishly spend political money are varied. Bloomberg's primary focus is on reducing gun violence. The DeVos family wants to expand public funding of private schools. The Koch brothers' wish list includes no healthcare expansion, less control of carbon dioxide emissions, lower minimum wages, lower taxes, less business regulation, more restrictions on voting and union activity, and privatizing education. Emily's List looks for and supports women candidates who are pro-choice on abortion. Gill Action funds candidates who support gay and lesbian rights. The National Rifle Association supports candidates opposed to all forms of gun control.

The list of organizations and super-rich individuals who pour millions into political campaigns grows every year. Their goals tend to be narrow and specific, and they are getting narrower and more specific. As a result, even though independent groups are generally associated with one party or the other, they are increasingly choosing to support a particular kind of Democrat or a particular kind of Republican. Both parties are experiencing more primary contests, as competing centralized interests fight over the "soul" of the party. In explaining the U.S. Chamber of Commerce's heavy involvement in an Alabama congressional primary, the chamber's political director told the *New York Times*, "We want to find candidates who come from the private sector, we want to find candidates who come from the *Chamber* family." A second outside funder added, "The goal is to elect not just a Republican, but the *right kind* of pro-business one" (emphasis added).

In the 2012 U.S. Senate race in Wisconsin, the Club for Growth, a national organization active in many Republican primaries across the country, worked hard to defeat Tommy Thompson, the popular former long-term governor, because he was not their kind of Republican. "Wisconsin Republicans should recruit a pro-growth conservative to run, not recall some big government, pro-tax Republican whose time has come and gone." Wisconsin Republicans rejected the outside advice and nominated Thompson. Weakened by the primary fight, however, he lost the general election.

Near the end of Bloomberg's tenure as mayor of New York City, *Time* magazine ran a cover story on his next career, which was described as "using [his] enormous private wealth to change government policies and shift human behavior." The story focuses on Bloomberg, but it mentions others with similar ambition: Mark Zuckerberg, Sheldon Adelson, George Soros, Peter Lewis, David and Charles Koch, Bill Gates, Eli Broad, and Jim Walton. The author concludes, "Over the past 30 years, the world has been transformed by globalization and technology, and from that tumult has emerged a new class of billionaires who profited by the change, innovators, business leaders and heirs. In the prime of their lives, many have turned their attention to remaking the world, often through policy and politics. It is a return to the era of great benefactors. . . . It is their world. You just vote in it."

Whatever the specific goal of an individual funder, the intent (mostly unspoken) is the same: to elect compliant legislators. When asked by the *New York Times* about those candidates who "might fear his financial might," Bloomberg essentially said that if they do *what he wants*, they have nothing to fear. He came close to bribery or intimidation when he told Senator Pat Toomey, as he claims in the *Time* article, "If you support reasonable background checks, I will support you, even though we have nothing in common on any other issue."

The reality of politics today is that no candidate can gather sufficient local resources to match those of outside individuals and groups. Candidates who are thinking of running for office naturally seek out organizations and individuals who will provide support—whether they come from within the district or outside of it. Organizations and individuals with particular interests seek out and recruit candidates who agree with them, regardless of where their districts might be. Politics has always been that way. It is the ultimate team sport. When the support is provided from outside the district, however, local voters are often left off the team. They are not part of the agreement. They become spectators to a contest waged by others. Unfortunately for local residents, officeholders who rely on outside interests to get elected tend to go along with those outside interests after they are elected, even to the detriment of their local constituents.

The trend is evident in Wisconsin where in recent years the legislature has removed or reduced local government control over the siting of wind turbines, the creation of voucher and charter schools, the responsibilities of landlords in regard to their tenants and the maintenance of rental property, oversight of mobile phone and commercial radio towers, soil erosion at construction sites, shoreline zoning, negotiating labor contracts, and setting residency requirements for their employees.

As the money comes increasingly from outside sources, political power flows from the local to the center. The community is no longer left to decide within itself what the community wants the community to be like. Voters are caught up in the national contest waged on their turf. There is little room for local dialogue that leads to a local solution. There are few stalls in the political marketplace where one can "buy local."

AS POWER MOVES TO THE CENTER, THE BOND THAT CONNECTS THE OFFICE-holder to local voters is loosened. Before even thinking about making the rounds to look for local support, prospective candidates travel to the state capital or Washington to meet with the state or national campaign committees, interest groups, and wealthy individuals to look for support and funds. They hope that the message will come back from the center to the local realtors, local union members, local NRA members, local Right to Life members, local members of Planned Parenthood, local members of the League of Conservation Voters: "This is our candidate. She will be good for us. He supports our issues." The group whose local members decide which local candidate should be supported is the exception rather than the rule.

This erosion of local influence makes it more difficult to address problems from the perspective of what is in a community's interest. Individuals, whether they are doctors, insurance agents, bankers, or restaurant owners, play a variety of roles in their own communities. The local banker is also father to a high school student, brother of the highway engineer, son to a mother with a long-term disability. His sister works at the nearby paper mill that is overloading the municipal treatment plant, and many of the bank's clients closed their doors on Main Street when Walmart opened a megastore fifteen miles down the road. In local discussions, the banker balances all of those interests. The banker is not just a banker. The banker is a banker who lives in Alma and is part of the community.

When the discussion shifts to Madison or Washington, however, it is taken over by groups with specific interests. The community interest drops out. At the center where political decisions are made, the banker is a *banker*, a member of an association that has only one interest—maximizing the profits of the banking industry. The bankers as an association have no interest in school funding, access to healthcare, maintaining the roads, or water and air quality. The banker with a child in the community votes for the referendum to increase local school property taxes. The bankers as an organized political action committee support tax policies at the center that make the referendum necessary.

Individual doctors may care about and want to solve the problems related to access, quality, and cost, but those issues don't surface in the questionnaires sent by the medical society to political candidates. Rather, the society wants to know if the candidate is going to be on its side in the fight with trial lawyers over malpractice issues and with nurses over scope of work issues.

Because PACs and other single-interest groups nurture an us-versus-them mindset, achieving any solution that requires compromise is increasingly difficult. The recruiting and fundraising messages they send out are always about conflict and fear. "Join . . . send money . . . they are after us . . . protect what we have . . ." I have yet to receive a letter from any organization I belong to that starts with, "We have just made a major compromise with [insert any opponent here], and we no longer need your money." Leaders work to energize their troops to fight the enemy, not to reach an accommodation. Conflict keeps organized interests financially healthy. Officeholders, locked into prior specific commitments to the committees that supported them, are not free to make necessary political compromises without those groups (whose membership and funding depend on being in a fight) first agreeing to the peace, and in doing so undermining their own organizational interests.

Consider the rhetorical exchange by Organizing for Action and the NRA after a congressional vote on gun legislation. The message from Organizing for Action: "Yesterday, 45 senators chose to ignore their constituents and stand with the gun lobby. . . . These senators had the nerve to get up there—right in front of victims' families from Newtown—and cast that vote against something that more than 90 percent of Americans support. . . . Those senators made a cynical calculation that, at the end of the day, the gun lobby would be louder and stronger than we are. Yesterday was just round one. We will keep fighting. . . . The special interests have been at this longer, and they can do a real good job at scaring people by distorting the facts they think we'll go away quietly. . . . We're going to keep fighting, and someday soon, we will win."

The president of the National Rifle Association delivered a similar fighting message to his members: "Our feet are planted firmly in the foundation of freedom, un-swayed by the winds of political and media insanity. To the political and media elites who scorn us, we say let them be damned. . . . We will never surrender our guns, never."

These messages from well-funded, centralized organizations focused on achieving one goal are typical. The words are heated. The opposition is demeaned. The specifics of the controversy are not mentioned. Principles that cannot be compromised are at stake.

No officeholder supported by the National Rifle Association will suggest a solution to the problem of gun violence (with the exception of arming more people) unless that officeholder is willing to lose the future support of the NRA. The political process, as we now find it, requires the formation of a new political action committee to make compromise possible. The American Hunters and Shooters Association, that "likes guns but thinks the NRA is too absolutist," was formed to back candidates "who oppose an outright gun ban, but who favor some restrictions." Little movement can be expected, however, unless the new organization demonstrates some political strength and candidates backed by Hunters and Shooters defeat candidates backed by the NRA. One can imagine that the NRA will put a lot more effort into defeating candidates supported by its compromising rival than candidates who oppose the NRA positions completely.

It is continuing conflict between extremes that keeps organized interests healthy. Wealthy individuals who feel strongly enough about an issue to contribute tens of millions of dollars to change the world to their liking are not interested in compromising or in supporting candidates willing to compromise. The new centralized power structure based largely on money tied to specific interests and narrow ideologies does not nurture agreement.

Back in the community, where the participants in the political discussion all had multiple interests and connections, where each was both a producer and a consumer, and where all shared in the benefits and the costs of whatever was decided, the positions were less polarized, the rhetoric less heated, and the solutions easier to achieve.

THE SHIFT IN POWER AWAY FROM LOCAL PARTIES TO NARROW CENTRALIZED interests also changed the normal political career path and the offices thought to be important.

Political parties built on patronage were interested primarily in local offices rich in jobs and local clout: the sheriff, county highway commissioner, tax assessor, mayor, and county clerk. State and federal legislative offices were important only to the extent that they provided state or federal jobs to local party members. The organization contested every office because each contributed to the strength of the organization. Officeholders got their start in less important offices and then moved up as they gained experience and name recognition. There was cohesion to the political structure as the local party organization, built around local officeholders, delivered the local vote for all of the party's candidates, from assessor to president. In contrast, money-media politics has no career ladder and little interest in local administrative offices that don't set policy. With the decline of political party organizations, and without any money interest, local races tend to become low-budget, nonpartisan, personal popularity contests, or they are not contested at all. Even where the local offices are officially partisan, most local officials play little or no role in the party organization, seldom even attending meetings except just before elections.

Since the deal is now money for policy, the new power structure is interested in the legislative and executive offices that make policy rather than the administrative offices with jobs. The campaigns for those offices draw the attention of the PACs and have become expensive, professionalized, and centralized. Even though local volunteers are attracted to work for specific candidates, they often disappear once the election is over. There is no longer an ongoing organizational structure that effectively holds together the local, state, and federal parts of the political system. Temporary coordinated campaigns may be created at the county level for each election, but these are generally run by field staff sent in by the candidate at the top of the state or national ticket, and all activities are directed from the center. There has been a complete reversal from the old political structure where the campaigns were run by the local party organizations and state and federal candidates climbed on board for the ride.

Name recognition has replaced political experience as the primary basis on which candidates are recruited. An individual pursuing a political career can still move up from local to higher office because the local office provides the name recognition sought by the central interests with money looking for a winner, but those interests don't really care if the candidate has had prior officeholding experience or not. Since they have no local political organizational goals, it is unimportant to them whether the name recognition of the potential candidate comes from holding a lesser office or doing something else that attracted media attention. Media personalities and media celebrities—television weather announcers, athletes, actors, talk show personalities—are increasingly being recruited to be candidates. Today, if one wants to start a political career, it probably makes more sense to spend two years doing the weather or news on local television than to spend two years as county clerk or local school board member. You get more exposure and don't have to do anything controversial. What is lost is the experience of dealing with public issues in the public arena.

The one alternative to relying on outside groups and money is to have enough money to fund your own campaign. Increasingly, wealthy individuals willing to spend their own money are starting political careers at any level they can afford. Money buys a candidate everything that is essential: attention, name recognition, media consultants, polling, research, image makers, advertising, telephone banks, and an internet presence. What money can't buy—a community-based political organization—is no longer considered necessary. It has to be your own money, however. There are no limits on what you can spend to get yourself elected. But campaign finance reform has put severe limits on what your siblings or your five closest friends can contribute to help you get elected—unless they do their own "independent" expenditures.

One of the advantages of running politics from the center is the opportunity it presents to think and act strategically. The leaders are very aware of how many legislative votes are needed for control and where the most likely places are to get them. They know that in Wisconsin it takes seventeen votes in the Senate and fifty votes in the Assembly to control the agenda and achieve the results they want. They know where they should concentrate their resources to maximize their chances of picking up those votes. They look for every advantage, from redrawing district lines to changing voting rules, whatever it takes to get the majority. They are always aware of the numbers driving their strategy.

This is often not the case at the local level. At a recent forum on education funding hosted by the local school board, members of the public clearly frustrated with the political process and their inability to achieve what they wanted were in a "let's have term limits, throw everyone out and start over" mentality—not thinking that they already had fifteen votes in the Senate, that they needed to keep those fifteen and figure out where and how they were going to get the other two. That kind of strategic thinking is more likely to exist at the center, where it is easier to see the whole.

AS TELEVISION BROUGHT AN END TO LOCAL, PATRONAGE-BASED POLITICS, does the internet, the new communication kid on the block, have the potential of changing politics in a way that brings power back to our communities where we can all access it?

Joe Trippi, who ran Howard Dean's presidential campaign in 2004, is among those who have argued that the internet will change everything. People will again become actively involved in making the decisions that affect their lives. Those who hold political office will be responsive to the needs expressed by the people, and money will have little influence. In *The Revolution Will Not Be Televised: Democracy, the Internet, and the Overthrow of Everything*, Trippi writes that there will be "a glorious explosion of civic re-engagement. . . . Americans will use it in the next decade to bring about a total transformation of politics, business, education, and entertainment."

Television brought a new political power structure because it proved to be more effective at changing votes than knocking on doors and made money the essential ingredient in winning campaigns.

Is the internet different enough from television to reverse the last fifty years, reducing the role of money and bringing power back to the local? For the answer to be "yes," the internet would have to prove itself more effective than television in influencing votes, the skills for its use would have to be accessible to more people, and the costs significantly less.

Trippi locates the power of the internet to change politics in its ability to do three things: raise money, organize people, and create community.

Howard Dean in 2004, Barack Obama in 2008, and Bernie Sanders in 2016 all demonstrated that the internet can be used to raise money—prodigious amounts of it—and in so doing made their candidacies credible. None of the three was a "typical" candidate. Each created an excitement that motivated large numbers of individuals to give who don't normally contribute to political candidates. The internet made the solicitation and contribution of those dollars easy.

The potential significance of internet-raised political money is that instead of a small number of individuals each contributing a large amount, a larger number of individuals each contributes a smaller amount. The connection between big money and specific policy payoffs can be broken. More individuals are involved in the central action and, as a result, broader public interests are served.

The idea is simple. As more people contribute, the influence of contributions tied to specific interests is weakened. As Trippi notes, "A hundred bucks from two million Americans. That's all it will take to . . . return America to the principles that it was founded on." The math is easy, but turning the math into real dollars is more difficult and has not been done very often. If the ability of the internet to raise political dollars from a lot of small donors is going to be revolutionary, it can't just work occasionally for a particular kind of candidate. It has to work in every election—for city council, the state senate, congress—and for the average candidate, because that is what the existing fundraising system does. The occasional successful use of the internet by an exceptional candidate in a high-profile race won't bring about a revolution.

Can we organize and recreate a local political community using the internet? Trippi is sure that with the internet people will talk to each other again. "We will build huge, involved communities around political issues and candidates." The internet very quickly demonstrated its power to create communities of people with like interests regardless of location. With several clicks of a mouse you can be playing chess with a Chinese master, discussing the latest theories of astrophysics with a Swedish colleague, or learning from fellow bird watchers where the northern hawk owl is hanging out. Environmentalists, healthcare-reform advocates, and political activists of all persuasions are connected with people of like mind through the internet. The conversations are largely within groups with the same interests and goals.

In a local political community, however, people of different persuasions and interests have to figure out in some collective way what kind of school to run, how many police to hire, whether there should be a library or a park, what taxes to pay, who should be prosecutor, who should be judge, what healthcare to provide, and how they want their representatives to vote when they get to the state capital or Washington. The internet has not proved useful in creating that kind of political community.

To be effective, local political organizations have to be built with local residents. The Howard Dean campaign was able to motivate and organize like-minded volunteers from across the country with the internet, but when they traveled by bus to Iowa to knock on the doors of strangers, they were ineffective because they came from outside the community. (The union members bussed in for Richard Gephardt in that same election were equally ineffective.) The strength of the old political machines lay in the fact that it was a familiar face that showed up on the front porch election after election. The precinct captain lived in the neighborhood, brought a six-pack to the annual block party, and had kids in the school around the corner.

The internet has the potential to help create local political communities. By its nature it is decentralized. The cost of setting up a site is almost nothing; there is no minimum audience that has to be attracted to cover costs; there is no marginal cost to expansion. It can be used with great effect in local organizing. With instant and costless messages, the internet can make it easier to recruit and energize volunteers, provide an organizational framework, give people things to do, provide resources, and fill rooms (and capitol plazas) with enthusiastic supporters. It is a way also for supporters to reach out to friends and neighbors with the kind of personal endorsement that can influence votes.

For elections to be won, however, believers have to get past talking to themselves and reach out to those who are not already persuaded. Trippi recognizes the difference when telling stories about his early campaigns: "Political organizing is all about finding those people who think like you do and drawing them into your organization any way that gets them involved—everything from canvassing to donating money to simply voting for your candidate—while at the same time trying to get your message out to the people who haven't decided yet."

The internet is magnificent in achieving the first part of the task—finding those people who think like you do. It falls short in the second—getting the message out to the people who haven't decided yet. As Trippi acknowledged, "It wasn't lost on me that after 11 months of showing how the internet would be the technology of future elections, in a few days we had been taken down by the technology of past elections—the TV attack ad." He seems to believe, however, that this will change as the internet matures.

It is not at all clear that the internet is sufficiently different from television to transform politics and break the tie between money and policy.

The internet as an advertising medium is not much different from television. The messages are more targeted, but the skills and resources required to produce them are similar. There is also little evidence that the internet reduces the amount of money needed to win or that the tie between dollars and winning will be loosened. (Advertising charges per viewer connected to the web are not much different than charges per viewer watching television.)

To bring about a revolution that changes the nature of the power structure, the connection between money and votes must be reduced. The game will change some, but not much, if the only effect of the internet is to bring more donors onto the playing field. The tie between politics and money will be loosened only if the web makes it possible to win with less money. So far that hasn't happened as the money flowing into campaigns continues to increase every election cycle.

The power of the internet to change politics may lie in its usefulness as a tool in organizing people to do things rather than in persuading people or raising money. It has been demonstrated many times that the most effective communication is person to person. With the internet it is easier to build neighborhood networks and provide the resources for volunteers to craft messages that will inform and persuade their neighbors. The 2008 Obama campaign, unlike the Dean campaign four years earlier, used the internet to organize supporters to work in their own neighborhoods, providing them with information, ideas, and materials as well as an easy way to communicate back to the campaign.

The internet facilitates communication. It is agnostic, however, about whether the messages originate at the center or from the local community. It can be just as helpful facilitating the increased centralization of political power as it is in mobilizing against that power. There is much evidence to support the accuracy of the insight by Marshall McLuhan, one of the first writers to examine the connection between communication technologies and social and political structures: "A speed-up in communication always enables a central authority to extend its operations to more distant margins."

It is interesting in this context to note that Trippi's populist grassroots revolution starts not at the local level, with local candidates, but at the top, with a president elected with the votes of internet-connected supporters following a campaign funded with internet-raised dollars. Congress will do the will of the president under the pressure of email messages from six million internet-organized individuals. "As soon as a candidate uses the internet to declaw the lobbyists and make our leaders be responsible by galvanizing the American people into a voice that can be heard . . . it's over. We'll have won."

Trippi's vision was the inspiration for Obama's Organizing for Action—the reincarnation of Obama's reelection campaign as a "social welfare group" under section 501(c)(4) of the tax code with no limits on contributions and no requirements to report contributors. Even though Trippi prophesied that the internet would turn politics upside down, shifting power from the top to the bottom and away from the center to the local, and despite efforts to make it appear otherwise, Obama's internet-based Organizing for Action is run from the top down, from the center. The organization's introductory email said, "We're a new grassroots operation. . . . Please chip in $41 or more to help build this new organization today . . . to help establish Organizing for Action as a real powerhouse in grassroots organizing. . . . Our first fundraising deadline is Sunday. . . . What happens between now and Sunday at midnight will determine what's next for this organization." A month earlier, however, the *New York Times* reported that the president's political team was busy raising $50 million "to convert his re-election campaign into a powerhouse national advocacy network . . . in support of Mr. Obama's second-term policy priorities." Half of the $50 million was to come from donors who would each contribute or raise $500,000 or more—putting those donors on the national advisory board of the grassroots organization. "The money [$50 million] will pay for salaries, rent and advertising, and will also be used to maintain the expensive voter database and technological infrastructure that knits together Mr. Obama's two million volunteers, 17 million e-mail subscribers and 22 million Twitter followers."

Television with all of its costly forms of entertainment assembles audiences and sells access to those audiences to anyone who can pay for the message they want delivered. Assembling an audience for internet-transmitted messages is also expensive, as it relies on proprietary information, data mining, and sophisticated software. Once the audience is assembled, however, access can be sold to those who have messages they want to deliver. It is not by chance that the advertisements appearing on your computer screen reflect your interests, the websites you visit, and your buying habits. There are huge costs and commercial and political advantages in assembling the databases that match name, address, telephone number, age, occupation, interests, buying habits, political inclination, history of voting, and email address. The money and resources required to build the databases, however, serve to further centralize political power. Those at the center with the money to build and own the databases can share them with favored local candidates, giving those candidates significant advantage. But, no one shares or sells the databases to anyone other than reliable allies.

Trippi also predicted that the American people will speak with "a voice" that will be heard. Despite its many accomplishments, the internet has not succeeded in reducing the many voices of the American people to a voice. If anything, the internet has amplified many of the unheard voices from the years when communications was dominated by newspapers and the three major television networks. Trippi expected the voice to be populist, but many of the voices have turned out to be corporate and conservative. More often than not the messages—regardless of their content—originate from the center, not the local.

DESPITE APPEARANCES TO THE CONTRARY, MANY GRASSROOTS ORGANIZA-tions are in truth top-down organizations, created by individuals or groups with specific agendas and supported with their dollars. Members are recruited and mobilized to accomplish the goals of the decision-makers at the center. They are motivated and kept active by the usual political messaging techniques. The "spontaneous" emergence of the Tea Party movement owed much to Dick Armey's FreedomWorks and the Koch brothers' Americans for Prosperity. Political action committees of all kinds generate messages to legislators that look like they come from voters in the home district but really originate from the center. "Action Alerts" direct organization members to immediately call or write their legislator. The request is urgent. The message is black and white and simple. Tell your legislator to vote the right way. Few details, if any, are included.

The legislator who gets the calls from the district and is faced with voting on a bill that is much more complicated than the simple portrayal in the Action Alert often finds that succumbing to the pressure to vote the "right way" is easier than trying to justify a contrary vote because the details don't match the Alert. When the Sierra Club was part of an agreement with the utilities in Wisconsin on an energy bill, it sent messages to all of its members asking them to call their legislators to vote for the "green energy jobs bill." Part of the bill, never mentioned by the Sierra Club, ended the state moratorium on nuclear power plants. When told by Kathleen that the bill included lifting the moratorium, most of the Sierra Club members who called her to vote "yes" on the basis of the Alert changed their minds.

Although presented as grassroots lobbying, the communication loop from the lobbyist to the hinterland and back increases the power of the center. The message and the information are controlled from the center. There is only the appearance that the message to the legislator is coming from the grassroots level. The internet has made organizing from the center much easier.

Even if the internet doesn't bring on the revolution some have forecast, it does have the potential for making our politics better. The internet has brought more volunteers and more donors into at least some high-profile races. The internet has also made a lot more information about candidates and issues readily available to anyone looking for it. The range of ideas that have credibility is broader. Public debate is more vigorous. It can facilitate the creation of neighborhood networks. The potential of many small donors funding a campaign might make more candidates viable.

To the extent, however, that the internet is just a tool for raising more dollars, an alternative medium for paid advertising, and a faster way for centralized single-interest groups to communicate Action Alerts to their members, it will support the continuing centralization of political power.

There will be nothing automatic about a revolution spurred by the internet. Political power that now rests securely at the center will have to be wrested away. In the struggle for power between the local community and the center, the internet is a tool that both can use. It will take concerted, intentional effort to bring political power back to local communities where the common interests are rooted in the same shared space.

WHAT WE HAVE LOST IN THE EXISTING POLITICAL POWER STRUCTURE IS local control of our elections. The important decisions on selecting candidates, funding candidates, planning campaigns, providing resources, and delivering votes are made centrally at the state and national levels. We have to bring those activities back to the local if we are going to take power back.

What does this mean in practical terms?

It means that the local political parties have to take charge of recruiting their own candidates, raising their own money, and delivering enough votes to win—regardless of what the groups at the center do.

It means convincing local doctors, lawyers, businesspeople, and union members to make their own decisions about which local candidates to support, rather than sending their money to their state or national organizations and then following instructions on which candidates to vote for.

It means putting people on doorsteps to persuade their neighbors and creating personal communication linkages to counter—in the only way possible—the influence of paid media messages created and paid for by the center.

It means persuading local activists of whatever persuasion to participate from the beginning in the local political process and not wait for instructions from their state or national organizations. It means local chapters of those organizations taking over the job of endorsing and supporting candidates.

It means raising or removing the limits imposed by campaign finance reform laws on local candidates and local political parties so that they can come closer to matching the resources available to the shadowy independent expenditure groups at the center who have no limits, are not accountable, have no local ties, are increasingly active in local elections, and whose influence is growing.

For the local media, it means paying more attention to local races and providing the resources necessary to give their audiences information about local candidates, their supporters, their policies, and their campaigns not contained in their advertising buys. Coverage of local races is now often limited to printing the announcement press release and, perhaps, running side-by-side answers to a few questions the week before the election. Voters are told far more about national and statewide candidates than they are about the local candidates who will be representing them in Washington, or Springfield, or Madison.

Above all, it means creating a mindset that decisions *will* be made by *us*. It means creating a local political structure that can carry out those decisions regardless of what those at the center do. It means gathering the local resources necessary to *win*.

None of this is easy. No one who has power is going to relinquish it voluntarily. No law or reform measure is going to return political power to the people at the local level. Saul Alinsky, who was a community organizer in Chicago, had it about right. To get power you have to fight for it. "Up against the wall . . . I am coming to get what is my own." Even then, success is not sure. So much of the existing political infrastructure facilitates centralization. It is easy to let someone else do it.

Nothing in politics happens automatically. Rebuilding local political structures capable of taking power back from the center will require time and effort. An agenda has to be agreed to and differences resolved. Credible candidates have to be recruited. Checks actually have to be written. Campaigns have to be planned and carried out. A majority of voters have to be persuaded.

WHY SHOULD WE BOTHER TRYING TO BRING POLITICAL POWER BACK TO the local?

Most of what we really don't like about politics as we now experience it has its roots in the centralization of power and decision-making. The list is long: the tight connection of campaign contributions to specific, narrow, economic interests, the power of lobbyists to dictate policy, the inability of elected officials to make the necessary decisions to solve problems and move on, the feeling that it doesn't really make much difference whom we elect, and the sense that there is nothing that we can do to change the course of events.

The local, spatial community is important because the quality of the lives we live depends on the characteristics of the particular community in which we live. The local community is where everything comes together. It is where the banker who wants to keep his tax incentive also wants a comprehensive curriculum in the high school his daughter attends. It is where the factory owner doesn't want pollutants discharged into the lake on which his family lives and where the CEO of Exxon joins his neighbors in a lawsuit against a fracking operation that would make the neighborhood a less enjoyable place to live. In the community, everyone has to live with all the results of the political decisions they collectively make. Both the benefits and costs are shared by everyone.

If we want our officeholders to represent the interests of the communities in which *we* live, then *we* have to make sure that *we* are the ones who ensure their election. *We* recruit them, *we* plan and finance their campaigns, *we* work for them, *we* persuade our neighbors to vote for them, and *we* elect them. When *we* have done that, power will be back in *our* hands. Politics will be local again when we take the responsibility to do the work.

4. WILL YOU BE *OUR* CANDIDATE?

They saw him as a young man of, at most, moderate ability, and this did not displease them. They had not chosen him because of his gifts; they had chosen him because, conceivably, he might win. . . . [H]e is amenable to the proper handling.

—Edwin O'Connor, *The Last Hurrah*

ALTHOUGH POWER BROKERS HAVE HANDPICKED CANDIDATES FOR PUBLIC office since the beginning of politics, the change in the political deal brought on by new communication technology in the latter half of the twentieth century has had profound effects on how and by whom candidates are selected, the nature of campaigning, and the experience of being a candidate.

Edwin O'Connor in *The Last Hurrah*, written in the mid-1950s at the very beginning of the revolution, described with great foresight the essentials of the modern political campaign. In it a small group of wealthy leading citizens selects and financially supports Kevin McCluskey, who is neither experienced nor gifted, to run for mayor. The strategy of O'Connor's fictional campaign has been copied time and again by "real" campaigns.

Their hope of success lay in preserving a decent distance between him and the public. A certain amount of direct contact was, of course unavoidable; any more than that would be, they felt, suicidal. They had not the slightest desire to see this pleasant, inexperienced man, of somewhat suspect capacities, compete . . . in that dangerous arena . . . where there were hands to be shaken, heads to be patted, solicitous familial inquiries to be advanced, and sudden, embarrassing questions to be answered on the spur of the moment. . . .

Here [on television] the candidate could address the electorate effectively, but at a safe remove.

The longtime incumbent mayor and his supporters are inclined to not take the young, inexperienced McCluskey too seriously—all except for one old ward leader who, recognizing the wealth of the supporters behind McCluskey, cautions, "with a couple more like that behind him our dummy is sitting on Fort Knox. And a rich dummy somehow don't look so dumb."

In *The Last Hurrah*, local people put up the money and run the campaign for their selected candidate. As money/media politics has evolved and become more dominant, the sources of money have become more distant and less connected to local voters. The campaigns their dollars buy are increasingly planned and directed by professional consultants, media advisors, and pollsters who are not politicians, who have never run for office themselves, and who often have no personal connection to the communities where their candidate is running. All of this has changed the experience of becoming and being a candidate.

When I ran for the Illinois legislature the first time, the strategy for winning was relatively simple. I was in charge of my own campaign. Nobody told me what to say, how I should spend my time, or what I had to do. The county Democratic precinct organization provided the workers. Donations came from friends, party activists, and groups and individuals long associated with the party. I spent little time fundraising. All the planning and activities were initiated and carried out locally. It never occurred to me that outside groups might spend money to elect or defeat me. No interest group asked me to swear allegiance to their issues as a condition of support.

The reality facing a prospective candidate today—particularly in a contested district—is far different. The high cost of media makes the need for money much greater. It is almost impossible to raise a sufficient amount from local donors. Local party organizations are far weaker and can't be depended on to produce the necessary votes to win. PACs routinely ask for commitments on specific issues as part of their endorsement process.

· As the candidate, you have a diminished role. Leaders of state and national organizations decide if you are a viable. From the day you are selected, there is pressure to run your campaign *their* way. Where previously you had to respond only to local influences, now you also have to navigate the often-conflicting demands from the distant sources of money. As the dollars have increased, so have the demands for control from those contributing the dollars.

The emphasis on money starts the day you first think about the possibility of running. You are told from the beginning how many hundreds of thousands or millions of dollars you will have to raise. More than one good candidate has decided not to run when recruiters repeatedly insist that raising money will be their primary task. Everyone adds to the exaltation of money. The press judges candidates on the basis of how much money their campaigns have raised or the personal wealth they are willing to put behind their own cause. Almost every political story includes some reference to money. Campaign workshops stress the absolute importance of money and the necessity of spending much of your time dialing for dollars. The political professionals associated with both parties are dismissive: "She can't win, she doesn't have any money." The professors of political science to whom reporters go for unbiased comment repeat the refrain. A friend summed it up this way over lunch one afternoon: "Whether you like it or not, money is the name of the game. If you don't have the money, you can't play."

Campaign strategy centers on raising money, mostly from out-of-district or out-of-state donors. Everything that happens, from the things your opponent says to the money raised by your opponent, is turned into a reason for needing more money. Recognizing, however, that the public views political money as corrupting, both parties portray the other as the pawn of big-money interests and themselves as the champion of the little guy—with the goal, of course, of raising more money. The messages are almost comical in their similarities.

Wisconsin Republican governor Scott Walker: "I am in the fight of my life against a notorious cartel of Madison Liberals, Washington Democrats, and East and West Coast Big Government interests. . . . Tom Barrett is pouring out a smokescreen of falsehoods about me and they can't go unanswered. We need to win this race both on the ground and over the air waves. . . . Rush your special contribution of twenty, thirty, or forty dollars to our headquarters."

Democratic Party of Wisconsin chair Mike Tate: "The sleazy money from special interest billionaires like the Koch Brothers is going to start pouring in even earlier and faster than we thought. That half-a-million dollar campaign of lies from Walker's corporate sponsors at Wisconsin Manufacturers and Commerce was just the tip of the iceberg. . . . We don't need corporate millions to beat Scott Walker. We just need you. Chip in $14 or whatever you can afford today to help us win in 2014."

Both messages, designed to elicit small contributions from the average party activist, evoke a David versus Goliath image. We can fight Big Money and win—if you send money. Homage is paid to the grassroots, but the underlying message is that money is what is really important. Despite the rhetoric directed at small donors, much of the serious fundraising by both parties is directed at large donors. In the real world, Tate abandoned his "We don't need corporate millions, we just need you" refrain, recruiting a millionaire to run for governor because she could self-finance her campaign and telling the media that the most important qualification is not the ability to do the job but the ability to raise "tens of millions."

And so the candidate spends time raising money, making the requests personally. Nobody parts with big money unless they get to talk directly to the candidate. The candidate is given a list of potential donors and call time is scheduled. Political operatives are hired to write the position papers, handle the press, plan the campaign, do the polling, script the ads, and make surrogate appearances at political and community events when the candidate has run out of time. The candidate raises money.

AS THE NEED FOR MONEY HAS CHANGED WHAT THE CANDIDATE DOES, EV-erything else in political campaigns has changed to fit the requirements of the communications technology. Campaigns have become little more than hugely expensive media-centered public relations efforts that follow all the techniques and strategies researched and practiced in the corporate world. The audience is mapped via data mining. The product is associated with images and words that poll well. The message is reduced to thirty seconds. Advertising buys get more news attention than policy proposals.

The need for dollars and the dependence on professional media consultants push candidates toward reliance on the center. Few local candidates have the money or the access to consultants to do polling or create effective political messages. There are few local people who have the personality and experience to manage a political campaign. So the candidate looks to the center for support and help, thus setting the stage for the almost inevitable tension that is created because the source of votes is local and the source of money and message is central.

It is understandable that those at the center who provide the money to run campaigns want to control the message and the strategy. They don't want their money "wasted" because of bad decisions by unprofessional locals not trained in modern campaign techniques. As the senate campaign committee told Kathleen, "We are going to help raise the money if we feel confident about the plans and buy-in."

Bad decisions, however, are not limited to the local level. There is the temptation at the center to treat all campaigns alike, to rely on techniques they are familiar with and reject strategies suggested by the locals based on their on-the-ground knowledge and experience. The political operatives and public relations consultants hired by the funders to run campaigns all went to the same training sessions, all ask the same polling questions, and all tend to run the same cookie-cutter campaigns. Most are reluctant to try anything new or different. What was done in past campaigns is repeated even though the campaign, the year, the district, and the candidate are all different. The same poll-tested talking points are used, and the same kinds of negative attack ads are launched. There is little creativity. Candidates who want to do something different are either stymied or left on their own. The consultants think the candidates are naive and idealistic. The funders think they are losers. The leaders think they are troublemakers. Kathleen was told, "We don't think you are all country bumpkins with no idea of what is going on. We know that you know this district and the people there. And we know you have campaign experience. But we have run hundreds of campaigns between us and know what it takes to play at the level we need to be at to compete with Ron Brown and his $500,000."

The socialization of candidates into acceptable behaviors starts early and continues throughout the campaign. New recruits are sent to two- and three-day training sessions in which they are taught what they have to do in order to win—everything from how to raise money to how to dress, what to say, and how to spend their time. "You may not like it, but this is what you have to do if you want to win."

Campaign managers are assigned and paid by the leadership campaign committee. A schedule is set for each day: so many hours knocking on these doors, so many hours on the telephone calling these people to ask for money. Literature, direct mail, radio, and television are designed and scripted by people hired by the leadership campaign committees. Candidates are told what they can and cannot spend money on. Without other experience to fall back on, they do what they are taught. Even when they don't like what they are being told and don't think the messages and script given to them will work for the voters in their districts, they don't have the knowledge, experience, or resources to think of, or carry out, a different way of doing things. The new candidate goes along because the direction comes from someone who has been trained in campaigning and is supposed to know.

Even incumbents have a difficult time cutting themselves loose, doing their own thing, and taking control of their own campaigns when they think that the message and strategy developed by the political operatives don't fit either them or their districts. After all, the advice is coming from "experts." There is rationality to the response by Mary Burke, who ran for governor in Wisconsin and whose only previous campaign was for the local school board. She told a person who thought her campaign for governor was not going well, "I have hired the best consultants [many of whom had worked in Obama's campaigns], and I am going to listen to them."

Some accept the direction readily. As one incumbent senator happily described his role to me, "I don't think about anything. I come in every morning, pick up my list, and go where I am told, and do what I am told." When I asked another incumbent about his literature, he replied he hadn't heard anything from Madison yet. Both ended up losing their races and expressing regret that they hadn't taken more control of their own campaigns.

Throughout Kathleen's first race for the state senate there was a constant tug-of-war between the funders in Madison and the local campaign over the manager, campaign activities, the candidate's time, direct mail, and media spending. In Kathleen's case, however, because she was willing to run without their support if necessary and always had a contingency plan ready to implement if they decided not to support her, it was possible to negotiate strategies that addressed both their concerns and hers. Not many first-time candidates can do that. And you have to be comfortable with being labeled troublesome, uncooperative, and not a team player.

Money is always used as the hook. In that first campaign, the morning after the campaign had agreed to the senate committee's offer to take over paying the salary of the campaign manager with "no strings attached," the call came from Madison to the manager wanting to know everything he had scheduled for that day. The following morning, a weekly report form showed up for the manager to fill in and return.

The explanation for the request: "That data helps all of us 'tell the story' down here of why and how Kathleen is going to win. So it helps with fundraising, endorsements, and the whole inside game. I would not think of it as 'checking up' or looking over your shoulder, but as getting us the information we need to help. A campaign that doesn't share that information, well, it leaves all of us here in a difficult position, where we have to say, well, 'Yes we've endorsed, but we don't know how many doors have been done, how many IDs have been made, or how much money has been raised, but hey, they tell us it's going well.' Not very credible. What people understand are numbers." The numbers they wanted, however, tracked the standardized campaign they had designed for all their candidates to run. Activities like coffees, house parties, and community conversations that were central to Kathleen's campaign were not included in the report form. They had no place in the cookie-cutter campaign.

The campaign canceled the agreement, telling the committee that there wasn't time to run two campaigns, theirs and ours, and we would go back to paying the manager from our funds and would run our own campaign. The committee stopped all of its activities on Kathleen's behalf, canceled a fundraiser, and had no contact with the campaign for three weeks. Then they got back in touch and resumed what had become a somewhat rocky relationship.

Most candidates don't have the experience to know that support from leadership committees and others at the center depend on only one thing—how they are doing in the polls. It doesn't matter whether they follow directions or not, or what commitments are made. Candidates can do everything they are told, but if they are not doing well in the polls, they will be dropped. On the other hand, if they ignore directions while doing well in the polls, there will be a scramble to help. A commitment from the center for continuing support is good only until the next poll.

The center also wants to control the message of the campaign—a message driven by polling that uses only the specific words that poll well. Kathleen called them "poll-tested pretty words." The strategy is simple: Don't say anything controversial. Stay with the "talking points." Talk only about issues that poll well.

The directive to Kathleen's campaign from Madison was forceful. "As for the Brown negatives, I'm going to be blunt here: I won't change them. These are not phrases or numbers that came in a dream. They are poll-tested in YOUR district. They are extremely reliable and extremely powerful. They show the greatest potential to move voters from her opponent to her side in the voting booth. We didn't hire the best pollster in the country to ignore the results. If we don't use the poll-tested negatives we gave to Kathleen's campaign, it will not be a positive result on November 7. If you trust nothing else I say, trust in that. I've been doing this for fourteen years and have won far more than I have lost, and the credit in every one of those wins goes to the poll and adherence to the tested language. When candidates ignore it they typically lose."

In large part because few words and phrases can be tested in a poll, candidates are routinely told to avoid policy discussions: just knock on doors, shake hands, make fundraising calls. On the hottest topic of the day in 2006, healthcare, Kathleen was told that she should limit herself to the most general of generalities: reform healthcare, cut costs, cover more people. Those were the words that had been tested. Never mind that healthcare was the topic everyone wanted to talk about and that they wanted to talk about the details of different proposals and how their families would be affected. In 2010, the Democratic senate candidates were told not to talk about school funding reform. In 2014, one senate candidate was told not to talk about anything because nothing polled well in her district.

Following the same strategy, Republicans also used platitudes devoid of substance to describe their anticipated replacement of the Affordable Care Act: "Free market reforms," "patient-centered," "turning more and more of the decisions of insurance back to individuals," "better coverage," "lower costs."

What the polling doesn't pick up, what Kathleen found in the many house parties she scheduled, is that people are knowledgeable, they want detail, they want a discussion of alternatives, and they are tired of political talking points that parrot the words that poll well. Voters want some confidence that the candidate has thought about the issues and has some intelligent ideas. What the consultants forget is that the politics they have contributed to creating has turned 85 percent of the people against politics. So the candidate is squeezed between what he or she experiences with voters and the directions from the center.

The reliance on polling has contributed to the proliferation of negative personal attack ads. If candidates limit themselves to safe subjects and pretty words, the primary selling point that differentiates one candidate from another becomes the candidate's "personal story" of achievement or overcoming adversity. It follows that if the personal story is the main selling point, then the personal attack is the preferred offensive weapon. If the personal story is what justifies election, then the personal story is fair game for attack.

Negative campaigns generally are easier to run. They require less thought and creativity. The candidate doesn't have to be able to talk substantively about controversial subjects. It is safer to attack since there is always more agreement on what we don't like than on what we think the alternative should be. The conventional wisdom is that you have to go negative to win. Certainly the overwhelming predominance of negative attack ads indicates the almost universal acceptance of that conventional wisdom. The negative campaign, however, leaves most voters unengaged, on the sidelines, watching the two candidates throw mud at each other. Since there is nothing in that spectacle that will affect them, their family, or their future, they don't care very much who wins. The number of voters declines.

In all of the discussion about the effectiveness of positive or negative campaigns, little attention is given to the *quality* of the campaign, whatever the underlying strategy. In one recent election in a western Wisconsin Assembly district, the Democratic candidate ran a positive campaign and lost. In the next election the Assembly leader told the new candidate that he had to run a negative campaign if he wanted to win. He followed instructions and lost. Perhaps the lesson is that we should take a lot of things into account when evaluating the effectiveness of any particular campaign. It is in the nature of things that when two campaigns compete, one has to win. The tendency is to label one a "winning" campaign and the other a "losing" campaign regardless of other contributing factors. Although both campaigns might have been run well or poorly, the winning campaign is the one that is copied, and the other is discarded. The same dynamic is in play when a message is not received well by the public. Other politicians and their consultants generally conclude that the topic should be avoided. But the problem might have been with the delivery and not the message itself.

THE FIRST STEP FOR EVERY CANDIDATE IS TO BE SEEN AS VIABLE, SOMEONE who has the chance to win. When I first started, this meant having the support of local community and party leaders. If you were interested in running, you spent time talking with people in the district who had influence. All of the recruiting was done by local people. Your viability was judged on the basis of your experience, your abilities, and your connections in the community. Today, the decision on whether you are viable is made by state and national party committees, leaders of state and national organizations, and individuals willing to fund a major share of whatever the campaign might cost. Most of the decision revolves around money. Can the candidate raise money? Can the candidate self-finance the campaign? In Kathleen's first race for the state senate, the statewide organizations and leadership committees decided to support her only after the first campaign finance reports showed she had raised three times more money than her primary opponent in half the time.

Increasingly, the deciders at the center also want candidates who agree with them on all issues and will follow directions in running their campaigns. There is far less room for disagreement on policy, rhetoric, and tactics than there was even ten years ago. Like professional sports teams, political organizations and committees have scouts looking for talent that fits into their game plan, talent that can be trained and bankrolled, talent that can deliver when the time comes. Wisconsin Progress, an organization dedicated to recruiting and training progressive candidates, is not unusual in saying that all of the candidates it works with "must score 100 percent" on its questionnaire and be committed to running a "viable campaign."

Conflict arises easily when organizations at the center decide that one candidate is viable and local leaders pick another. Twice in recent years the Senate Democratic Campaign Committee based in Madison recruited and endorsed candidates in rural districts who had little or no local community connections despite the fact that there were other candidates with those connections already running. Those local candidates were not supported because they didn't have ties to the Madison-based interest groups important to the party leaders and were therefore deemed incapable of raising enough money or running the right kind of campaign. They didn't fit with the Madison political in-group. The results were predictable. In both cases, the candidate that won the primary lost in the general. When the local candidate won the primary, the interest groups with the dollars stayed out of the general. When the centrally supported candidate won the primary, there was not enough local enthusiasm to win in the general.

There is collateral damage that comes from the desire at the center to find amenable candidates they can control. Individuals with an independent mindset and a well-developed sense of self who might otherwise run become reluctant. Individuals who do decide to run have the added burden of figuring out how to balance local interests with central demands. In Kathleen's first race, the struggle to find this balance took up an immense amount of time and energy that could have been spent more usefully elsewhere.

The search by the funders for a viable candidate is made easier because the campaign messages and strategies that are planned and paid for at the center can be adapted to any candidate. Little is said about what the candidate is planning to do if elected. Nothing is said about the interests of the individuals and groups who put up the money to pay for the messages. The funders believe—and there is evidence to support their belief—that they can elect anyone given their cash, the technologies they can buy, and the strategies they can use. Their interest is not so much in their own particular candidate and his or her qualifications as in defeating the groups and individuals who are funding the other side. Those are the real opponents, the ideological enemies. As seen earlier in the fundraising requests, Scott Walker's opponent wasn't Tom Barrett but the "cartel of Madison Liberals, Washington Democrats, and East and West Coast Big Government interests." Tom Barrett's opponent wasn't Scott Walker but "special-interest billionaires like the Koch brothers . . . [and] corporate sponsors at Wisconsin Manufacturers and Commerce."

The funders, both the individuals and the groups, increasingly see themselves as partisans in an ideological war. They get their identity not from their participation in a particular campaign but from their role in that bigger fight. We have become so used to our politics being this way that groups feel compelled to project themselves into a larger war even when one doesn't exist. We saw this in Buffalo County when one outside group declared victory over another in our county board supervisor races, even though neither group played any role in the election. Wisconsin Progress claimed in a fundraising letter, "We beat the Koch brothers in Buffalo and Trempealeau counties, electing progressive county boards that put an end to unregulated frac sand mining." When board members were asked about any involvement by Wisconsin Progress in their campaigns, only two recalled any contact. The executive director of Wisconsin Progress was present at two meetings they attended. That was the extent of campaign activity by Wisconsin Progress in Buffalo County. There was no activity at all by the Koch brothers. And subsequent to the election, the county board didn't change any frac sand regulations. But the significance of the letter lies not so much in its reinvention of reality as in the fact that the reinvention mirrors much of what politics has become: a fight between centrally organized competing ideologies, good and evil personified, fueled by the need for funds to keep the organizations alive and the fight going. As a fundraising letter, it was probably successful.

THE UNDERLYING ASSUMPTION OF THE CAMPAIGNS BASED ON THE STRATEgies used in commercial and corporate advertising and driven by polling and the collection of personal data is that decisions are made individually. Vast resources are poured into compiling huge databases that contain as much personal information as possible on the targeted population: from age, voting history, interests, and occupation to religious affiliation, magazine subscriptions, and anything else for which there is a public record or a private source willing to sell its data. Just as Starbucks can send an ad to the smartphone of a coffee drinker walking within three blocks of its establishment, so campaigns can send messages to single women between the ages of twenty-six and thirty-five who live in selected zip codes, subscribe to upscale women's magazines, and have a hunting license. As one campaign consultant noted, the profession is very near to achieving the "Holy Grail" of being able to send individualized messages to individual voters.

The messages are not intended to persuade or change minds, or to engage voters in a dialogue. Rather, the effort is designed to deliver messages that associate the candidate with ideas and values already held by the target or messages that associate the opponent with fears and prejudices of the target. As one consultant told me, "Much of this is intended to give voice to the doubts that already are in people's heads. They don't think about politics that much, and so we use poll-tested lines that we know they already have some belief in and parrot them back to them. And they become truth in their minds." Commercial advertising has followed this formula for decades. The difference today is that the databases are much more robust, the amount of information known about each individual is much greater, and the communication techniques are more grounded in scientific studies of learning and perception.

This conceptualization of the campaign also drives how candidates are told to spend their time. Even when the candidate sets out to meet the public, not much of the public is included, and the give and take of conversation is frowned on. All the emphasis is on maximizing the number of voter contacts and adding information to the database. The candidate is told by keepers of the database, "Here's a walk list of doors to knock on; don't waste time on those who vote the same way in every election or on those who didn't vote in the last election. Don't spend more than thirty seconds at a door, keep moving. When you get done with your walk list, start phoning the donor list to raise money to pay for media. At the end of the day, send in your report with the number of doors you knocked on and the number of phone calls you made." Those are the metrics that rule your life for the months of your campaign.

There is an alternative way to conceive of campaigns, one that is easier to run with local resources. That is to think of the election as a decision made by a community, not by individuals isolated from each other who respond only to their own values and beliefs. The campaign becomes a dialogue between the candidate and members of a community about the community's values and goals. Not only does this approach result in more a civilized campaign there is also much communication theory to support its effectiveness.

Kathleen's campaigns from the beginning were based not on maximizing the number of voter contacts but on maximizing the number of *quality* voter contacts. Five minutes of conversation on a front porch was thought to be better than ten introductions and a hasty goodbye, an hour and a half of dialogue with thirty people at a house party better than ninety phone calls. The thinking was that a quality contact was much more likely to result in conversation by that person with their friends and neighbors and produce ongoing ripple effects—multiplying the candidate's efforts long after the candidate has moved on to other places. The campaign's focus was on creating as many concentric, growing ripples of conversation as possible in the community.

The approach reflects the communication theory that ideas spread in a two-step process. Ideas are first adopted by opinion leaders, who then pass them on to others. The Rand Corporation found in an experiment on energy usage in Los Angeles that the only message that actually got people to change their usage practices was, "Your neighbors are doing it." Corporations, advertisers, bloggers, hucksters of all kinds work for all the "likes" they can get to help spread their presence through cyberspace, one circle of friends at a time.

The campaign becomes centered on communities. The question changes from how to appeal to a specific demographic, like single women between twenty-six and thirty-five who read *Cosmo* and hunt, to how to increase your vote by twenty in Alma Center, by four in Bluff Siding, and by fifty in the third ward in Eau Claire. The emphasis shifts from appealing to individual beliefs and prejudices to addressing community concerns. The electorate is not seen as being segmented by race, religion, gender, age, education, and wealth but as being grouped in communities that have community interests.

The other usual way of thinking about voters is that they exist on a continuum from conservative to liberal and elections are won by winning the "moderates" in the middle. This conception affects everything about a campaign. Contact is limited to those who voted in previous, similar elections. Talking with non-voters is a waste of time. Turnout is assumed to be fixed. The campaign focuses on winning the 5 percent or so of undecided voters in the middle, either by moderating the candidate's own earlier positions or characterizing the opposition as too extreme. Both approaches run the risk of failing the "genuine" test.

An alternative way is to think about voters as existing on a continuum from "completely engaged" at one end to "I don't give a damn" at the other. With this thinking, the campaign becomes focused on moving voters from being less engaged to becoming more engaged, from being regular voters to helping in the campaign or putting up yard signs, from voting occasionally to voting in every election, from not voting at all to voting this once. The target audience goes from the 5 percent of voters who are undecided to the 50 percent or so of adults who don't vote.

The campaign faced with the task of motivating people to vote begins to address what matters in people's lives and has to convince them that voting will make a difference to them and the quality of their lives. As the candidate, you have to talk about things that matter. You have to know what you are talking about. You have to be able to talk about what you know in a way that is both understandable and compelling. Talking points and poll-tested pretty words are not enough. You have to make the connections between what people experience every day and the decisions made by their elected officials, building an understanding that the results on Election Day affect what happens to them and their families the other 364 days of the year. The goal is to bring people into a conversation about what their community is going to be like, what their lives are going to be like this year, next year, and the year after.

In some ways this kind of campaign is easier to do; in some ways it is more difficult. The campaign is not dependent on expensive databases and polling. The campaign needs less information about individual voters and more information about policy choices that impact the quality of life in a community. There is less dependence on dollars and more dependence on people willing to organize the neighborhoods in which they live. There is less dependence on media messages and more dependence on personal messages. There is less emphasis on "messaging" and more emphasis on having a message.

The campaign works to establish a physical presence in communities and neighborhoods and create visual evidence of support. The candidate spends time in those communities talking with opinion leaders, holding house parties, and sitting down with the regular morning coffee drinkers at the local café. The most important conversation that takes place in a campaign is the conversation that occurs when the person in the coffee shop or bar turns to the person sitting on the next stool and asks, "What do you know about the senate candidates?" Who are you going to vote for?" The answer that comes back determines the result. The campaign wants to dominate that conversation. The focus is on achieving a *collective* decision in favor of your candidate.

This kind of community-based campaign fits comfortably into a setting where the candidates are recruited by local leaders, the resources for running the campaign come largely from local sources, and the focus of the campaign is building connections. The poll-driven, data-based campaign, on the other hand, has to be the strategy of choice for the committees, consultants, and funders at the center because that is the only kind of campaign they can run from a distance.

We are not going to turn the clock fully back to the days when candidates were selected and campaigns were run locally. The groups and wealthy individuals at the center looking for local candidates are not going to withdraw from politics. But we are not facing an either/or proposition—all controlled from the center or all controlled locally. Candidates with a local base of support who are recruited and funded from the center can resist the pressure to conform. The most common complaint of new legislative candidates in Wisconsin is that the campaign strategies and messages crafted in Madison did not fit them or their districts. But if you are the candidate, you don't have to do what you are told. You don't have to be afraid of saying no. It is a dance from the beginning. You can lead. You can trust your own judgment. You can ignore the fear of failing. Despite the unavoidable conflict and tension, you can know it is coming, you can be ready for it, and you can learn to cope. All of which becomes easier as you build your own base among your own voters and increase your own support structures within your local community.

If the relative bargaining power begins to shift from the center to the local, the question changes, ever so subtly perhaps, from "Will you be *our* candidate?" to "How can we help *you* win?"

5. IT'S A PLAY, AND YOU ARE THE LEAD ACTOR

I CAN STILL HEAR THE ADVICE MY CREATIVE WRITING PROFESSOR GAVE TO the class: "Don't tell your readers something is exciting or beautiful. Create excitement. Show the beauty."

Likewise, politics is not just words. Politics is a play, words embodied in a person acting out a story. The audience comes to understand you and relate to you by what you do as the story unfolds. You can say that you are independent, courageous, or different, but to make the audience believe, you have to *be* independent, *do* something courageous, *act* outside the norm.

The story ties your acts and words together into a narrative that resonates with the audience. In your story, you are the protagonist; your opponent is the antagonist. Your story gives each of you particular characteristics, beliefs, and a role. The curtain goes up and the story begins, weaving events and dialogue together, giving them meaning, and reinforcing who you are and who your opponent is.

But yours isn't the only political play running on Main Street. Your opponent has a play too. The stories are different, the roles assigned to the actors are different, and events are woven together in ways that support a different ending. In your campaign, you want your opponent to act in *your* play, to take on the role assigned in *your* script. You don't want to act in your opponent's play. You want your play to dominate, to be more believable, to tell the story that the voters buy into. The lead actor in the play that resonates more with the audience wins the election.

As many scriptwriters have found, it is not easy to write a play with believable characters, strong dialogue, and a compelling story line. In a campaign play, the scriptwriter can't create a completely imaginary character. The longer the candidate has been on the public stage, the more the scriptwriter is limited in creating a role. As in any play, the dialogue and the characters have to be believable, the suspension of disbelief by the audience has to be maintained, and there is a limit on the number of times that costumes and masks can be changed. Scriptwriters have more latitude with new candidates the audience is seeing for the first time.

The play has to fit. It has to be internally consistent with itself and with the outside world. Most importantly it has to fit the candidate. Although the script can be somewhat fictional, it has to be grounded in reality, building on the background, experience, interests, and skills of the real person running for office. (If the candidate is young, the story is about energy, vitality, and change, not experience, judgment, and reflection.) As on the stage, everything—the costumes, the set, the lighting, the supporting cast, the movements and gestures—contributes to the story and the overall impression left in the minds of the audience. Although it is a play, its effectiveness depends on the characters being genuine, the events appearing real, and everything fitting together.

One of the headlines we used in print pieces during Kathleen's first campaign read, "Not your ordinary politician." The picture we used to go with the message was a black-and-white family photo of Kathleen in her milking clothes and barn boots, Nathan on a tricycle with oversized sunglasses, with Maggie the family dog and calves in the background. The political people thought the photo was terrible. She didn't look "senatorial"—which was precisely the point. They wanted instead to substitute the most typical of political pictures— Kathleen in a suit shaking hands with the governor as they both smile into the camera—but still use the same headline, "Not your ordinary politician."

All of the pictures her opponent used of himself said clearly, "I'm a politician." Even in his candidate-on-farm-talking-to-farmer-with-tractor-in-background picture he was wearing white pants. The presidential campaign pictures of Michael Dukakis in a tank and John Kerry on a bicycle didn't work because they were false and left the two men open to ridicule. Scott Brown, who won Ted Kennedy's Massachusetts senate seat after Kennedy died in office, carried out the "everyman" role successfully, in part by always showing up in a brown farm jacket and driving a pickup truck.

The evening before one election, I listened as Michael Bakalis, the Democratic candidate for Illinois governor, talked with a few friends about the campaign he was just finishing, a campaign that had given him the one opportunity for fulfilling his lifetime ambition. Early in the campaign he had hired two consultants from out-of-state. The script they had written called for him to play a conservative Democrat running to the right of a liberal Republican. It was not a role that he played willingly or well. Looking back over the campaign on that last night, he said with obvious regret, "I went through this whole campaign and never once talked about anything that I was really interested in." The script didn't fit the candidate, and the candidate wasn't a good enough actor to appear genuine in a false role. The next day when the votes came in, he lost.

Dan Walker was a LaSalle Street lawyer, an attorney for large corporations, before deciding to run for governor of Illinois as a Democrat. He had never run for office before and was largely unknown outside of Chicago where the original Mayor Daley then ruled both the city and the state Democratic Parties. Walker began his candidacy by saying that he would neither seek nor accept the endorsement of the Democratic Party. He described himself as a reformer, an independent, opposed to the mayor and the machine. He would make his case directly, he said, to ordinary voters and not to the political bosses. The story line for the primary campaign was David against Goliath, the independent against the boss, the common person against the establishment. The play opened with Walker pulling on jeans, tying a red bandanna around his neck, lacing up a pair of hiking boots, and walking the 425-mile length of the state from Cairo to Rockford, following a winding route that touched every media market. His campaign pollster knew they were ahead when the polls showed that more rural and small-city folk could imagine themselves living next door to the Chicago corporate lawyer with the walking boots and red bandanna than to Paul Simon, his primary opponent, who actually came from Downstate and had lived all his life in a small town.

Simon had been an independent and a reform-minded member of the state legislature for almost twenty years. On the strength of that reputation, he had been elected lieutenant governor as a Democrat in a year the Republican candidate won for governor. But four years later he asked for and received Mayor Daley's support for governor. Throughout the primary against Walker, Simon struggled with his role as the machine candidate. He had always been an independent, but he believed he needed the support of Daley and his organization to have a chance of being elected governor. He went out of his way to avoid offending the mayor, even going so far as to refuse to endorse some of his oldest independent friends who were in primaries of their own against machine candidates. He ran television ads stressing his independence. But that old script didn't fit the new situation. As long as the play was about an independent fighting the machine, Walker was the hero. If independence was important, Walker was the choice. What Simon needed was a whole different play, a play not about being independent, but a play with a story line in which he was the hero for another reason, a play that could compete with Walker's play. Once he settled for competing with Walker for the lead role in a play about independence, he was in danger of losing.

In political campaigns it helps if the candidate in real life resembles the character in the play. It is easier to be genuine. When the real character of the candidate and the character of the play diverge, the candidate is limited to stage appearances and scripted lines. The greater the divergence, the more important it becomes for the candidate to have both the willingness and the ability to be an actor. The incentive and the ability to remake the image of one's self by acting out a drama should not be underestimated. In a media world in which chemical companies transform themselves into stewards of the environment and lumber companies become protectors of forests, actors in real life can become televised presidents. But the script has to be believable. The acting has to be good. The feeling of falseness cannot be allowed to creep in. Voters have consistently demonstrated they will vote for a candidate who is "genuine" even if they disagree on important issues. The genuine candidate produces a feeling of confidence: "You know where he stands." This is why so much negative advertising is aimed at proving the candidate is not what he appears to be. Not that he is wrong, but that he is false and untrustworthy. Character is the issue, not policy. Image is the goal, not substance.

Over the years, many real political television ads have only been sophisticated variations of the fictional ad described in *The Last Hurrah*, written in the mid-1950s at the very beginning of the television era. The candidate is in his living room, "neat sandy hair, large earnest eyes, and a boyish smile[,] . . . Irish setter stretched out sleepily in front of the fireplace[,] . . . on the rear wall . . . a portrait of Pope Pius XII. . . . [Mrs. McCluskey] places the milk and cookies on the coffee table[,] . . . little Valerie . . . toddles over to her father and, in the process of hauling herself up onto her father's knee, seems to get stuck . . . the cute little baby bottom shootin' right up into the camera." One of the funders comments, "Ah, that's grand stuff . . . the little behind is worth a thousand votes. . . . What decent mother could vote against the lovin' father of that little behind? He's a good lad, that McCluskey! A grand family man."

THE BEST PLAYS REFLECT A STRATEGIC PLAN BASED ON ANSWERS TO TWO fundamental political questions: how many votes are needed to win, and where will they come from? With the answers to those questions in hand, you will know the audience for your play. Knowing the audience, you are more likely to craft a story that makes the play successful. When done well, the characters, the story, and the set all mesh in a performance that moves the audience and produces enough votes to win. The strategists for Dan Walker, in planning his campaign for governor, conceded all of the usual primary votes to Simon. Simon was well-known and popular and had the support of all of the county party organizations, and there was no realistic way for Walker to cut into that support. The planners concluded that Walker's only chance to win was to motivate enough new primary voters to double the normal primary turnout. In the play they created, everything they did was designed to attract new voters and increase turnout. They succeeded. Twice the normal number of voters went to the polls, and Walker won by a narrow margin, much to everyone's surprise.

When looking for additional votes needed to win, there are two relatively easy audiences you can appeal to: those who are not strongly partisan but make a habit of voting and have voted for candidates like you in the past, and those who are not in the habit of voting but believe as you do and would vote for you if they could be persuaded to go to the polls. In the first group, you have to persuade the minds attached to feet already headed to the polls. In the second group you have to motivate the feet to get up and go to the polls. Plays created for these two different audiences would be substantially different. Knowing the audience to go after and what strategy to use depends on local voting patterns that don't change much over time.

In Kathleen's first race for the state senate in a nonpresidential off-year election, the statistics for the district made the choice easy. Historically, the larger the turnout, the more likely it was that the Democratic candidate won. Of every four additional voters motivated to go to the polls, three were likely to be Democrats. In some wards the ratio was much higher. At the same time, the percentage of habitual voters not already committed to a particular party was quite small. The strategy of increasing turnout was successful. Although her opponent got two thousand more votes than he did when he had won four years earlier, voter turnout increased by seven thousand. Five thousand of the additional voters cast their ballots for Kathleen, enough to give her the victory. As predicted by the statistics, three of every four additional people who went to the polls voted Democratic. The campaign play was written to energize people who agreed with Democratic Party values. The organizing effort was directed at wards where more than half the Democrats who normally voted in presidential elections did not go to the polls in off-year elections.

Once the audience for the play has been decided, a message has to be crafted. The message should be significant and simple. It should address a primary concern of the audience. It should explain the origin of that concern and point a way forward. In short: this is what you are feeling, this is why you are feeling it, and this is what needs to be done. The candidate becomes identified with the solution to a perceived problem.

In campaign training sessions, however, the emphasis is on "messaging," which shifts attention from the substance of a proposal to goals and values. The techniques recommended by all the consultants are spelled out in the AFL-CIO playbook: emphasize outcomes, appeal to values, keep it simple, and stay on message. "We frame complex and nuanced issues by focusing on one aspect . . . and building our message around that. . . . Deliver your message and stick to your issue frame. . . . Stay on message. Repeat your message."

Using polling data and focus-group results, media consultants told participants in a workshop sponsored by Clean Wisconsin, the oldest and largest environmental organization in the state, what to emphasize, what values to attach policies to, even what specific words to use in talking about and selling environmental programs to policymakers and the public. "Recognize the dominance of economic concerns, and highlight the job-creating benefits of sound energy policies. . . . This is the challenge: connect clean energy with jobs now; show that jobs are blue, white, pink collar jobs; explain these are jobs they can get; push government's role [as a catalyst] to create jobs." How many jobs should be talked about? "How about a thousand? . . . People are not moved by companies hiring less than a hundred. . . . But don't oversell! . . . They do not believe clean energy is the economic engine to create a lot of jobs."

And the specific words to use? "Clean energy jobs not new energy jobs or green jobs. Clean is good, requires accountability." "Reliable" or "renewable" can be included between "clean" and "energy." One should also talk about jobs, not the economy. It is more direct, more concrete.

There is nothing new, secret, or sinister about any of this. The techniques are taught in every advertising 101 class. In politics, as in advertising, they can be used with more or less integrity, with more or less intent to deceive.

The reliance on polling and messaging, however, can work against crafting a significant message and delivering it in a simple way. In Kathleen's first campaign, the issue that everyone wanted to talk with her about was healthcare: the cost of health insurance, the difficulty of getting coverage, and access to care. People had their own stories, and they wanted to know, often in some detail, how things could be fixed and made better and how their circumstances would change under different proposals. They were aware of the complexity—they were not looking for easy answers. The staff working on messaging for the Senate Democratic Campaign Committee didn't want Kathleen to go beyond the poll-tested words: "Reform that would cut costs by 15 percent, cover 98 percent of Wisconsin citizens, and make businesses more competitive."

Those lines took equal billing with other poll-tested language on lower gasoline prices, middle-class tax cuts, landfill fees, mercury in fish, and traditional marriage, all of which the staff included in drafts of direct-mail pieces. The strategy seemed to be, if people agree with it, say it. But there was no narrative that pulled these nuggets together into a coherent story. They were just listed under headline clichés like "Putting Our Families First!," "Fighting to Save Our Farms," "Together We Can Get It Done." Kathleen argued for direct-mail pieces that were solely about healthcare reform, and explained why it was needed and how it could work. During the campaign, she held community forums on healthcare; much of her advertising was about healthcare; most of her press releases were about healthcare. Her opponent countered that it was "unfair" to ask the legislature to fix healthcare. By the end of the campaign, even though she talked occasionally about other issues (primarily education), she was known as the healthcare candidate. She had presented a solution to a significant problem and created an identity that people could relate to. The campaign was a play with a lead character and a coherent message.

Pollsters tend to forget the limitations of their art. The math can be difficult, as some creativity is required to accurately connect results from the sample to the population the pollster is interested in—those who will vote in the election. But it is the art involved in choosing what to ask and how to ask it that separates the better pollsters from the average ones. In looking at poll results, we need to remember that the individuals being polled are only responding to a limited set of questions asked in an artificial setting, and we know nothing about their attitudes toward anything not asked.

In one of Kathleen's races, the pollster selected by the senate campaign committee had put together a series of questions about effective strategies for creating and protecting jobs. He included the usual suspects: cutting business taxes, reducing regulations, investing in infrastructure, developing renewable energy, and providing tax incentives. I wanted him to include "making sure our schools are good and our communities are safe" in the list of possible strategies for improving the local economy.

After several days of back and forth he finally agreed to include a variation of that answer in the poll. It turned out that "good schools and safe communities" topped the poll, five percentage points higher than tax incentives for new businesses, seventeen percentage points higher than reducing taxes on businesses, and twenty-two percentage points higher than reducing government regulation of business—opening up a whole new way of thinking and talking about economic development. If only the original possibilities had been included, the poll results would have showed that people think tax incentives and reduced taxes are the most effective strategies for creating jobs. Most questions are not asked. We don't notice what is not there to be noticed. Polls don't tell us about the whole of reality. Most polls are put together from the perspective of "accepted wisdom." Often there is little creative thinking that goes into framing the questions.

Polls can also blur the perception of what is important and what is not important. Think of the last time a pollster called you on the phone, making a variety of statements and asking you how strongly you agree or disagree with them. Some of the issues, like landfill fees, you would never think of in your daily life, but standing there in that moment and assessing the statement, you strongly agree with it. Other issues, like healthcare reform, you have given a lot of thought to because they affect your family and your income, and you don't agree or disagree with them as strongly because you know more about the pros and cons. Reading the poll results, the campaign adviser tells the candidate to talk about landfill fees, but you, the voter, want to know what the candidate thinks about healthcare reform. You might agree strongly about landfill fees, but you probably don't care very much about them. In Kathleen's first campaign, landfill fees polled high, but no voter ever brought the issue up in any conversation with her. As a character in the play, the candidate must have a significant message. The play must be about what is important to the audience, something the audience has to deal with every day.

The message has to be simple. That is to say, you must be able to deliver the essence of the message in a simple, declarative sentence. True, you will have to spell out reasons and results in longer explanations, but these are only expansions of the simple, essential thought. You should have a three-second version of the message (the time it takes to glance at a direct-mail piece before tossing it in the wastepaper basket), a fifteen-second version (time for a press conference sound-bite), a thirty-second version (time for a radio or television commercial), a five-minute version (time for a stump speech), and a full version (for house parties, policy junkies, experts, and editorial boards). The simple version makes it easier to focus the longer versions.

Most people will hear and remember very little of what you say. They will come away with a general impression of what kind of person you are and what you are interested in. It is the impression that lasts, not the memory of anything particular that you said. Kathleen became the healthcare-reform candidate who was knowledgeable, worked hard, and did her homework. I remember a friend who came up to me one day when I was a representative, smiling and congratulatory. "You were great on television last night," she said. "You made a lot of sense." I hadn't seen the news and wanted to know what the station had chosen to show of what I had said, so I asked, "What did they have me saying?" My friend tried to but couldn't articulate a response, and she started to become embarrassed. I rescued her from the conversation, but the exchange intrigued me. For the rest of the time I was in office, whenever anyone told me they had seen me on television, I asked them what I had said. No one was ever able to tell me.

One of the purposes of the story of the play is to give meaning to what people are experiencing by linking the random events and facts of life together in such a way that it explains why things are the way they are and points to how they can be made better. People feel the hurt of not having a job or not having health insurance. The story tells them why they don't have a job or health insurance. Government has gotten too large, taxes are too high, regulations are too strict, and private-sector initiative has been stifled so much that the economy no longer works to provide what is needed. Or, alternatively, they don't have a job and they don't have health insurance because the private sector has run amok, with Wall Street firms sinking the financial system with speculative fever and insurance firms making huge profits by refusing to write health policies for those who need it the most. Or some other story. But the facts are the same: no job, no health insurance. The stories by which we understand the facts are entirely different. We can't address the facts without a story. We have to understand why there is no job and no health insurance before we can craft a solution that will create the job or produce the health insurance. If the story is false, the solution we choose will not be effective.

So the story told by the play provides both an understanding of the issue and a direction for taking action. The play that resonates with the audience, that connects best with what people are experiencing and provides a reasonable way forward, wins. The crucial element in all of this is getting people to accept your definition of the problem. If your definition of the problem dominates, the solution that you want naturally follows. Once your opponent says "yes" to the problem as you have defined it, it is difficult to say "no" to the obvious solution. "Yes—but . . ." is not a winning slogan.

In the 1960s and 1970s the problem was largely defined by the Democratic story of opportunity, or lack thereof. As the narrative went, everyone should have the opportunity to go to college, the poor should have decent housing, seniors should have healthcare, the unemployed should have access to job training, and blacks, women, and the disabled should be able to participate as they chose in every activity. The Republican position was one of "Yes— but . . ." Yes there is the problem of inequality and lack of opportunity, but we shouldn't go so far or spend so much. Medicare, Medicaid, the War on Poverty, and Pell Grants for college students all passed and became law. Opportunity all across the population spectrum expanded.

Around 1980 the Republicans began redefining the problem as one of high taxes: a story that over the last several decades has become the generally accepted definition of what is wrong. The Democrats moved to the "Yes—but . . ." position. Yes, taxes are too high, but we shouldn't cut them so much (particularly on the wealthy); tax cuts should go to the middle class; or tax cuts should be targeted to selected industries to maximize growth. Over the years, few proposed tax cuts at any level have been defeated, and tax cutting continues apace. With government revenues declining, the War on Poverty has disappeared, Medicare and Medicaid are poised for severe surgery, and Pell Grants cover less and less of college tuition. The programs that Republicans couldn't defeat when the old story about opportunity dominated are now being whittled away. The new story about taxes has changed our way of looking at things, changed the prescribed cure, and changed the result. The stories we tell each other both reflect and change the way we think. This *New York Times* observation after one of the presidential debates should not be surprising: "The two parties do not just disagree on solutions to domestic and foreign policy issues, they do not even agree on what the issues are."

THE MOST EFFECTIVE PLAYS ARE THOSE IN WHICH THE CHARACTERS EMBODY the message and actions carry the story. Demonstrations and symbolic acts can be powerful. Young blacks sitting in at all-white drugstore soda fountains changed the face of the South. Gandhi leading a march to the sea to make salt effectively brought an end to the British Empire. The fourteen Wisconsin senators who left the state to prevent a vote on a bill to end public-sector collective bargaining reenergized a political movement.

One can't always write such dramatic scripts or produce such powerful visuals, but the aim is always to combine the person, the message, and the action into a single story. This is why the place where a message is delivered and the visuals that go with it are as important as the details of the message itself. If the adage "A picture is worth a thousand words" is true, then the visual in a 30-second television ad that has no more than 150 words, is 85 percent of the message. We remember George Bush on the aircraft carrier under the sign "Mission Accomplished." Who remembers the words he spoke? Would we remember anything if he had said those same words in the White House briefing room?

The campaign's play is not the only one out on the public stage. The opposition campaign has its own play. The media, think tanks, pundits, bloggers, commentators of all kinds have their stories of what the campaign is about. Everything you do, everything your opponent does, is interpreted and explained through the stories they tell. You win when your story dominates, when your story resonates most with the audience. You do everything you can to stay within your story, to stay out of your opponent's story, and to lure your opponent out of his story and into your story. When questions are asked that reflect a story that is not yours, you reframe the question in a way that allows the answer to fit your story. You stay on your own message, you talk about what you want to talk about, you refuse to be diverted.

You stay in control of your own story by limiting the possibilities for the media and others to create a different story out of what you do or say. As a candidate and as governor, Dan Walker was a master of the practice. His printed news statements were always brief. They contained only the single point he and his media advisors wanted on the evening news. The reporters were never given an opportunity to choose what was going to be covered. If they were going to cover Walker at all, their stories had to carry the message he wanted them to carry. At the news conference, Walker read the statement and answered questions; but regardless of what reporters asked, Walker's answer always made the point of the day. He was very disciplined. He always followed the script.

Adlai Stevenson III, who ran for Illinois governor against Jim Thompson in 1982, was the opposite. He prided himself on being candid and having the integrity to give real answers to whatever questions were asked. His reason for calling a news conference and the point he wanted to make there, however, were often buried in the subsequent news stories. Reporters naturally gave primary coverage to the answers he gave to *their* questions, which were usually not related at all to the issue he originally addressed. Issue development in the campaign was driven by the random sequence of questions that popped into the minds of reporters or were planted there by the opposition. As a result, the story line in his play wandered, and Stevenson lost the election. It is not easy to be both genuine and follow the script.

Staging your play has become more difficult now that the audience has started to fragment and gravitate to media outlets more intent on making your play a part of their play than in providing a relatively impartial stage. More voters view your play through an ideological prism over which you have no influence. In addition to media becoming more ideological and more strident, more attention is given to the sensational and outrageous. When a fan disrupts a sporting event by running onto the field, reporters turn the cameras away from the bad behavior. In response to the same dynamic in politics, political reporters rush to capture every antic. Not surprisingly, bad behavior increases as candidates adapt to get coverage. News organizations with a smaller audience and less revenue have fewer resources to cover the content of your play, so they limit themselves to the much easier reporting of tactics, who is ahead and behind in the polls, and who is raising the most money. Policy discussion drops into a black hole. Producing a successful play takes ever more ingenuity and creativity.

In the heat of a campaign, it is easy to forget that the audience is the audience. The other campaign is not the audience. It is the audience's reaction to what is being said and done that you want to be sensitive to. Any response to what your opponent says or does, particularly any attack, should be directed to the audience's reaction rather than to the initial attack. If the audience has no reaction, there is no reason to respond. It is always tempting to hit back at your opponent, but you want to do so only if hitting back fits into the play that you are putting on for your audience.

The play should be built around the candidate's strengths, emphasizing the experiences that reflect the experiences of the audience and fit the overall story. Events should be planned that showcase the candidate's talents. Situations in which the candidate is not comfortable and does not perform well should be avoided. If the candidate speaks well and is familiar enough with issues to go beyond canned talking points, then debates, community gatherings, group discussions, and neighborhood coffees should be on the schedule. If the candidate doesn't perform well in those venues, they should be avoided. If the candidate is personable, and does well one-on-one, schedule a lot of door-knocking and shaking hands on Main Street. If the candidate doesn't interact well with people, raise money to buy media to carry the story line.

With the best plays, everything fits together. The script takes into account the personal strengths and interests of the candidate, the political and demographic makeup of the voters in the district, the particular problems that people are struggling with, and the communication tools available to reach the voters. Each candidate is different. Each campaign is different. Each play should be different.

6. POLITICS IS A TEAM SPORT

MANY OF THE SHORTCOMINGS POLITICIANS ARE CHARGED WITH—COMPRO-mising too much, succumbing to pressure, following the party line, selling out to contributors—are rooted in the most fundamental rule of democracy: you have to have majority agreement to make decisions. The game is a game of 51: get 51 percent of the vote, and you win the election; win 51 percent of the legislative races, and you have control; with 49 percent you get nothing. Politics is a team sport. One individual acting alone may get something started, but success depends on reaching out and building a majority. Unlike the lone hero in an old western who rides off to battle the bad guys with nothing except his own ingenuity and skill with a gun, the politician requires a posse to get the job done.

Stepping onto the political playing field for the first time can be daunting as you begin to realize how many other players there already are, players with greater skills and more years of experience than yourself, players who have known each other for a long time, players who all have their own agendas, their own cheerleaders and numerous fans, and who have already formed coalitions among themselves. You want to know which players can help you get to 51; they want to know how you can help them get to 51.

Just getting acquainted with everybody takes time. Finding out what each one wants and how they play the game takes more time. Relationships go in every direction and are always changing as participants jockey for position and influence. Lobbyists and interest groups play an active role in the selection and election of legislative leaders. Interest groups ask the legislative leaders for recommendations on which lobbyists they should hire. Interest groups funnel contributions to candidates through the leaders and recruit influential members from the local community to talk to the candidate about their issues. You begin to realize that even though your future depends on winning the support of local voters, many of those local voters are influenced by out-of-district organizations. The game you have gotten involved in is played in multiple places and on multiple levels.

The local political parties are naturally the first place to go to look for team-mates. The parties have the image of being monolithic, powerful institutions—the *Eau Claire Leader Telegram* called the leaders "party moguls"—but if you go to a local party meeting you find a bunch of friendly, outgoing individuals who like to work in campaigns, who take government and politics seriously, and who share similar views on the economy, government, and social norms. The choice of which party to align yourself with sends the first message to voters: this is the way I think, these are my values, these are my teammates.

For people who identify with a particular party, the party name is enough to get their votes. But the local party organizations, with a few exceptions, don't have the power anymore to deliver enough campaign resources and votes to win. The muscle within each party is now provided by a coalition of interests that over time have aligned themselves under each party's banner. When Kathleen first ran for state senate, she cultivated local party activists and built a grassroots organization of individuals within the district, but the single most important meeting took place in Madison almost a year before the election when she met with the leaders of statewide groups associated with the Democratic Party. As a result of that meeting and several others, she was supported by Progressive Majority, AFSCME People, Wisconsin's Citizens' Action, Wisconsin State AFL-CIO, and the Wisconsin Education Association Council in the Democratic primary. Those endorsements not only helped define who she was but also conveyed the message that she was a strong candidate and capable of persuading others to join her.

In today's politics the messages about first-time candidates typically come from groups associated with the party and not from the party itself. In some states, including Wisconsin, Democratic Party organizations are prevented by their own rules from becoming officially involved in the very primaries that are designed to select the candidates who will represent the party in the general election. In Kathleen's race it was the progressive organizations telling their members that Kathleen was progressive, the unions telling their members that Kathleen was good for workers, consumer groups telling their members that Kathleen was on their side, and the Education Association Council telling teachers that Kathleen was a strong, knowledgeable sup-porter of public schools. There was no message from the Democratic Party to its members telling them that Kathleen was a good Democrat. As a result, candidates and officeholders often feel a tighter kinship with the groups that first supported them than with the party itself.

If you survive the primary, your party gives you the beginnings of a winning team in the general election but also limits where you can go looking for additional teammates to get to the magical 51. If you are running as a Democrat, you have to sound like a Democrat or risk losing Democratic votes. The same holds for Republican candidates. One goes looking for help to get to 51 from those voters who don't identify themselves as belonging to either party and from individuals who don't usually go to the polls, always keeping in mind that it does little good to add some votes at the expense of others. One also starts talking with the leaders of organized groups that actively participate in elections.

BECAUSE WINNERS TAKE OFFICE WITH A SET OF ATTITUDES AND BELIEFS shared by the teammates they campaigned with, all the important decisions are made on Election Day. Taking the oath of office is not a conversion experience. People get it wrong when they characterize legislation as "payback" for campaign support. The candidate alone didn't win, the team won, and the whole team shares in the spoils of victory. There is little difference between those who help win the election and those who help govern. The team members who were active in the campaign remain members of the team after the election.

In 2008 in Wisconsin, when for the first time in many years the governor's office, the Assembly, and the Senate were all controlled by Democrats, the major initiatives were changes sought by the trial lawyers and the teachers' union. In 2010 the governor's office, the Assembly, and the Senate all switched to Republican control, and the major initiatives became repealing what the Democrats had passed and enacting the wish list of Wisconsin Manufacturing and Commerce, the most politically active business group in the state. Governing is an extension of campaigning. The teams don't change at halftime.

Within the team, however, there is an inherent conflict in the roles of members who are public officials charged with representing the public interest and the private members whose only responsibility is to pursue their own interests. Arriving at a partnership in which the different roles of officeholder and supporter are appreciated by both can be difficult. This relationship is similar in many ways to a romantic one. At the beginning we are on our best behavior, we see only what we want to see, and our expectations are high. The wedding night with the election returns is euphoric, but then comes the swearing in, and we begin to live with each other and notice the messy details of what each of us wants and what each of us is willing to give, all of which has to be worked out in public. Reality seldom meets expectations. Disappointment creeps across the threshold. As in any relationship, mutual understanding of a common interest can degenerate into submission and domination.

The tendencies to submit and to dominate are troubling. Something is awry when public officials act as nothing more than cheerleaders for the programs pushed by the private members of their team. We don't want our legislators to be wholly owned subsidiaries of private interest. We don't want the answer I once received from a Republican member of the House when I asked him to vote for one of my bills. He cut the conversation off fairly quickly with, "What does the chamber of commerce say? Whatever they say, that's how I'll vote."

It is not uncommon for members of your team to think your vote belongs to them. Many individuals and organizations who vote, endorse, or donate really do expect you to vote for *all* of their interests *all* of the time. And they can be crass and blunt about expressing that opinion.

One day I was talking with the president of the state AFL-CIO who was standing by the third-floor rail in the capitol rotunda outside the House chamber. A crucial vote in the House of Representatives was being lost because a Democratic member was "defecting," and the president was furious. "Doesn't he know he is ours? We supported him. We put him in there. He can't do that."

Even though Kathleen in her first four-year term disagreed with the trial lawyers on only one of their many issues, they refused to support her campaign for reelection. One previous donor wrote cryptically in response to a fundraising letter, "Can no longer help. Very disappointed with Vinehout."

Groups want to control their issues and become the recognized authority on what is "environmental," what is "feminist," what is "right to life," what are "Second Amendment rights," or what is "campaign reform." By controlling the definition, they control the debate. The goal of each group is to be the keeper of the canon and arbiter of what is heresy. The Sierra Club chooses the votes that determine whether a legislator is 100 percent for the environment or just 60 percent for the environment. The NRA decides what is pro-gun. NARAL defines pro-choice; Right to Life defines pro-life. The Wisconsin Democracy Campaign decides what campaign reform is. If you can attach the label, you don't have to talk about the specifics. The message that goes out against a candidate is not that you disagree with a particular Wisconsin Democracy proposal but that you are against campaign reform.

Your teammates also want to exercise the legislative function of deciding whether, how, and when to make the necessary compromises to solve problems. They don't want their legislators to "freelance" and think and act for themselves. Kathleen, in her first term as senator, was publicly chastised by Wisconsin Planned Parenthood for "turning her back on Wisconsin women" when she proposed a compromise on dispensing contraceptives. That same language in Illinois had been called "a thoughtful solution" by Illinois Planned Parenthood. The Wisconsin organization was not ready to solve the problem, and so it sought to punish those who acted without their sanction. Two years later, when they were ready to solve the problem, they supported the Illinois solution and praised the legislators who voted for it.

Groups have multiple objectives. Not only do they want to achieve policy goals, they also want to expand and strengthen their organization. At times, their decisions on legislation are driven by their organizational goals, and they keep a political fight going in order to energize their members and increase contributions. Legislators who are on the team but want to solve the problem and move on are caught in the middle.

For a legislator, there are rewards and sanctions that come with every vote, and you reflexively begin to weigh costs and benefits. "If I vote with the nurses, will the Medical Society put up a lot of money to beat me in the next election? Will my supporters still contribute if I don't give them the vote they want?" When it is a team sport, the political question is not "What does this law do?" but "Who wants it?" When you choose among ideas, you are also choosing sides. It is the second choice that gets attention. Regardless of the merits of whatever was being discussed, I always found myself deciding between the small banks and the large banks, the unions and the manufacturing association, the doctors and the nurses, the dentists and the denturists, the developers and the environmentalists. It was always tempting to simply side with friends and supporters, because that was easier—it saved the time necessary to study and understand the issue, and I could avoid the anger generated when I had to explain to friends why I thought they were wrong on a particular issue. Saying "no" to your friends is the toughest decision to make.

LEGISLATORS, IN ADDITION TO BEING A PART OF THE TEAMS THEY CAMPAIGN with, become part of a small, select team—the Assembly or Senate caucus made up of fellow members from their own party. Caucus members become tied together by bonds of shared experiences and shared goals, sometimes under extreme pressure that no one who has not been elected can fully appreciate. Walking into a caucus meeting is like walking into an exclusive club with guarded doors. A feeling of importance, exclusiveness, and gravitas takes hold.

The caucus provides a forum for party members to select their leaders, discuss issues, argue, shout at each other, posture, arrive at a party position (or not), and devise strategy. It allows leaders to get collective feedback from members and provides a powerful venue for exerting peer pressure on members reluctant to follow the party line. From the beginning, the caucus impresses on you that you are part of a team. Where you sit, what office you have, what committee assignments you get are all determined by your place within the team and your relationship to the team's leaders.

You vote for the bills sponsored by your fellow caucus members, they vote for yours, and the team wins. The numbers within the caucus are small, and everyone knows everyone else. Every defection is noticed. It is hard to resist a teammate who begs you for a vote with tears in his eyes. It is difficult to be the one vote that defeats a bill sponsored by a friend who has consistently supported you in the things you have asked for. The narrower the margin between the two parties, the greater the pressure to stick together and always support your leaders. More than anything else, party leaders want to be able to count on the votes of their members. Reliability is the most prized political attribute. Reliability is encouraged with rewards and punishments.

The pressure to vote with the caucus is always greater when your party is in the majority. Whichever party wins, it is expected to deliver on its programs. In some states, that can be difficult. Not only do members have different interests and personalities but they come from all parts of the state, and the teams and voters who put them into office can be quite different. Typically the cities are safely Democratic, the suburbs safely Republican, and the rural areas a mixed bag depending largely on history, habit, and early immigrant settlement patterns. Each party carries its own base area, and whichever party carries the more evenly divided, less ideological parts of the state (usually a small city/rural mixture) wins the majority.

Party programs and platforms are typically crafted by the more activist and ideological members who live in strong party enclaves. The party's legislative leaders also typically come from those same areas primarily because they tend to have the most seniority. (It is almost impossible for a member to lose in any subsequent election once they are in office.) But party leaders are faced with a dilemma. In order to gain the majority and be able to pass the party program, they have to win the contested districts where the party ideology is not strong. If newly elected members from contested districts follow the party line, they are in danger of not being reelected, and the party will lose its majority. What is passed this year will only be repealed after the next election when the other party wins back the majority. At the same time, the more activist and ideological voters want to see their party's program passed, and if the leaders don't move on that program, they face the displeasure of their strongest supporters and the danger of being defeated in the next party primary by a more ideologically pure candidate.

Members from swing districts feel the most pressure in the caucus because there is more at stake for them personally; they are much more likely to lose the next election if they vote for everything the party leaders and groups associated with the party want. The pressure on the members from swing districts to support the party doesn't just come from the legislative leaders in the capitol. The pressure also comes from the strong ideological party members who live in their districts, who are probably among their strongest campaign supporters, and who want to savor the fruits of victory—not considering that doing too much can lead to defeat.

In the 2006 and 2008 elections, the four legislative seats in the Eau Claire area that had been held by Republicans were won by Democrats. Of the four new Democratic members, Kathleen was the only one to publicly question the party leaders and break with the caucus position on a few high-profile votes. She was also the only one to win reelection in 2010.

When Kathleen challenged the Democratic leadership for the way the budget was being handled, the press in the district was strongly positive. Among the editorial comments were these: "We applaud Vinehout for standing up to the leaders in the legislature—even those in her own party—to do what is right: represent the people of her district." And this: "Whether you are a Republican or Democrat, you should cheer Vinehout's honesty and support her call for change."

The voters in swing districts tend to expect their legislators to fight "Madison" or "Chicago," resist the blandishments of their leaders, act independently, and above all represent the district. These voters are generally more moderate, more pragmatic, and less ideological. And some of it, because these districts tend to be more rural and distant from the capital, comes from a general distrust of everything urban and a belief that their district gets only the leftovers when state goodies are given out. In Illinois, a member of either party from Downstate can run against Chicago. Being perceived as too friendly to

Chicago is a negative. Similarly, any rural Wisconsin legislator can tap into strong local feelings by running against Milwaukee or Madison.

Barbara Gronemus, a longtime Democratic Assembly member from western Wisconsin, routinely got 70 percent of the vote by cultivating a plainspoken, hell-raising, constituent-serving, bureaucracy-bashing, nonideological image. Her vote could never be counted on by the Democratic leaders. More than once they talked about trying to find someone to oppose her in the Democratic primary, but she could always count on support from the voters in her district. The talk in the local bars was that she was "feisty." It was a good word.

There is a price to pay, however for not being a reliable vote in support of party programs and party leaders. The implication of the message that goes out to party members is not that you disagreed with the party position but that you are not really committed to the party's goals. During a primary campaign after Kathleen voted against the governor's proposal to extend health insurance to low-income families, she was attacked for being "the only Democrat" to vote against the bill. It didn't matter that the program had already failed because it was poorly designed—flaws that Kathleen had pointed out when voting against it. Those details weren't discussed. The message to the party faithful was that she was out of step with the party. The attack—"She isn't one of us"—is simple and lends itself to the thirty-second sound-bite. It is more difficult to explain that a program with a good goal isn't going to work because it is poorly designed and the incentives are wrong.

The legislator who has a strong local team of supporters and his or her own voter base has much more freedom in deciding how to vote at the capitol. When you know you have local support and you are not dependent on centralized groups, you don't have to agree with your leader when he or she says, "Our friends want this." You have the capability of responding, "They are asking for too much." It is a balancing act. It helps, however, if you know there is a local counterweight to the political power from outside the district that can be used against you. Most of the efforts to remove incumbents in primaries are led by "friends" from outside the district who have not gotten everything they wanted. If they know they can't take you out, not only can you be more independent but they will also be less demanding. Local interests will be better served.

Team leadership, team dynamics, and team chemistry are as important in politics as in sports. Sometimes you have to take one for the team, submerging your own welfare, because the goals and success of the team are more important. At the same time, it is only by saying "no" that members of the team can keep the team and its leaders from self-destructive, excessive acts.

The choice of whether to stand with your team or not is difficult. It is most difficult when you are part of the majority and your choice decides whether your team wins or loses. If you are in the minority, there is little effect if you differ from your leaders; the outcome doesn't change. Only when members of the majority go against their party's position is there a different outcome. The pressure within the majority to go along can be intense.

Wittingly—or unwittingly—the media contributes to the pressure by reporting the results of a vote as a win for one leader and a loss for the other. The tactics and the politics are the story, not the policy. So in addition to weighing whether your party's policy is wrong, you have to decide if it is wrong enough to give the opposition a victory and your own team a loss.

For the new member, the arm-twisting by leaders and peer pressure from the caucus is disconcerting and coercive. The leaders themselves, however, are judged not on the basis of how democratic the process is but on their ability to deliver votes. As Mike Madigan, longtime Speaker of the Illinois House, gained power at the beginning of his career, he was affectionately dubbed "the Velvet Hammer" by reporters who were impressed by his command and his ability to deliver results. We don't like arm-twisting, we don't like vote trading, we don't like negotiations behind closed doors. We do like independence, we do want our representatives to stick to their guns. But we also get upset when nothing happens because a majority can't come to an agreement. The lesson for anyone who wants to become known as an effective leader of a winning team is: get your program passed. Whatever you do to achieve that goal will be forgotten. The lesson for members is: show your independence. Get everything you can, then get in line.

In her first term, Kathleen helped to bring together a group of senators and Assembly members from western Wisconsin. Dubbed the "Rural Caucus," they developed a program to help schools and local governments in the more rural parts of the state. They were attacked in both Senate and Assembly Democratic caucuses for being renegades and not team players. At the end, their votes were needed to pass the budget, so even in a year that began with a $6.5 billion deficit they were able to get $100 million more for rural schools and local governments than the governor originally proposed. The leaders found a way to do it because without the Rural Caucus they didn't have the votes for what they wanted.

You have to be careful, however, to not put too high a price on your vote. There may be alternate ways to get to 51, other votes that can be wooed, other teams that can be put together, even temporarily.

At the beginning of my third term in the Illinois House, the Democrats had a one-vote majority, and I figured my one vote gave me enough leverage to change the House rules to reduce the control by leaders over the flow of legislation and give more power to individual members. I assumed that even if I were not joined by any other Democrats in reducing the power of the Democratic Speaker, all the Republicans would vote with me, making a majority and getting the job done. The Speaker sent an emissary: "What are you trying to accomplish? What do you want? Chair of the Appropriations Committee?" I replied that I wanted to change the way the House operated. I wanted a *revolution*. That ended the conversation. The Democratic and Republican leaders got together and agreed on rules that retained the existing prerogatives of leadership. The revolution died. The opportunity to be appointed chair of the Appropriations Committee vanished.

It is easy to feel intimidated by pressure, to believe that if you don't vote with the team today you will be ostracized and marginalized. The fear passes when you begin to realize that there will always be other roll calls, tomorrow and all the days after. As long as your vote is needed, you will be a valued member of the team.

POLICYMAKING IN THE EXECUTIVE BRANCH IS ALSO A TEAM EFFORT, SHARED by agency personnel and the interests that come within the purview of the agency. Almost without exception, agency directors come from, or are recommended by, an affected interest that takes an active part in electing the winning gubernatorial candidate. If a Republican is elected governor, utilities and insurance companies expect a sympathetic friend to be put in charge of regulatory policy and enforcement. If a Democrat is elected governor, consumer groups expect one of their own to be appointed.

Every agency has formal or informal advisory groups, made up of team players, where policies are worked out. No agency official will initiate a significant policy change without their approval. The players for an agency are those interests or individuals who benefit from the dollars that flow through or are subject to regulation by the agency. The players for the Department of Transportation are the highway contractors, the heavy equipment dealers, the highway engineers, the asphalt and concrete companies, the truckers, the railroads, the laborers union, the heavy equipment operators, and the mass transit companies—all the people who benefit from the money being spent.

The players for the Division of Developmental Disabilities are nursing homes, long-term care facilities, rehabilitative workshops, daycare facilities, case coordination agencies, and parent organizations. Only the parent organizations represent the people for whom the programs exist, the "consumers" of the agency. All of the others are "providers," those who get money from the agency to provide services to the consumers. Because it is their business and their full-time livelihood, providers are almost always better organized and have more influence than consumers over policy decisions of an agency.

One director of state developmental disability programs responded this way when I asked about giving individuals with disabilities and their families more influence over planning the assistance they received: "This is a provider-driven system. Providers assume ownership of the money appropriated to provide programs for people with disabilities. They talk about *my* community living arrangements, *my* workshops. We have lost sight that the purpose of programs is to serve the people. . . . How do you create a culture of change? How do you get people to begin to think differently? . . . It can't all be changed at once. It would be defeated from the beginning. . . . Providers and the political process are what is impeding change. The department is not going to take a leadership role. Change has to come from the bottom up. It is only as families begin to make a noise that the legislature will listen. . . . They have ways of putting *me* in the closet if *I* make a noise."

Securing legislative approval of executive policy changes is also a team effort, as those who benefit from the proposed change are recruited to help round up the votes to get it passed. Although the focus is on the governor and the legislative leaders to get their program passed, everyone who benefits becomes part of the process. Responsibility for getting the necessary votes to translate a policy proposal into law is coordinated and shared. Highway contractors, engineers, asphalt manufacturers, heavy equipment dealers and manufacturers, and the unions representing the workers who build highways will be involved with the Department of Transportation and the governor's office in any effort to increase the gasoline tax to build and repair highways. School boards and teachers' unions will play a lead role in any effort to increase funding for education. Physicians, hospitals, nurses, and insurance companies will be recruited to help look for votes on changes in health policy that enhance their position. All of these players are effective because they and their members also played on the teams that elected the legislators from whom they are now looking for votes.

VOTERS DON'T GET THEIR WAY EITHER UNLESS THEY ARE PART OF A TEAM. They have to ask themselves the same questions that candidates and officeholders face. How much am I a member of a team? How much am I an independent? How much of my personal beliefs and goals will I forego to join others in an effort to get to 51? Is it worth getting to 51 if I don't get everything I want?

Political parties are established and hold together when enough members form a majority that collectively meets their desires. Members can depend on each other, and the rewards of this cohesion can be great. Increasingly, however, in politics at all levels, we are inclined to go our own way, acting as individuals and pursuing our own goals. We are impatient with the time and effort required to round up a posse to ride with. The percentage of people who identify themselves as being Democrats or Republicans is the lowest since the 1940s, at the beginning of public polling. Back then, 80 percent attached themselves to a political party. Since then, the percentage of individuals who describe themselves as independent has doubled. The rate of increase has accelerated in recent years, and now there are more independents than either Democrats or Republicans.

The evidence for the decline of the parties is not just in the numbers. When I first ran for office in the 1970s, almost all yard signs, literature, and advertising included the candidate's party identification. One now looks in vain for the words "Democrat" or "Republican" in political advertising and has to intuit the candidate's allegiance by the presence of code words. The seventeen Republican candidates for president in 2016 wrestled constantly over who was more "conservative." None argued they were more "Republican" than the others. On the Democrat side, a self-identified "independent socialist" came close to winning the party's nomination. Bar talk is almost all about the individual qualities of the candidates, not much about the party or policy. "I vote for the individual, not the party," is the common claim.

By their nature, political parties, particularly in a two-party system, are broad coalitions of disparate parts. The forces tugging them apart are as powerful as the forces holding them together. Over time the coalitions form and reform. The Democratic and Republican Parties both had their origins in the 1800s, and each was defined for a long time by the Civil War and its aftermath. In addition to the usual economic and class distinctions between the parties, their current incarnations have their origins in the divisions of the 1960s and 1970s that centered on war, race, sex, gender, and religion.

The Democratic coalition that elected Franklin Roosevelt president four times brought together the "solid South" (reliably and completely Democratic since the restoration to power of the white oligarchy in the years after the Civil War), the urban political machines dominated largely by second- and third-generation European immigrants, and the unions which, over several decades, had successfully organized a third of the workers in the country.

The Republican coalition in the first half of the 1900s included much of the educated and economic "upper class," the commercial and industrial interests, much of the relatively conservative Midwest, "good government" reformers and progressives, and those who still identified with the "Union" and its goals.

The Democratic Party's hold on the South began to loosen in 1948 with the adoption of a civil rights plank in the party's platform and the subsequent candidacy that year of Strom Thurmond, Democratic senator from South Carolina, as the nominee of the breakaway States' Rights Democratic Party. The split widened after the passage of the Voting Rights Act of 1965 by President Lyndon Johnson and a Democratic Congress that brought federal oversight to elections in the South. Richard Nixon's "southern strategy" in 1968, with its emphasis on appealing to white voters in the South, accelerated the shift in southern allegiance from the Democratic Party to the Republican Party—a strategy slowed only temporarily by the candidacy of Jimmy Carter, the peanut farmer from Georgia. As southern white voters became increasingly Republican, African Americans, responding to the same set of events, became increasingly Democratic.

The questioning of traditional values and societal, religious, and political norms resulted generally in the Democratic Party welcoming those on the side of change and the Republican Party embracing the traditionalists. Over time, feminists, the LGBT community, and environmentalists have mostly found their way to the Democratic Party, joining African Americans, Hispanics, and other minority ethnic groups. Members of Christian denominations adhering to traditional theological beliefs have mostly become Republicans. These allegiances are layered on top of the basic economic divide between the two parties, with the Republican Party generally supportive of Capital (a market unhindered by government regulations will produce the best results for the most people) and the Democratic Party generally being supportive of Labor (if left on its own, the market will exploit workers, defraud consumers, and harm the environment).

Both parties struggle to hold together factions more motivated by economics and those more motivated by ideology. Although the Democratic coalition at present seems to be more cohesive than the Republican coalition, both parties struggle to bridge the gulf between the source of their votes and the source of their money. As with all generalizations, there are exceptions, but funders tend to have more interest in putting together a majority and winning, while core party voters tend to want more ideological purity, thinking they have already lost if they compromise too much just to win an election.

It is becoming more common for disappointment to cause former teammates to actively oppose incumbents and try to replace them with friendlier candidates. Incumbents marked for elimination in their own primaries are usually perceived as "not Democratic enough," "not Republican enough," or not sufficiently supportive enough of values and goals important to one or more members of the original team. Environmentalists and women's groups in 2010 successfully replaced a Democratic state senator from Milwaukee because he had voted too often with the power companies and for restrictions on abortions. The Republican leader of the Wisconsin Senate was defeated in the 2006 primary in her suburban district because she wasn't sufficiently opposed to the tax increases included in the Democratic governor's budget.

The decline in influence of the official party teams is reflected in the takeover of party functions by other groups. The Wisconsin Prosperity Network, a coalition of more than a dozen new organizations along with a few older ones, with a proposed budget of $6.4 million, was formed in 2009. As reported by *Capital Newspapers*, the purpose of the network, which would exist outside the Republican Party, was to "recruit candidates for local and state office, mobilize voters on Election Day, use lawsuits to pursue conservative policies in the courts, research public policy issues and fight perceived media bias." The main organizer and fundraiser of the network was the president of the state chapter of Americans for Prosperity, the primary political arm of the Koch brothers.

Capital Newspapers went on to note that "liberal groups like One Wisconsin Now, the Greater Wisconsin Committee and Advancing Wisconsin have been working together in recent years with the liberal group America Votes to coordinate research, independent political ads and voter turnout that benefits Democrats. The effort in Wisconsin is part of the Committee on States, a little known national program to create a political infrastructure in some states to help Democratic candidates at the polls."

In 2015, Citizen Action of Wisconsin started "organizing cooperatives" made up of dues-paying members who pooled their monthly contributions to hire a full-time community organizer. The appeal to participate went to union members, environmental supporters, public education advocates, healthcare consumers, and political activists. The purpose is to advocate for issues and win elections.

When the parties were strong, they brought together teams that were broad enough to both win elections and govern. As they have weakened and split into factions, they are losing the ability to govern. Governing will become even more difficult if political power continues to move away from the parties to more private groups with narrow agendas and few roots in any community.

PUTTING TOGETHER THE VOTES TO GET TO 51 IS MORE DIFFICULT NOW THAN it once was. More voters see themselves as independent and unconnected. In Kathleen's first campaign, one person, even though he acknowledged that he would agree with her 95 percent of the time, was emphatic in saying he wasn't going to vote for her because of one issue he felt strongly about. He thought there should be a better alternative. Maintaining a belief was more important than achieving most of his goals.

We are all becoming more like that individual. We have less sense of community. Increasingly, organized interests and individuals are motivated by a single cause, and they will support candidates who support that cause—or oppose candidates who oppose that cause—without regard for other policy goals. Candidates are left to cobble together their own teams in seeking election. The number and variety of political skills required to put together a team capable of achieving a majority and moving forward have become much greater.

7. YES IS ALWAYS THE RIGHT ANSWER

IT WAS THE DAY BEFORE THE ELECTION FOR CHAIR OF THE COUNTY PARTY organization, and I was on the telephone rechecking commitments. I was concerned about one precinct committeeman in particular with whom I had talked two weeks earlier. We had reached an understanding about how he was going to vote, but I was uneasy enough to double check. The committeeman, an elderly, part-time Baptist preacher, answered the phone. He didn't say anything as I recounted our agreement and asked if it still held. There was a long pause before he answered. "You know that I am a religious man," he said. "And I try to do God's will. I have to talk to Jesus about which of my commitments I'm going to keep."

In politics, *yes* is always the right answer. *Yes*, I understand your problem. *Yes*, I agree with you. *Yes*, I will support you. Say *yes* and you have a happy constituent, a friend, and a supporter. Say *yes* and you are part of the group making policy. *Yes.* The day for delivery may never come; you may never have to talk to Jesus about which commitment you are going to keep.

No is always a wrong answer. *No*, I can't do that. *No*, I don't agree with you. *No*, you can't have my vote. *No* creates friction. *No* puts you in opposition. A *no* today makes an enemy today. A *no* postponed may be a *no* that never needs to be said.

You can only say *no* so many times before you stop getting elected. People don't like to be told *no*. They take it personally. They think they have been singled out for negative treatment while others are favored. They think you are on the other side for political reasons. They get angry. Anger is a much stronger emotion than approval or gratitude. It lasts longer. It is much more likely to motivate a person to take political action. The urge to defeat is always stronger than the urge to support. So the *no*'s have to be given out sparingly.

People say they would rather be dealt with honestly and be told *no* if the answer is *no*, but *no* is too personal, too final, too direct. The anger in reaction to a direct *no* is stronger than the disappointment felt when you don't follow through after a *yes*. The disappointment is tempered by the hope that you might still follow through, that you were sympathetic and may have tried but just weren't able to do it because you got tied up with other things. Even if these things are only imagined, it leaves the impression that your intent was good.

Yes is always the right answer. *Yes* brings support. *Yes* avoids opposition. *Yes* gets things done.

"What do you agree to?" is the central question of legislative politics. *Yes* is the vote that moves things along. The agreements supported by a majority determine what policies will be followed and what actions will be taken. Without enough *yes* votes to make a majority, there is no action, there can be no government.

Coalitions are built when you cooperate with someone else so that both of your goals are achieved. A common ground has to be found, one that is held together by *yes* votes. It is in the nature of things that only *yes* votes can be traded. "I'll vote to solve your problem, if you vote to solve mine," "I'll vote for your project, if you vote for mine," "I'll compromise here, if you compromise there." You can move forward only if both sides say *yes*. Only positive actions can be traded.

Nothing is achieved by trading *no* votes. "I'll vote against your bill if you vote against mine" is a common threat and often occurs, but retaliatory *no* votes lead to deadlock. A *no* vote has no political currency. You make friends and build coalitions with *yes* votes; you make enemies and isolate yourself with *no* votes.

Politics is like economics. You have to bring something to the marketplace that someone else wants in order to get something that you want. You can bring cash, your labor, or a product to the economic market. You bring your *yes* vote to the political market. If you are not willing to use that vote, you might as well stay home.

Walking out through the doors of the House of Representatives on the third floor of the Illinois State Capitol, one sees across the rotunda the high mahogany doors that give entrance to the Senate chambers. Small groups of people stand talking beside the polished brass rail that circles the rotunda. The people are mostly lobbyists, legislators, and staff. The rail is a favorite place to lean against and talk, because you are talking into 160 feet of space where there are no listeners and no microphones. When not working a bill, a lobbyist's favorite pastime is listening to and passing on the latest gossip: what's happening on the big issues, who's got the votes, what's the schedule, who are the possible swing votes and how can they be delivered. The good ones have a keen sense of the character of each individual member, the political history, the personal motivations, and what it takes to change that member's vote. One of the more dismissive appraisals I heard at the brass rail was this: "He is not a player; he always votes *no*."

Vote-trading per se is frowned on. Some legislatures have rules forbidding it. Under Wisconsin law, trading votes on separate pieces of legislation is a Class 1 felony. You can't say, "Vote for my bill, and I will vote for yours." But agreements confined to a single measure or conflicting provisions of different measures are permissible. You can say, "If you agree to my amendment, I will vote for your bill." (Since the Wisconsin tradition is to include everything important in one omnibus "budget" bill, the law in practice is less restrictive than it appears.) Even so, the ban on vote-trading has little practical effect. Human nature and necessity being what they are, an "understanding" of how one is going to vote replaces the outright trade. The result is the same. In a system in which the essential dynamic is adding votes to get to a majority, there are some natural results. More laws are passed. More money is spent. For every additional vote you have to bargain for, one more item is added to the approved list. One can hardly blame legislators for insisting on taking care of their interests, the interests of their constituents, when they are asked for their vote to solve someone else's problems. As voters, we are not going to keep reelecting someone from *our* district to represent *us* if he or she takes care of others but doesn't get anything done for *us*. As taxpayers, we don't tend to be altruistic. We want to make sure that we get "our share" back from Washington or the state's capital. The only leverage that a legislator has to get what her constituents need is her vote. It needs to be used carefully and wisely.

Only those willing to provide the necessary *yes* votes on final passage will have any influence over the contents of a proposed law. There is no reason for the sponsor of a bill to include your ideas unless he picks up your vote in return. If the idea isn't good enough to get your vote, it is not worth it to the sponsor to add your language. In considering whether or not to vote for proposals that you don't like, you are always faced with the choice of continuing to oppose a bad idea that might pass regardless or switch and have the sponsor agree to an amendment that makes the bill " less bad" in return for your *yes* vote. On the other hand, as the sponsor of a bill, you want to keep the language as close as possible to what you really want and still get enough *yes* votes to assure its passage.

Even though *yes* is always the right answer, there is some political advantage to not having your *yes* taken for granted. When the *yes* is not automatically given, it is more earnestly sought—by both sides when an issue is in dispute. The undecided votes are always the focus of attention in political fights.

Even though *yes* is always the right answer, political judgment is required in making the decision when to say *yes*. A *yes* delayed is not a *no*. A *yes* delayed is a *yes* with increased potential trading value, one that is more earnestly sought. A *yes* delayed too long, however, becomes meaningless if there are enough other *yes* votes to make a majority. Nobody is going to trade for a *yes* vote that isn't needed. Political power comes from knowing how to position yourself to be among the final *yes* votes needed for passage.

SINCE *YES* IS ALWAYS THE RIGHT ANSWER, LEGISLATIVE PRACTICE IS STRUCtured in such a way as to maximize the ability to say *yes* to as many groups as possible and reduce the necessity of saying *no* to a minimum. The question commonly asked by legislators in committee hearings and floor debates is, "Is there any opposition?" If there is no expressed opposition, discussion is usually perfunctory and the *yes* vote is almost always unanimous.

When there is opposition expressed by an interested group, the first response is to see if an amendment will remove the opposition. If the sponsor and the opponent can agree on wording that satisfies both, then the amendment is offered and everyone votes *yes*. If a simple amendment that removes the opposition can't be agreed to and significant interests are involved, voting on the bill is delayed and the opposing groups are asked to work out their differences and come back to the legislature with a bill to which everyone can say *yes*. If there is no agreement, particularly on important legislation on which major groups disagree, nothing happens. The bill is held without a vote ever being taken. The dynamics change when the competing interests are each aligned with opposing political parties. Then the majority party may happily pass the agenda of its allies over the objections of the minority party and its allies.

It is a rare legislator who will oppose an agreement negotiated by the affected private interests because the provisions are not "right." When it comes to laws affecting the private sector, most public policy is simply the ratification of decisions that have previously been reached in the private sector. Most of the real legislative work—the discussion of the alternatives, the negotiation of provisions, and the writing of the final language—is done by the lobbyists and lawyers representing the private interests. The legislators wait for the signal that an agreement has been reached and it is okay to vote *yes*.

This was the process followed when the Illinois legislature had to renew the laws governing various healthcare practices. The "practice acts" regulate, among other professions, physicians, physician assistants, nurses, pharmacists, dentists, and optometrists. Each of the practice acts specify who can provide what kind of care, in what settings, and the standards that have to be met. When the practice acts came up for reauthorization, there were serious problems with the availability of healthcare in the state. Medical resources, particularly those needed by pregnant women and newborn babies, were unequally distributed. Many rural physicians had stopped providing obstetric services, forcing some women to travel out of state. Women living in rural areas received less prenatal care, and many rural counties had above-average infant mortality rates.

Although the practice acts play a primary role in determining the quality, cost, and availability of healthcare—issues of primary importance to the public—those issues were not discussed during the yearlong effort to rewrite the practice acts. Agreement on changes, mostly procedural and mostly of internal interest to the professions, was reached in negotiating sessions between the professional associations and the state regulatory agency. There was no public legislative debate. The statement on the floor of the Senate by the sponsor of the bill changing the practice act for physicians was typical and consisted of three sentences: "This is the compromise that was worked out by the various affected interest groups. I believe it addresses the concerns of virtually all those who have been contacting us on this particular bill, and I believe it is a reasonable compromise. I don't think that everybody is totally happy, but I think it is something that all sides can live with and probably will give us a little peace at least on these issues for a year or two."

Those three sentences constituting the total legislative debate on the law governing the delivery of healthcare by physicians capture the politics of the process. Policy is made by the private groups that are affected. Legislators vote *yes* on something that has been agreed to and will leave them in peace at least for a time. The effect on the public is not a concern.

The reauthorization of the Nursing Act presented difficulty to the legislature because the Illinois Nurses Association wanted a significant change that affected the interests of other professional groups and was controversial even among its own members. Parties to the bargaining did not reach an agreement, and as the deadline for action approached, the proposed changes were dropped, and the existing law was reauthorized.

The most controversial proposal by the Illinois Nurses Association was to create two levels of licensed nurses: (1) professional nurses with four years of training who would be granted increased authority to provide health-care, and (2) technical nurses with two years of training who would not be given any increased authority. Licensed practical nurses would be phased out. The groups involved in the discussion and their particular interests included the following.

The Illinois Nurses Association, in addition to creating two levels of li-censed nurses, wanted improved salaries and increased independence for nurses, including authority for professional nurses to develop patient plans independent of doctor's orders.

The community colleges wanted to protect their investment in two-year associate degree nursing programs that resulted (under existing law) in fully licensed nurses.

The Illinois Hospital Association opposed all changes designed to increase the salaries or independence of nurses. Instead, the hospitals wanted to in-crease their own authority over all health professionals and, at the same time, shift liability for bad decisions from themselves to the health professionals.

The Chicago Black Nurses Association wanted to maintain full access to the nursing profession with an investment of two years of training. The association felt that a four-year requirement would disproportionately affect African Americans.

The Illinois Medical Society agreed not to take sides in the minimum entry dispute in exchange for veto power over other provisions in the Nursing Act.

The state regulatory agency wanted standardized regulatory language, enforcement powers, and fines across all the practice acts.

The Illinois Council on Nursing wanted to give nurses more authority over regulating their own profession.

The assistant majority leader of the House of Representatives was assigned the task of working out an agreement on the Nursing Act. She described her goals this way: to negotiate a resolution, to keep the issue from spilling out onto the floor, and to avoid forcing members to choose sides on a "philo-sophical" issue. It was also something of a woman's issue for her. "They [the nurses] should be able to negotiate it out like the other professions." As time ran out after two years, the Nurses Association, facing defeat, gave up on most of what it wanted and settled for a few small changes everyone agreed to. The legislature was not "forced" to choose sides. At no time was it even contemplated that the legislature was the appropriate body to debate the question and make a decision.

As the last part of any agreement, the participants often pledge to oppose all amendments to what has been agreed. You can't come late to the bargaining table. If you want your concerns considered, you have to be part of the discussion from the beginning.

In Wisconsin, the effort to extend the ban on smoking to all public places, including bars, was finally passed when the Tavern League and the groups aligned with Smoke Free Wisconsin unexpectedly worked out a compromise that exempted outdoor additions. As the bill was moving through the legislature, people involved with veterans homes and nursing homes suggested that veterans and seniors who had smoked all of their lives and might be in their last years really should have some place set aside where they could smoke in comfort and with dignity. The veterans and seniors hadn't been part of the negotiations, however, and the amendment to provide a solution for them was voted down. One senator commented after voting *no*, "That was a really good idea. I would have voted for it if there hadn't been an agreement."

In theory, each legislator is elected to represent the public's interest at the bargaining table when the decisions are made. But if issues are kept from the floor and legislators wait to vote *yes* for whatever is decided by the private interests who are at the bargaining table, the public does not get represented. If decisions are negotiated in the private sector and only ratified in the public sector, only those who are big enough and organized enough to claim a place at the negotiating table are represented in the political decision-making process. Those who don't organize themselves are not represented. The unorganized, general community interest (if there is such a thing) is not a part of the discussion.

The public is told repeatedly by legislators and executive officials alike, "If you want to be heard, get organized." The world the legislator sees is one made up of competing interest groups. In that world the legislator plays the role of referee, overseeing the outcome of the contest rather than getting in the middle of the fight and representing the interests of the unorganized public in the negotiations. When *yes* is always the right answer, the legislator wants to be in the mode of listening rather than acting. It then becomes the responsibility of everyone else to take the initiative to be heard. If your interests are not taken into account, it is your fault. You didn't get organized.

It is not easy in practice to represent the unorganized public interest. There is the philosophical problem of knowing what the public interest actually is. There is the practical problem of determining what the specific policy and legislative language should be to achieve that public interest if indeed it were known. (Every group claims that the public will benefit if the group gets what it wants.) Then there is the political problem. Saying *yes* to the unorganized public means saying *no* to the organized private interests. The unorganized public for whom you are saying *yes* will never know that you are trying to support them. The *no*, on the other hand, is said to the organized private interests—they are paying attention, and they *know* you just said *no*, and they are not happy with that *no*.

Most legislative issues receive no publicity. The issues that do get publicity are usually not covered in sufficient detail for the public to determine where its interests lie. The organized interests on the other hand, to whom you have said *no* in your pursuit of the public's interest, have kept track of all of your votes, and come election time they let their members know how you voted on their issues. The legislator never gets to make a case to the members. Usually the members are not given the details but are simply told that their legislator voted 75 percent of the time against family farms, or against dentists, or nurses, or insurance agents, whatever the group is. The message is direct, simple, and clear: he voted *against you.* The legislator who votes with the organized group is endorsed, and the message goes out in organization mailings, "He was with us 90 percent of the time." There is a picture of the legislator shaking hands with the group's leaders, receiving a "best legislator" award, or addressing the group's annual membership meeting. The communication with the membership is always controlled by the group's leaders. Membership lists are never shared. The leaders want the legislator to deal only with them, to say *yes* to them, to agree with what *they* negotiate. A legislator's political problems are minimized when decisions are made in a private-sector negotiating process. *Yes* can then be said with the knowledge that the *yes* will be recognized and rewarded by those to whom it is said.

The legislator who has worked to protect the public interest cannot effectively capitalize on that work in a campaign. All candidates say that they listen to the public. The public, with no way of determining the accuracy of those statements, discounts all of them as self-serving. In the meantime, the legislator who has listened to the organized interests gets the donations to fund campaign messages and benefits from all of the private messages that he or she is "*for us.*"

Long-standing private-sector conflicts finally get solved when the effects spill over and begin to sufficiently inconvenience the general public. The trial lawyers and the doctors are forced to reach an agreement when the size of malpractice premiums results in whole areas of the state being left without obstetric care. The chamber of commerce and the state AFL-CIO are forced to compromise on workers' compensation and unemployment compensation laws when premiums get to the point where businesses are closing and union members are losing jobs. The electric utilities and the electric cooperatives are forced to finally divide territory when competition between them significantly limits economic expansion. In these cases the public sector provides a forum to resolve private differences and gives the stability of law to the agreed solution. The public officials involved want to see the solution negotiated by the interested private parties. The private parties have an incentive to negotiate a solution; there is always a fear, not often realized, that if they do not negotiate a solution themselves, a solution less to their liking might be legislated.

When a problem *has* to be solved and the interest groups directly affected cannot negotiate a solution, or if all potential solutions are politically unpalatable, the common response is to appoint a prestigious commission to study the issue and make recommendations. A commission is another way of structuring a *yes* vote. It has the advantage of bringing to the table the voices of recognized experts who don't have a direct vested interest in the outcome and can pressure the interests to make compromises that they would not make on their own. The appointment of a commission also raises the public profile of an issue. With increased media attention, the interests involved can't be quite as crass in their demands as they might be in a more closed setting. A study commission can be successful, however, only if the commission engages all the interested parties in the process and there is sufficient urgency to force agreement.

The amount of pressure on private groups to negotiate in good faith and give up some of what they want depends on whether there is public perception that something has to be done. Unemployment gets too high. Too many jobs are lost when too many factories close. Medical bills skyrocket and health insurance becomes increasingly unavailable or too expensive. Property taxes become unaffordable. Too many rivers and lakes begin to stink and get slimy. Too many potholes send too many automobiles to the repair shop. The legislative incentive to do something increases when a challenger who gives voice to public dissatisfaction defeats an incumbent and the dissatisfaction was a factor in the outcome.

When *yes* is always the right answer, it pays to ask for what you want. It pays to have a legislative agenda. It pays to be proactive. It pays to plan how to change the law to what you want. The legislature is not going to take it upon itself to imagine a better way of doing things. The legislature listens and responds. It doesn't act on its own. But it is waiting to say *yes*—if there is no opposition.

When *yes* is always the right answer, it is absolutely essential to pay attention to what your competition is asking for. If you don't know that your interests are being harmed by their requests, and if you don't object at the appropriate time and place, those requests will get the ritual *yes*, and you will have to live with the results.

When *yes* is always the right answer, it is essential to have a lobbying presence in the legislature. Without someone keeping track of what is going on all the time and being prepared to advocate for your interests, you will find it difficult to play the political game. Once you establish your presence and sphere of interest, however, you will be routinely consulted and included in the discussion when legislation affecting that sphere is considered. You will have a place at the table.

YES PLAYS MANY ROLES. *YES* IS THE ESSENTIAL INGREDIENT OF SUCCESSFUL politics that allows government to function. *Yes* is a way of avoiding responsibility. *Yes* supports the established order.

8. WHAT DO I KNOW ABOUT THAT?

ONE OF THE FIRST IDEALS THAT A LEGISLATOR HAS TO GIVE UP AFTER TAKING the oath of office is that he or she is always going to know what is in a bill before being asked to vote on it. After a while you develop an instinct on how to vote, but the expectation that potential effects will be clearly stated and fully debated before you are called on to vote will not be realized. Even when the leaders are not trying to manipulate your vote with speed and secrecy, the variety, volume, and complexity of issues make informed decisions difficult.

Being rushed, distracted, entertained, romanced, and lobbied are all parts of the job. There are letters to answer, telephone calls to return, constituents who want to talk with you, organizations that want you to come to their meetings and report on what is happening at the capitol, groups that walk into your office unannounced on their "lobby day" and take up an hour of your time. There are lengthy committee hearings that require attention. Leaders will give you assignments. Innumerable reports will land on your desk. What you are not given is time to study, think and weigh alternatives. Hundred-page amendments will be dropped on your desk only minutes before you have to vote on the contents, and you can never be sure that the explanation provided by the sponsors will be accurate or complete.

The volume of proposed laws is overwhelming. In Illinois, when I was a member of the House, approximately five thousand bills were introduced every session, adding up to a five-foot stack of legal-sized paper printed on both sides. Amendments created a similar stack. If I had been a speed-reader without anything else to do, I could probably have read everything before voting on it. Finding the time to do the necessary homework to figure out what the proposals actually did was almost impossible.

Understanding what a bill does often requires the knowledge of an expert. For example, what do these four comparatively simple proposals that were introduced one session actually do? What problems do they solve? Why are they needed?

- Exempt from the sales tax qualified technological equipment as defined in Section 168(c)(3)(B)(iv) of the Internal Revenue Code that was purchased by a lessor who elected to pay the sales tax based on the gross receipts from leasing the equipment in the state to a lessee for his or her use and not for the purpose of a sublease.
- Increase the threshold share ownership level before a shareholder is considered to be an interested shareholder from 10 to 15 percent.
- Remove the application of the rule against perpetuities to trusts created by an inter vivos instrument and trusts created by will or through the exercise of a testamentary power of appointment where the testator has died.
- Reduce from five to three years the time that a trust fund orga- nized under the Religious and Charitable Risk Pooling Trust Act must be active before it may reorganize into a mutual insurance company or a reciprocal.

Knowing what one is voting on is only part of the job, one that often gets squeezed out as the more immediate political demands—paying attention to all the people who want to talk to you—take up the hours of the day. Your constituents want to tell you what they think, and they want you to listen. They telephone, they write letters, they email. They want a conversation. They want your attention and your time. You also need to initiate contact, talking with those affected by what is being proposed, discussing the poten- tial results, and exploring alternatives. Then there are all the lobbyists who want to tell you their stories and your fellow legislators with whom you have to build relationships.

Social work is part of the job. People ask for help with all kinds of per- sonal problems and problems they are having with public agencies. The cer- emonial part, being present and participating in community events, is also necessary—and can be fun. You have to keep up with what is going on in the state, what the press is reporting. You have to know what the state agencies are doing, how dollars are being spent, which programs are effective, which are in trouble, and the choices that are being made. If you want to see your own projects accomplished, the ones you talked about in the campaign, you need to nurture them with time and attention. The fights, internal debates, and decision-making within your party caucus can sap the energy of even the most enthusiastic. The press always has questions. And the relationships necessary for political effectiveness don't get built in a week. Politics is not a part-time job. As one freshman legislator reported at a chamber of commerce legislative breakfast, "This is the hardest eighty-hour-a-week part-time job I have ever had."

With all the tasks and demands, there is little time left to read the two-hundred-page bill that will be voted on the next day along with forty-five others, much less figure out what the technical language at the bottom of page thirty-six really means.

Enter the lobbyists who want to help you understand. The information they provide, however, is designed to persuade rather than inform. The good ones will find answers to your technical questions or refer you to a knowledgeable source within their industry, but like other players on the political field, most stick to their talking points. They are hired for their political experience, their contacts, and their knowledge of the legislature, not their technical knowledge of the issues. Lobbyists who do have that knowledge, however, can be very helpful.

There is little incentive for a legislator to dig around in the details of complicated bills—or much payback. It cuts into the time you can spend with your constituents. The media won't give you the time or space to report what you find. Your opponents won't like you any better. Even your friends don't want you messing with the details of their bills. They much prefer you to stick to the talking points and leave the details to them. If you don't like their details, they are not reluctant to accuse you of not being their friend any longer.

When our local member of Congress suggested some changes to the payment structure in the Affordable Health Care bill, I got urgent emails to call him because he was wavering in his support and getting ready to jump ship. There was no hint that what was at stake was only a difference of opinion over a detail, and no explanation that would let me make up my own mind about the particulars. When Kathleen didn't support the Clean Energy Jobs Bill because, among other things, it lifted the moratorium on nuclear power plants, she was labeled "anti-environmental" by the environmental groups who had agreed to the bill.

With time constraints and practical politics both working in the same direction, it is much easier to make your decision to vote for or against a bill based on who is for it and who is against it. You dance with those you came with. As the chief lobbyist for the Illinois State Medical Society told me one day, "Discussions with legislators are not very issue oriented. They will say, 'Just tell us what you want, what's your position.' They don't have time to read research papers. Sometimes I send one over for the impact of the headline, but anecdotes work much better than research."

Because so much of the debate over substance is reduced to talking points, there is always the temptation to not bother with substance at all and just rely on talking points. As one leader explained his jobs program to his caucus, "This is about politics, not policy." Words are used to manipulate, not inform. The inheritance tax becomes the death tax. Coal becomes the new clean energy. Oil companies are the instruments of energy independence and national security. Lower corporate taxes and less business regulation come wrapped in the messages of liberty and self-sufficiency. Jobs are currently the ultimate value that all issues are attached to. What you support will create jobs and strengthen the economy. If you are against it, it is a job killer. Even same-sex marriage legislation was predicted to "strengthen the Illinois workforce . . . and boost economic development."

The Video Competition Act in Wisconsin, written to the specifications of AT&T, was described as a bill that would, "increase competition . . . lower prices, make customer service better, . . . facilitate the development of new exciting technologies, . . . and to top it all off, . . . create thousands of good, high-paying jobs across the state as new video providers move in." Not mentioned are any of the actual provisions of the bill, which among other things shifted control from local governments to the state, reduced consumer protections, cut funding for community television, and contained no requirement for the provider to offer service to all residents in a service area.

It is not just the interests and the politicians who embrace "messaging." Much of the media and the "talking heads" don't go any further than David Walker, advocate for fiscal reform, head of the Comeback America Initiative, and former U.S. comptroller general. Warning about the "ticking debt bomb" in a speech in La Crosse, he listed the six values that should underlie the "tough choices" that have to be made—pro-growth, socially equitable, culturally acceptable, mathematically accurate, politically feasible, with bipartisan support. Not a tough choice in sight.

The diversion of attention from the specifics of what is being proposed to values that may or may not be connected make reasoned public discussions and decisions more difficult to achieve. The values—which most people agree with—are not being legislated, but rather specific requirements and standards for which there is much less agreement. Facts become more difficult to ferret out, knowledge harder to achieve for both legislators and the public. The legislator who does know the substance has the problem of convincing a public that has heard only the values messaging.

WITH THE VARIETY AND COMPLEXITY OF ISSUES, UNDERSTANDING THE SUBstance requires effort. For legislators who want to do the work and make it a priority over other demands on their time, digging around in details can pay off in increased influence. Knowledge can be power. But knowledge is never certain. There are competing claims. Experts can disagree. When you don't have personal knowledge of a subject area, even if you read the bill, you can only guess at what it means and what effects it will have. In the fight over lifting the limits on crude oil exports, the major oil companies, who were in favor of doing so, argued that increased exports would lower the price of gasoline. The refining companies, who wanted to keep the limits, argued that *not* exporting would lower the price of gasoline. Both sides had reputable economists to back up their different stories. Every issue comes at you the same way. You study. You learn. You begin to figure things out. But it takes time.

Legislative staff, particularly those who have been around for years and have developed expertise in a subject area, can be of great assistance, but they still may not be a match for the lawyers working for the interests who wrote the language. As the Wisconsin Legislative Council noted at the beginning of its sixty-five-page analysis of the Clean Energy Jobs Bill, "Three statutes that are affected by the bill, the energy efficiency and renewable source programs (s. 196.374, Stats.), renewable portfolio standard (s. 196.378, Stats.), and the statute relating to the review and approval of new nuclear power plants by the Public Service Commission (PSC) (commonly referred to as the 'nuclear moratorium' statute) (s. 196.493, Stats.), are particularly difficult to follow in the bill, due to extensive renumbering of provisions and some reorganization of those statutes."

Even full-time specialists can have difficulty. When AT&T added a two-hundred-page amendment to its original two-hundred-page communication bill, the lobbyist for Sprint told Kathleen, "It took our lawyers two weeks to figure out what AT&T was doing to us."

A couple of times when I was in the House, I tried to convince professors at public universities to get involved in the legislative process and contribute to committee hearings by providing their knowledge and additional background information. It was clear from those discussions that the academic and political worlds don't fit well together. Interests are different. Incentives are different. Professional rewards are different. Even timelines don't mesh. One of the reasons why full-time lobbyists are hired to hang around the capitol is that there are few things less sure and more changeable than legislative hearings. No professor wants to take the time to research an issue and travel to the capitol to testify at a hearing that can be delayed for hours, postponed to another day, or canceled at the last minute. For the legislator, on the other hand, research that takes three weeks to complete isn't useful when the vote is the next day.

In recent years, think tanks have sprouted up all over the political landscape with the intent of providing an academic imprimatur to policy research and program recommendations. Some do better research than others, some are more objective, but all, to at least some degree, select issues, reach conclusions, and publish reports that reflect the interests and biases of their funders.

Using Wisconsin as an example, there are several broadly based think tanks on opposite sides of the philosophical spectrum. The Wisconsin Policy Research Institute advertises itself as "Wisconsin's Free Market Think Tank" and is "guided by the belief that competitive free markets, limited government, private initiative, and personal responsibility are essential to our democratic way of life." Its board of directors comes from Wisconsin corporations. The Institute for Wisconsin's Future does "policy research in the public interest" with a mission "rooted in the belief that an educated and engaged citizenry is key to improving individual outcomes." Its board comes from unions and educators.

Among the many think tanks with more specialized interests, there is the Wisconsin Environment Research and Policy Center, "dedicated to protecting our air, water and open spaces." Its mission is "to investigate problems, craft solutions, educate the public and decision-makers, and help the public make their voices heard." Two analyses of the Clean Energy and Jobs Act, one done by the Policy Research Institute and the other by the Environment Research and Policy Center, came to completely different conclusions as to the potential effects on the Wisconsin economy. It is not surprising that politicians regard the conclusions of think tanks as no more than another form of lobbying. The legislator is left to judge the merits of competing arguments and claims. Quite naturally you choose which reports to believe based on who paid for the report and your confidence in their reliability. You believe what you already thought. You dance with those who brought you.

The dance, however, is sometimes a masked ball, and you don't know who your partner really is. The trial lawyers in both Illinois and Wisconsin funded consumer groups who advocated for trial lawyer–friendly issues. AT&T funded TV4US to collect names and addresses on a petition to support lower cable rates and more competition in the cable industry—a list that was then given to Wisconsin legislators purporting to show popular support for a particular AT&T-sponsored bill. The president of the Gay and Lesbian Alliance Against Defamation supported the merger of AT&T and T-Mobile as being good for gays and lesbians, not bothering to note that AT&T had contributed substantially to the organization. Coca-Cola, maker of sugary drinks linked to obesity, contributed more than $100 million over a five-year period to dietary and health-related groups. Academics are a favorite of interests looking for a mask. The *New York Times* quoted correspondence from the vice president of a public relations firm working for the biotechnology industry to one of the professors he had hired to do research: "Professors, researchers, and scientists have a big white hat in this debate and support in their states, from politicians to producers. . . . Keep it up!" There were times when the professor simply adopted what had been written by the industry as his own conclusion. The source and credibility of the information you are given can be difficult to determine.

ALTHOUGH TALKING POINTS MAKE UP THE SUBSTANCE OF PUBLIC DISCUSsion, debate, and media coverage, the details are at the center of attention for those drafting the language in the back room. The individuals sitting around the table—pens in hand, adding words, scratching out lines—are the ones making the important decisions. They decide what is in, what is out, whose objections are taken care of, whose are not, always keeping in mind a nuanced appraisal of who has the clout to take votes off the board if what they want is not included. When their work is done, the finished product is turned over to the legislature to be passed.

As a legislator, you can only truly develop your own expertise on a few issues. You can insert yourself into the writing of the details on those issues, and you can make a difference, particularly if you have some seniority and have developed a reputation with your colleagues. If you can't influence votes on the floor, however, you won't have influence in the back room.

It doesn't take long for everyone in the capitol to figure you out—what you know, your interests, your habits, your motivations, how reliable you are—and they act accordingly. At the same time, you are making the same assessments about everyone else and deciding who you can believe and who you can't, whose judgment you can trust and whose you can't, who thinks like you do and who doesn't. You begin to rely on the expertise of those you trust when you don't know the details yourself. You can make a quick, somewhat informed judgment on many bills by knowing the origin of the bill, who the sponsor is, who the supporters and opponents are.

Knowledge is a problem for the public as well as for legislators. The devil may be in the details, but details don't get much news coverage from reporters who are attracted to outrageous statements and who are more interested in who is winning the fight than what the fight is about. Major issues are increasingly taken public in commercial media advertising campaigns. Political debate becomes a battle of simple slogans delivered in ten-second sound bites and thirty-second television commercials.

Can details become part of the public discussion? It is impossible with broadcast television and radio and most mainstream newspapers. Public television and radio provide some opportunities to get beyond sound bites. Alternative newspapers will do in-depth stories on issues that interest them. The internet allows anyone to search out everything that anybody knows about any topic—and every variety of opinion that may or may not be based on fact. But, in general, the answer is no.

Are people interested in the details and complex policy discussions? Yes, some are. Probably more than most political consultants believe. This was first impressed on me when I attended a weekend retreat put on by the United Auto Workers for its rank-and-file members. I sat through a three-hour Sunday morning session featuring detailed discussions of arcane issues. The audience was interested and engaged throughout. Coming from a background of listening to sermons that lasted no more than half an hour, I wasn't expecting such attention to rather dull subjects.

I have seen the same interest exhibited in neighborhood coffees during my and Kathleen's campaigns. People who attend are knowledgeable and want very much to discuss not just your goals but also the specifics about how you are going to achieve them. Their questions cover a wide range of topics. They are not hesitant to challenge you. They are reluctant to stop when the time is up. There are few venues, however, for such discussion and interchange in today's political culture, and none that reach a significant segment of the voting public. The legislator who is persuaded by the details and who rejects the simple sound-bites is faced with the task of conveying those details to the public without an effective way of doing so.

YOUR PRIMARY—AND MOST DIFFICULT—TASK AS A LEGISLATOR IS DECIDING state law and policy. The volume and complexity of issues are bewildering. There is no sure source of reliable information. Nobody is satisfied with leaving you alone to make up your own mind. Your leaders will schedule a vote on language you haven't had a chance to read. The rules limit what you can do. The House, however, will still be called to order in five minutes. The gavel will fall whether you are ready or not.

9. THERE OUGHT TO BE A LAW

THERE OUGHT TO BE A LAW: THE WAITRESS, SERVING UP PANCAKES, SAUSAGE, and eggs over easy in the small-town café, was not happy over something that had happened to someone in her extended family. It might have been related to insurance or health. I forget the details of her problem, but the cure she prescribed was familiar: "There ought to be a law..."

Get the government off our backs: The owner of the same café was not happy as she sat down at the table to rest for a minute. She and her husband had run the place for forty years. They had made a living and a life. Theirs was the only place to get coffee or a meal in town. A day earlier, the county health inspector had told them that all their kitchen equipment and prep tables had to be stainless steel, an investment they couldn't support with the current business. The Health Department was enforcing its rules more stringently after a case of food poisoning caused by raw eggs in salad dressing had occurred at a new restaurant in the city. Stainless steel isn't going to keep raw eggs out of salad dressing, but the government was taking action. It didn't matter that the café had never had any problems.

In the conflict between there "ought to be a law" and getting the government "off our backs," there "ought to be a law" is usually the winner. The typical response to tragedy, adversity, or even a simple problem is, *there ought to be a law.* A child on a bicycle without reflectors is killed on a rainy night ... *there ought to be a law.* A driver throws an empty can out of the window ... *there ought to be a law.* Lake Springfield is showing traces of atrazine ... *there ought to be a law.* A six-year-old playing with a gun accidentally kills his four-year-old brother ... *there ought to be a law.* It's the last two minutes of the game and the telephone rings—it's someone calling to sell you something ... *there ought to be a law.* Property tax bills go up 15 percent ... *there ought to be a law.* My liquor-distributing franchise is threatened by consolidation among breweries and distillers . . . *there ought to be a law*. I can't get health insurance . . . *there ought to be a law*. How often have we said it? *There ought to be a law*. When we feel unsafe, wronged, insecure, indignant, or have taken a hit in the pocketbook, our reaction almost invariably is, *there ought to be a law*. That the law might not have any material effect on the problem doesn't matter—*there ought to be a law*. In addition to those who think their particular problems should be solved with a law, there are those who see the law as a way of achieving their own economic or philosophic goals. From them the message also comes, *there ought to be a law*. It is only in the abstract that we think there should be fewer laws.

WHERE DO ALL THE BILLS COME FROM? WHO SITS AROUND THINKING UP ALL this stuff? The answer, if you can find it, is the beginning of wisdom. If you know who wants something, you can start to figure out why they want it, who will be affected, and what some of the results might be. Very few bills originate in the legislature itself. Almost all are brought to the legislature by people who think there should be a new law or changes in existing law.

There are some useful ways of thinking about proposed laws that helped me understand their underlying purpose and the motivation of their sponsors, and to decide whether to vote *yes* or *no* on a particular bill.

The basic assumption about how we all get along together under an organized system of self-government is that government should be limited and individuals should be free. In theory, how this works is relatively simple. State agencies, municipalities, townships, schools, and all other public bodies can do only those things that the legislature says by law that they can do. Individuals (and businesses), on the other hand, are free to do whatever they want, unless the law forbids it. Bills then fall generally into two types: they give specific directions to state agencies and local governments about what they can or must do and how they must do it, or they specifically limit what private individuals and businesses can do. The legislator has to decide what public bodies should do and what individuals and businesses should not do.

In a single two-year session, about three-fourths of the bills introduced in Illinois were government bills and one-fourth affected the private sector.

The limits imposed by law on the private sector tend to be either in the form of *thou shalt not*, or *if you are going to do it, you have to do it this way*. You can't steal, you can't murder, you can't drive drunk, you can't burn leaves, you can't ride in the back of a pickup truck, you can't smoke in restaurants or in airplanes. To practice medicine, you have to be a licensed physician. To fix toilets, you have to be a licensed plumber. To offer consumer credit, you have to provide written disclosure of all finance charges. To start an insurance company, you have to have so much capital. If you hire employees, you can't discriminate on the basis of age, race, or sex. If you discharge waste products into the air or water, you have to remove pollutants to a specified level. If you ride a bicycle, you have to wear a helmet. If you hunt or fish, you have to have a license, and you have to follow the game laws.

Government bills have to do with the way state agencies and local governments are organized and how they function. Most are proposed by the agencies and governments themselves and involve problem-solving or housekeeping issues that exist because the law doesn't specifically authorize the actions officials want to take. Examples from the Illinois legislative session alluded to earlier included the following: allowing cities and counties to regulate parking in commercial or industrial parking areas under contract with the owners; requiring applicants for a position in a city's fire or police department to be under thirty-five years of age; allowing a particular forest preserve district to sell land within a two-year time period if the land is less than fifteen acres, it contains a structure that is no longer suitable for its original purpose, and the district board approves the sale by a two-thirds vote; and allowing the Animal Disease Laboratory in the Department of Agriculture to charge and collect fees for analysis of nonagriculture samples. About 60 percent of the government bills concerned state agencies, about 40 percent affected local governments. The areas that generated the most bills were the courts and prisons, taxes and spending, employee pensions, and education.

Although most of the government bills in any session have to do with the details of running agency programs, some address broader policy questions, such as how to ensure a good education, provide affordable healthcare, keep the environment clean, or maintain high employment levels—all concerns that raise the fundamental question about the proper role of government and the appropriate relationship between the public and private sectors. What activities should be completely public? What activities should be paid for publicly but carried out privately? What activities should be left to the private sector?

Of the private sector bills introduced that session, about 80 percent affected actions by business; 20 percent affected actions by individuals. Most of the individual bills involved traffic regulations (cell phones in automobiles have to be usable without hands), family relationships (a sixty-day waiting period is required before marriage unless the applicants for a marriage license have completed a premarital education program), the creation of new crimes (so-licitation of a minor by computer), or the imposition of new responsibilities (a private swimming pool must be enclosed with a forty-two-inch-high fence; an unconfined cat has to have a rabies shot).

The business bills dealt with how a business should interact with customers (a bank can't foreclose on a mortgage without appropriate notice; a barber has to wear protective gloves), with employees (pay can't be withheld; unions can't be excluded), with the community at large (the site for a factory must be appropriately zoned), and with actual or potential competitors (realtors can't write land contracts; banks can't sell insurance; nurses and pharmacists can't write prescriptions).

Consumer groups have long fought for government assistance for consumers in the marketplace, particularly against fraud. The industries impacted by consumer-protection bills reflect the areas in which consumers have the least bargaining power and feel the most insecure. (In a recent year, one-fourth of the business-related bills had to do with healthcare, and another quarter dealt with utilities, insurance, and financial institutions.) Consumer bills typically impose quality and safety standards on products and disclosure and fairness requirements on the practices of sellers.

Consumers need government help, the rationale goes, because in a centralized, impersonal market increasingly dominated by large entities run by people in faraway locations, there is little incentive for a business to treat customers as individuals. The customer has little recourse when things go wrong. The foreclosure practices of a local bank run by local owners with all local customers will be much different from how Bank of America acted during the last housing crash when it foreclosed on thousands of mortgages that to the bank were merely investment instruments that could be bundled and sold in international financial markets. As the bargaining power of the individual consumer has decreased, pressure for the government to weigh in on the side of the consumer has increased.

The unions have a much longer and more militant history than the consumer groups, and a lot of blood has been shed over the years in the fight over the appropriate relationship between a business and its employees. The fight has always been partly political as each side has sought to use the law to protect and advance its position. Bills dealing with the workplace generally set out the rules that employers and employees must follow in competing for their share of the revenue and benefits that together they produce. Uniform standards are often imposed when labor doesn't have much negotiating strength or when a company would be particularly disadvantaged if competing companies didn't face the same costs.

The relative economic and political strength of business and labor has varied over time, but neither side has been reluctant to use whatever means it had to gain advantage. The ultimate economic weapon of both employers and employees is to withdraw from their mutual relationship that makes production, and therefore wages and profits, possible. Companies can close or move. Employees can strike or quit. In the global economy, capital has become much more mobile than labor. With this increased mobility and the willingness of business to relocate production facilities, the relative economic strength of business has grown while labor's has declined. Businesses have achieved their goals by moving or threatening to move. Unable to compete economically, unions are moving away from economic competition—strikes have become rare—and increasing their political activity. Changes in workplace conditions are being made by law rather than by collective bargaining. Unions have pushed for family leave and higher minimum wage laws. The chamber of commerce has pushed for laws that would dilute the requirement for overtime pay, allow companies to set up worker groups outside the union structure to discuss working conditions, and make it more difficult for union dues to be spent for political purposes.

Environmental laws are a prime example of laws that govern the relationship of business to the community at large—all the residents of the neighborhood. The goal is to ensure that economic activity is carried on in such a way as not to impair the communal quality of life. The political fight here is not between economic contestants over sharing the gains from a mutual economic activity; rather, it is a fight over values, the kind of community residents want, and who will pay the costs of maintaining the agreed-upon standards. The goal generally is to make sure that the environmental effects of an economic activity are taken care of by those who participate in the activity so that the community at large is not burdened by environmental degradation and doesn't have to pay the cost of restoration. The spirit of environmental laws can be summed up by my mother's admonition, "Clean up the mess you made." The economic principle involved is expressed in language that is more erudite: "Maximum efficiency is achieved when all costs are internalized and reflected in the price." Environmental groups are as strong now as they ever have been, and they continue to exert pressure to limit the adverse impact that business activity can have on the aesthetics and living conditions of the community at large. There is general political agreement that the environment should be protected. Both Republicans and Democrats agree that the land, air, and water shouldn't be polluted, but there are continuing battles over what amount of pollution is permissible, what kind of controls should be implemented, what cost is appropriate, and who should pay the cost. Those arguments keep generating legislation.

Bills that affected the relationship of competing businesses to each other in the marketplace were always fascinating. In the abstract, business lauds competition as the engine that makes the economy work, but the reality is that no business or profession likes competition. If the competition can't be beaten, bought, controlled, or diminished by economic means, then the law can be used to minimize competition and protect or increase one's share of the market. These bills that originate from producers almost invariably seek to gain economic power in the market either at the expense of other producers or at the expense of consumers. This can be done by imposing minimum requirements to enter the market, by limiting the number of those who can provide a service, or by requiring that a particular product be used. Although these bills originate with and are supported by producer groups, they are marketed as bills that will benefit consumers—by improving product quality and increasing the professionalism of vendors.

In one year the list of businesses and occupations that asked to be licensed and regulated, thereby making it more difficult for startups to compete, included repairing and remodeling homes, printing checks, leasing employees, interpreting for the deaf, mediating divorces, fitting orthotics and prosthetics, hypnotizing, handling fireworks, repairing roofs, electrical contracting, providing home medical equipment, tattooing, professional designing, real estate appraising, reviewing healthcare utilization, dental hygiene, auctioneering, surgical assistance, and psychological counseling in schools.

The bill requiring all bicycles to have reflector strips originated with 3M Company, manufacturer of the reflective material. Most of the bills requiring the installation of safety equipment on school buses originate with the companies that manufacture and install the equipment. The Illinois Medical Society got a bill passed prohibiting the practice of telemedicine without being licensed under the Illinois Medical Practice Act. The Illinois Education Association wanted a law to prohibit school nurses from exercising instructional judgment or educational evaluation unless they were certified as teachers.

I remember when the manager of the second-largest manufacturing plant in my district invited me to a meeting with their top personnel. The plant, which made tachometers and other metering devices, was facing financial difficulties. Their proposal was simple. Would I sponsor a bill to require all commercial trucks and buses licensed by the state to install tachometers? Their argument was that tachometers would result in improved highway safety and efficient fleet management.

The president of the Family Practice Physicians Association in the county was perfectly frank when I asked him if the physicians would support a bill to license nurse practitioners as a way to provide more medical care in rural areas and the inner city of Chicago. He said, "If we could license nurse practitioners to practice only in the rural areas of the state and in the ghetto areas of Chicago, we would, but you can't license someone to work in only part of the state." He didn't have to add that family doctors didn't want to compete with nurse practitioners for patients in the prosperous areas of the state where physicians tended to locate.

Millions of dollars are often at stake in the fights that pit one group of businesses against another as they all seek advantage in the market. Both sides hire lobbyists to talk to legislators and spend incredible amounts of money on public relations and advertising campaigns to persuade the public to convince their legislators. Often it is unclear who, if anyone, other than the winner of the fight, will gain. Both sides argue, however, that if they win, the public will win.

The bitter struggle over branch banking in Illinois was a classic example. When I was in the legislature, a bank could have only one main office. The big Chicago banks wanted branch offices to expand their business into larger communities around the state and follow their customers moving to the suburbs. Their argument went like this: competition would increase, more banking services would be available, loans would be easier to get, and larger projects could be financed. Banks located in the midsize cities didn't want the Chicago banks moving into their markets, but they did want to put their own branches in the smaller communities that surrounded them. The smaller community banks didn't want branches of any kind, arguing that big banks would only suck money out of the community, make loans for smaller local projects more difficult to get, and give strangers in faraway places decision-making power over the financial future of the community. No matter how I voted, the public would be better served—or not! The two largest international legal publishing conglomerates fought huge fights over the copyright law governing the arrangement and printing of state statutes.

Telecommunications law "reform" has been a brawl in the mud involving AT&T, Sprint, Verizon, long-distance carriers, satellite companies, companies that own local lines, telephone cooperatives, and cable companies.

In the liquor industry, the manufacturers, distributors, and retailers continually fight over how markets and dollars will get divided. An indicator of how much money is at stake: the lobbyists hired by one Illinois distributor to work one bill over one year included a former governor, a former senate president, a former house majority leader, two former federal district attorneys, a former legal counselor to the governor, seven former legislators, and three former legislative staff.

The number of bills seeking to make the marketplace more compatible to one's own interests has increased with the rise in the number of groups that have formed political committees, have hired professional lobbyists, and participate actively in the legislative process. Once established, the political committees, staff, and lobbyists create their own work, ensuring their own survival. Their legislative agendas tend to grow; there is always some problem that needs to be solved, another advantage that can be gained, or some proposed change in the law that needs to be defeated. This story may be apocryphal, but it has the ring of truth: looking for a way to keep his usefulness and maintain employment with his clients, one lobbyist would get a friend of his in the legislature to introduce bills harmful to his clients' interests, making sure that there was always something his clients would want him to work against.

The trial lawyers and the medical society have an ongoing battle over the rules governing malpractice lawsuits and the damages that can be awarded. The labor unions and the manufacturers' association struggle over wages, working conditions, safety requirements, job security, workers' compensation, and unemployment compensation. Dentists and denturists fight over the line dividing what each can do. Banks, savings and loans, credit unions, currency exchanges, insurance companies, brokers, mortgage finance companies, independent insurance agents, real estate agents, and a host of others all have limits to what they can do that need to be defended or expanded depending on the year and political conditions. The select few who hold casino licenses fight any effort to expand the number of casinos.

As more groups get into the game to increase their advantage in the marketplace, it becomes necessary for others to join to defend themselves. Human nature being what it is, defense quickly morphs into offense.

THE GOVERNMENT BILLS AND THE PRIVATE-SECTOR BILLS MAKE UP MUCH of the legislative workload, but they usually don't get the media attention paid to the smaller number of bills dealing with politics, cultural values, and the hot topics of the day.

Since the vote is the unit of power in a democracy, the contested political bills are related in some way to elections and the election process, changing the rules to give advantage to one party or the other, or to the two major parties at the expense of new parties and independent candidates. Every election bill, whether it changes the requirements for voter registration, the hours that polls are open, voting procedures, getting questions on the ballot, becoming a candidate, fundraising, spending limits, financial reporting, reapportionment, or who gets to vote, gives advantage to one party and takes it from the other. The political bills often occupy center stage in a public production with high dramatic values, since the political life or death of at least some of the players hangs in the balance.

The deep split in the electorate over cultural values also generates high-profile bills that mix politics, religion, and sex together into a potent brew. The fundamental questions of what are the appropriate roles of the individual, the state, and organized religion in determining behavior and establishing norms are continually revisited. With beliefs running as deeply as they do, and Democrats and Republicans generally on opposite sides of the cultural questions, the bills become very partisan. The political parties and private groups play on their members' fears that the other side will prevail, both to raise money for their organizations and to generate votes in the next election. Rhetoric becomes heated, and believers on both sides feel compelled to push the law further in their direction whenever they have a legislative advantage.

The temporary hot topics of the day, by definition, get a lot of attention. There is an ebb and flow to what is hot, and the forces that heat up an issue generally lie outside the legislature. Media attention, events of the day, circumstances, disasters, economic disruption, public anxiety, and insecurity all play a role, and the process is never certain. Legislative response depends on the potential to use the issue to further a political agenda, gain points by solving the problem, or pin blame for the problem on the opposition. Shootings in schoolyards, factory closings, hospital closings, newspaper exposés, deaths from food poisoning, toxic chemical spills, serial killings, rising healthcare costs exacerbated by declining insurance coverage, welfare expenditures, and poor results of public education have all been hot at one time or another, prompting partisan fights over proposed legislation.

The hot topics tend to be treated in one of two ways. Either the political parties use a problem and the proposed solutions to define and differentiate themselves from the other party (in which case the issue becomes controversial and partisan) or everyone climbs on the bandwagon of doing something and the proposed solution passes nearly unanimously. At times, the details of the solution will be fiercely fought over, but the final vote will be nearly unanimous as no one wants their opponent in the next election to charge them with being "for" the problem.

Regardless of the subject or purpose, however, almost all legislation originates from outside the legislature: from executive agencies, local governments, organized groups, economic interests, constituents, and think tanks pursuing their political vision of the way the world ought to be. Identifying the specific source is the first step in discovering the purpose and probable effects—regardless of what the stated purpose is.

WITH AN ANTIGOVERNMENT MOOD IN THE ELECTORATE, WHY DO SO MANY of the bills pass? What is the motivation for legislators to pass what is presented to them?

On one level, the answer is quite simple: that's what legislators do. Legislators make laws. The highlights of a legislative career are the major bills sponsored and passed. An incumbent seeking reelection points to the laws she or he can take credit for. A challenger points out that no major law bears the name of the incumbent. A primary measure of individual success is the number of bills passed; a measure of failure is the lack of any bills passed. At the end of Kathleen's first session, the local media ran a scorecard showing the number of bills each legislator introduced and the number of those passed by the legislature and signed into law by the governor. Several recent Republican presidential candidates, who habitually voted *no* during their terms in Congress, struggled to answer the question, "What have you accomplished?" Every legislator's obituary recounts the important laws he or she sponsored and passed, not the bills that he or she voted against.

On a second level, a legislator cannot acknowledge a problem and be against the proposed solution. It is always the problem that drives the debate. Are you for or against solving the problem? There is little reasoned discussion about the relationship—if any—of the proposed solution to the problem.

That won't work is seldom a compelling argument. *We have to do something* is more persuasive. The legislator who votes against a solution is left open to the charge of being for the problem—even if the solution won't work.

When *there ought to be a law* becomes *there is a law*, why, so often, does so little change?

In part because that is the nature of things. The law follows. The law does not anticipate problems that have not occurred. The law comes along and closes the barn door only after the horse has left. The law can't anticipate where and how the next horse will break out. The law can't cover every eventuality, and those who don't like the law are always looking for and creating new ways to evade its intent. Few catastrophes can be prevented. You can't legislate against stupidity.

In addition, the solutions that pass tend to be simplistic. There are a number of reasons for this. Simple solutions are easy. They are easy to think up. They have intuitive appeal. They don't deal with complexities. They deal with symptoms rather than underlying causes. They don't change anything fundamental; they don't trample on any entrenched toes. They are easy to pass. Health Savings Accounts did as little for healthcare as No Child Left Behind did for schools and DARE did for teenage drug use. On the other hand, solutions that actually change the way things are done are incredibly difficult to pass.

Laws by themselves are largely symbolic. They are only words on paper that will not drive any significant change unless people and resources are assigned to make the law work. There has to be a budget. Where there is money, something real happens: people are hired, contracts are let, offices are rented, computers are bought, plans are made, actions are taken, goals are set and strived for. Where there is no money, there is no action—nothing happens. If you want to kill a program, it is just as effective to cut the funding as it is to repeal the law, and you leave fewer fingerprints at the scene of the crime. The legislator is always tempted to do the symbolic, to pass the law and not worry about whether anything real happens. The legislator running for reelection doesn't have to explain the difference between a law that is symbolic and the allocation of real resources. The law was passed. The problem was solved. It is time to take credit. The bureaucracy is to blame if nothing changes in the real world.

Finding the money to address a problem by taking a significantly different approach usually requires taking money away from existing programs and ending what is not producing the desired results. This stirs up opposition from all those who benefit from the way things are done, and as Machiavelli pointed out a long time ago, changing the usual way of doing things is the most difficult of all political acts.

The classic legislative way of achieving the appearance of moving in a new direction without really changing very much is to include a "hold harmless" clause when creating a new program. There is a new goal, and a new way of allocating money, but no current recipient and no existing program gets a cut in funding. When existing programs are grandfathered in and new programs have to be funded with new dollars, there is little change. Because there is little change, opposition is diminished, if not eliminated.

For years, Illinois law and official state policy required that programs and supports for individuals with disabilities and their families be characterized by "individual choices, empowerment of individuals and families, full community inclusion, and responsive and uniquely tailored [for the individual] supports and services." Few programs, however, were actually designed to provide choice, empowerment, and inclusion. Even though those programs were the ones highlighted in budget summaries and agency annual reports, the actual dollars supporting the new way of doing things was minimal. More than 90 percent of the budgeted dollars went to programs characterized by regimentation, segregation, and group programming. There was no political will to actually change the existing way of doing things by reallocating dollars even though the law and the policy had changed.

The simple solution and the small incremental change are often all that are achievable. To do anything more would require mobilizing public and legislative support, not only for the idea of change and the specifics of the particular proposed change but also for allocating additional real resources (e.g., raising taxes) or taking resources away from already entrenched interests. The existence of a crisis and real effort on the part of lawmakers and others would be necessary to accomplish either. Changing business as usual is not easy, not the least because many people are comfortable with business as usual.

The simple solution tends to address the political problem that arises from a social problem rather than the social problem itself. The political problem is the fear, uncertainty, insecurity, and unhappiness of voters. These emotions can often be addressed without solving the underlying social and economic causes. The social and economic problems are much more difficult to address because there is little public understanding of their dynamics and interconnectedness, little agreement on the appropriate solution, and little patience for the effort necessary to make real change work. People will feel better if they think *something* has been done. In such a setting it is tempting and much easier to increase penalties and build more prisons than it is to make communities safer by building the social, economic, neighborhood, and family structures associated with low crime rates. It is easier to require national tests than to improve teaching skills, provide resources, change dysfunctional administrative structures, attract the best and brightest to the teaching profession, and create parental support for local schools. It is easier to require stainless steel kitchen equipment than to figure out how to keep raw eggs out of salad dressing.

If outcomes are not as good as they could be and the program does not produce the results that are expected, there is often little political pressure to make changes. For the most part, individuals who have neither the resources to complain nor the standing to be heard are the ones most affected. It is the person with disabilities who has to stay in the workshop program when skills are not taught. It is the poor who have to live with the broken fixtures when cheap materials are used in the construction of public housing. It is the criminal on parole or probation who has to go back to jail when their case officer is overworked and becomes negligent. It is the drug addict who goes back to the street when the counseling program is disorganized. It is the patient who suffers when the doctor prescribes the wrong medicine.

Evaluating the quality of programs is difficult. It is not easy to determine whether the cause of failure lies with the design of a program, the execution of a program, or the person the program is designed to help. Our bias is to listen to the providers who run the programs and have little incentive to place the blame for failure on either the design of the program or their own performance. The individuals who have "failed" don't have the time, the resources, or the standing to get organized and therefore are seldom heard. When we place responsibility for failing on the person being helped, we have no reason to tackle the more difficult problems of changing the program if it is not designed well or improving performance if the design is good but the execution is poor.

THERE OUGHT TO BE A LAW TO MAKE LAW-MAKING MORE RATIONAL.

10. MAKE THE RULES, WIN THE GAME

I LEARNED EARLY THAT YOU DON'T HAVE TO CHANGE SOMEONE'S VOTE TO change the result. It is possible to get the result you want by changing the rules. In 1972 I was a member of the Illinois delegation to the Democratic National Convention, and our first task was to elect an additional six at-large delegates. Mayor Richard J. Daley's six candidates lost, coming in seven through twelve, whereupon the state chair announced that the top twelve would be elected and each would be half a delegate with half a vote.

Because getting the number of votes necessary to win by using persuasion can be difficult and time-consuming, those in power are always tempted to control the voting process itself. You don't have to go to the trouble of changing a vote when you control who can vote, what gets to be voted on, how many votes it takes to win, and by whom the votes are counted. With favorable voting rules, winners can institutionalize the power they have gained.

Even small changes can influence the result. When the proposal was made to extend voting hours in Illinois from 6:00 P.M. to 8:00 P.M., Democratic legislators discussed whether the extra two hours would increase Republican votes because Chicago suburban commuters would have time to vote after taking the evening train home. Before the U.S. Supreme Court claimed jurisdiction, the 2000 presidential election hinged on whether the rules in Florida allowed punch-card ballots with "hanging chads" to be counted.

The delegates to the 1787 constitutional convention in Philadelphia knew instinctively that the voting rules they established would directly affect how power would be allocated in the new republic they were creating. The specter of votes being spread equally across the population scared both the small states who feared being dominated by the large states and the aristocrats who feared being overwhelmed by the votes of common people. Their solution was to divide legislative power between two bodies: a House of Representatives, in which votes would be based on population, and a Senate, in which each state would have two votes regardless of population. Representatives would be elected by popular vote. Senators would be selected by the various state legislatures and thus insulated from the demands of common folk. The president was also to be insulated from the common folk, selection resting on the votes of electors appointed in a manner determined by each state's legislature, the number of electors in each state being equal to the state's representatives plus its two senators. (In two of the last five presidential elections, the outcome of the Electoral College vote was different from the popular vote.)

The effect of those rules on where power lies today is seen in these numbers. California, with a population of 37 million, has two votes in the Senate. Wyoming, Montana, North Dakota, and South Dakota, with a combined population of three million, have eight total votes in the Senate. If California's population were spread out in a way that matched the smaller states, they would have forty-four votes in the Senate instead of just two.

The 1787 constitution left it up to the states to decide which individuals would actually have the right to vote in elections—participation was typically limited to white males who owned property. Over time, as others pushed to be included within the meaning of "equal," constitutional amendments were adopted forbidding states to use race, sex, or age (if over eighteen) as a qualification for voting. Poll taxes and literacy tests were outlawed. Even though the allocation of two senators to each state remains in place, they are now elected by popular vote and no longer insulated from the common people.

Even though every citizen over eighteen has the constitutional right to vote, exercising that vote can be made easier or more difficult. Since voting is like riding mass transit—the easier and more convenient you make it, the more people participate—the kind of voting rules you want depends on your calculation of whether winning is more or less probable if more, rather than fewer, voters show up at the polls.

Usually, a larger turnout helps Democrats; a smaller turnout helps Republicans. Democrats want warm sun on Election Day. Rain keeps people home and dampens turnout, helping Republicans. In Kathleen's senate district in western Wisconsin, the vote in nonpresidential years is slightly Democratic. However, in presidential elections when the turnout is larger, the Democratic margin goes up, as seven out of every ten additional voters who go to the polls usually vote Democratic.

Paul Weyrich, one of the fathers of the modern conservative movement, was very clear about not wanting a large turnout in elections. "I don't want everybody to vote . . . our leverage in the elections quite candidly goes up as the voting populace goes down."

It is not surprising then that in states where they hold power, Democrats have passed laws making voting as easy as possible: longer voting hours, fewer and shorter residency requirements, same-day registration, automatic registration, mail-in balloting, few restrictions on early or absentee voting, and minimal identification requirements.

Republicans, on the other hand, have passed laws in states where they are in power to make voting more difficult, particularly by requiring voters to present approved photo identification at the polls before being allowed to vote. In Wisconsin, after the 2010 election in which they took control of the Senate, the Assembly and the governor's office, the Republicans tripled the number of days a voter had to be resident at his or her current address, eliminated absentee voting the weekend before the election, limited the authority and the number of deputies who can register voters, and eliminated the use of witnesses to corroborate a voter's residency, all in addition to requiring a state-issued photo identification card.

In Ohio, where Republicans eliminated early voting the weekend before the election except for members of the military and their families (who tend to vote Republican), the courts threw the provision out, saying that the law could not treat some voters differently from others. In Cleveland, where many African American churchgoers (who typically vote Democratic) often vote after church on the Sunday before the election, turnout that Sunday was greater than normal. As one pastor was quoted in the press, "Many of those who showed up were galvanized by the Republican drive to end weekend voting. When you try to take away something that somebody already owns, then you inspire them to protect it." In Pennsylvania, a Republican legislator was candid about the desired effect of requiring photo identification—it would make the Republican presidential candidate a winner in Pennsylvania.

Those who physically run elections and count votes can also be crucial to determining the result—a fact well understood by the old political machine bosses. Huey Long in Louisiana, Tom Pendergast in Kansas City, Ed Kelley and Richard Daley in Chicago, Big Bill Tweed in New York, Dan O'Connell in Albany, James Michael Curley in Boston, and Ed Crump in Memphis all seemed to know that if their people ran elections and counted the votes, then their candidates had a better chance of winning. Some of their more energetic and creative ward captains reported vote totals that exceeded the number of residents in their wards. As Tweed is quoted by a biographer, "The ballots didn't make the outcome. The counters did." Elections don't end when the polls close; counting the ballots is part of the contest. The fear that the counters will make the outcome underlies the concern many have expressed about modern computer-based voting systems, particularly those systems that don't include a paper trail. Faith in programmers and their programming is fragile. Confidence that those in charge of the election machinery will play "fair" is minimal.

Outright fraud is now rare, but if you are in charge of running the election, there are still simple ways to affect the result. Judges can be helpful, or not, in explaining what documents can be used to verify residency. Not assigning enough voting booths and election clerks to a high-turnout polling place where your opponent is likely to do well slows the process, creates long lines, and reduces the number of votes. In Kathleen's first election, I saw college students walk into the polling place on campus, take one look at the line and a possible two-hour wait, and walk right out again. The lawyers watching the poll for the party were chatting amiably. Things were quiet, no laws were being broken, they saw nothing wrong. The fact that voting was being inhibited by administrative action (rather than force or intimidation) did not register in their minds as a problem. Vigorous complaining brought additional voting booths and clerks. The lines shortened and disappeared. But votes had not been cast.

You can also "make the outcome" by choosing the people eligible to vote in the race you want to win. Elections are tied to place. Everyone who lives within a particular geographical boundary gets to vote for the office defined by the boundary. Everyone within the city limits can vote for mayor. Everyone in a ward can vote for a city council member. Everyone in a senate district can vote for the senator. It is not rocket science to figure out that if you move the boundaries so that the mix of voters inside the boundaries is different, you can get a different result.

Therein lies the art of redistricting. If one knows the voting history of every precinct (people's voting habits don't change very much), then it is relatively easy to change the result by changing the boundaries to include areas that historically vote the way you want and exclude areas that historically vote the way you don't want. The overall strategy is to maximize the number of districts you can win by spreading your strength across more districts while concentrating your opponent's strength within fewer districts. Those who draw the lines win the election.

The city of Eau Claire, in Kathleen's district, generally votes Democratic. Historically, it has been split between two Assembly districts giving Democrats an edge in winning both seats. In the latest redistricting, when the lines were drawn by Republicans, all of Eau Claire was put into one district, giving the Democrats one sure seat but dividing up the voters in such a way as to make the surrounding districts more likely to elect Republicans. In Illinois, Democrats have gained legislative seats over the years by extending Chicago districts out into the suburbs, absorbing Republican voters into reliably Democratic territory.

Even though it is an accepted part of the political game that you can draw boundaries in such a way as to dilute the voting strength of the opposition party, the Voting Rights Act and subsequent court decisions have ruled that boundaries cannot dilute the voting strength of an ethnic or racial group by dividing members of the group among several districts, keeping them a minority in each. Springfield, like other cities with councils elected at-large, had to move to a council elected from wards when a federal judge ruled that electing all council members by citywide vote effectively deprived African American voters from representation of their own choosing. When I lived in Louisville, the members of the city council had to live in the ward they "represented" but were elected by citywide vote, leaving minorities feeling disenfranchised as voters outside their wards could override their preference of who should represent them on the city council.

ALL OF THE RULES THAT GOVERN WHO GETS TO VOTE MATTER. THE RULES that apply to what we get to vote on also matter. When we walk into the polls, our choices are not unlimited. We get to vote only on the choices that are on the ballot in front of us. Political power lies in getting to decide who and what is on that ballot. Who has that power and how broadly that power is shared makes a difference.

Choosing the candidate who will carry the party's label on the ballot is one of the main functions of a political party. For many years, the decision was typically made by party leaders at party conventions held at city, county, state, or national levels depending on the office being filled. Conventions have mostly been replaced by primaries, giving voters the power to choose party candidates. Even though primaries are intended to give "power to the people," not many people participate. Turnout is relatively low, usually less than a fifth of those eligible, as political parties are not held in high regard and the number of people who identify themselves as members of any party is diminishing.

Primaries are in-group events where people of like mind decide who will carry their banner in the general election. But who is part of the group? Answers vary and the rules are more or less restrictive. In some states voters have to be registered members of a party to vote in its primary. In others, like Illinois, voters have to publicly declare which party's primary they are going to vote in when requesting a ballot. In Wisconsin, the voter makes that choice in the privacy of the voting booth. In all cases, however, the voter can vote in only one party's primary at that election. The restrictions placed on who can vote in a party's primary stem from the fear that if voters aligned with one party voted in the other party's primary, they would vote to nominate a weak candidate who could then be more easily defeated in the general election.

The timing of primaries conveys advantage. Early primaries, as in Illinois where primaries historically have been held in February or March, nine months before the November general election, benefit established party organizations whose business is elections. In these instances, petitions for candidates to be on the ballot have to be circulated over the Christmas holidays (something the party professionals are more likely to do), and only the most disciplined and motivated voters are going to brave late-winter slush and snow to go to the polls. By the time most people realize there is an election coming up, the choices that will appear on the ballot have already been finalized.

It is generally easier for candidates of "established" parties to get on the ballot than it is for candidates of new parties. In Illinois it takes a petition signed by twenty-five thousand voters to be recognized as a new party. To maintain continued access to the ballot, a party must get 5 percent of the vote. In Wisconsin, it takes ten thousand signatures to be recognized as a new party and 1 percent of the vote to stay on the ballot for the next election.

Getting on the ballot as an independent candidate is also more difficult. In Illinois, party candidates for most state and local offices can get on the primary ballot with petitions signed by 0.5 percent of their *party's* vote in the previous election. Independent candidates have to have signatures totaling 5 percent of the *total* vote in the previous election. The hurdle is higher for legislative candidates. Party candidates for the legislature need 1 percent of their party's vote in the previous election; independent candidates need *10* percent of the *total* vote. In a typical state representative district, a party candidate needs about 180 signatures to get on the ballot; an independent candidate needs about three thousand. In Wisconsin, independent candidates can get on the general election ballot with the same number of signatures required for party candidates to get on the primary ballot: two thousand for governor and other statewide offices, two hundred for Assembly members.

Independent and third-party candidates are rare in presidential races because, in part, to have a credible chance of winning, they need to qualify to be on the ballot in most of the fifty states, a daunting task as the requirements and timelines are all different.

The rules by which presidential candidates of the major political parties get on the ballot are largely set by the political parties themselves. Delegates to each party's national convention are the ones who get to vote. The number of delegates from each state and the method of selection are set by each party's rules. In the old days, delegates were largely selected by state party leaders, delegates were not necessarily committed to any particular candidate, and the party's choice emerged out of the convention only after a lot of discussion and horse-trading. Today, delegates are chosen in party primaries or caucuses open to average voters, and those delegates are bound by law or party rule to vote at the national convention for the candidate who won the state's primary or caucus.

Democratic Party rules require delegates from each state to be elected from districts that are no larger than congressional districts. Delegates must be allocated to presidential candidates based on the percentage of votes they receive in the district. To get any delegates, however, a candidate has to get at least 15 percent of the vote. Electing delegates at the congressional level potentially gives minorities a greater voice in the party—groups that are a majority in one congressional district may very well be only a small part of a statewide vote.

Republican Party rules are somewhat different. About half the states have some form of winner-takes-all rule. If you come in first, you get all the delegates, regardless of how close the vote totals are. In some states the winner has to get 50 percent of the vote before getting all the delegates. Although many states select delegates at the congressional district level, the national party does not require them to do so.

In the political game, those who don't like the outcome are prone to blaming the rules, expending more effort on "reforming" politics than designing a better game plan or building a stronger team to compete under existing rules. The proposed reforms, which include eliminating the electoral college, reducing the influence of parties, ending winner-take-all, limiting the terms a person can serve, and providing multiple options for casting and counting votes, all have as an intended result the election of a different kind of winner.

In recent presidential elections, the almost total attention focused on the eight to ten states in which the vote was expected to be close has fueled calls for electing the president by national popular vote. Since, with the minor exceptions of Nebraska and Maine, all states have winner-take-all Electoral College voting, it makes sense under the current rules for candidates to spend all their resources winning the few states where the vote will be close. A direct election would require a constitutional amendment, but the same result could be approximated by allocating a state's Electoral College votes on a proportional rather than a winner-take-all basis, or by allocating the votes by congressional district rather than by state. Those changes could be made without a constitutional amendment, as each state can decide by law how its Electoral College votes are apportioned. The outcome of who is elected president could be significantly affected if rules were not substantially the same in all states—particularly if, for example, a group of states allocated their votes on a proportional basis and the rest allocated their votes on a winner-take-all basis.

Since, with only a few exceptions, the results of the national popular vote and the Electoral College vote have been the same, a national vote for president might make little difference to the result, but it would change campaign strategy. Attention and resources would shift from "swing" states to major media markets. There would be more fundraising and fewer personal appearances. There would be less talk about regional and rural concerns and more emphasis on a national advertising campaign. Urban problems would dominate.

A national popular vote might change the result, however, if turnout increases because everyone, regardless of where they live, would feel their vote might make a difference. The increase might be particularly noticeable in urban areas of states in which—under the present rules—the statewide outcome is certain, there is little incentive to vote, and neither party tries to increase turnout. Those voters would be a prime target if the presidency was decided by national popular vote. A vote in New York City, or Los Angeles, or Houston would become just as valuable as a vote in Iowa or Florida or Wisconsin is now.

Other reforms have as a goal the election of more moderate and less partisan candidates. One proposal would eliminate separate party primaries and create in their place a single primary in which all candidates competed, with the top two vote-getters, regardless of party affiliation, moving on to the general election. Proponents of the change believe that with a single primary it is less likely that the two most partisan candidates would make it to the general election, as is now often the case when each party conducts its own primary and voters in each are among that party's truest believers.

Single primaries are commonly used in nonpartisan elections to narrow the field to two candidates, but the system could be used for partisan elections. California has adopted such a system. In the single primary, candidates are identified on the ballot by party, but the race is everybody against everybody, with the top two vote-getters—even if they are of the same party—facing off against each other in the general election. In such a single-primary system, more candidates would probably consider running, and more voters would probably participate. The mix would certainly be different. Depending on how turnout changes, there could very well be an incentive to appeal (as in the general election) to a wider audience than just the base of one's own party. It would also be more difficult, but not impossible, for the partisans of one party to purge their own incumbent for not being "pure" enough. At the very least, a single primary would require new strategies for winning.

Another proposal would eliminate winner-take-all in congressional and state legislative races by creating three-member districts, with the top three vote-getters all being elected. The authors want to broaden representation, arguing that winner-take-all leaves the 49 percent of the voters who voted for the loser without any representation. In a race where the top three candidates win, 25 percent of the vote assures election.

When I served in the Illinois House, we did have multimember districts, with three representatives being elected at-large from each district. There was also "cumulative" voting. Every voter had three votes that could be divided among the candidates in three different ways: three votes to one candidate, one and a half votes each to two candidates, or one vote each to three candidates.

Cumulative voting in a multimember district affected elections in several ways. The first was intraparty rivalry. Usually in competitive districts, two Democrats ran against two Republicans, with three of the four being elected. As a practical matter, then, you were assured of winning if you ran ahead of the other candidate from your party regardless of how you ran compared to your opponents from the other party. Trust was not common—particularly since you could take votes away from your "running mate" by persuading your friends to give you all three of their votes.

Second, there was little incentive to be moderate. You were more likely to be elected with enthusiastic support and three votes from a minority with strong feelings than with more tepid (and split) support from a broader electorate.

Third, since each party was almost guaranteed at least one representative from each district, both parties had to pay attention to all parts of the state. The Republicans could not ignore Chicago because one Republican was elected from each of the largely Democratic Chicago districts. The Democrats could not ignore the suburbs because a Democrat was elected from each of the largely Republican suburban districts. Neither party could be particularly ideological, or focus solely on the problems of one part of the state, and still keep all of its members in line.

Instant runoff voting, in which voters rank their preferences, has also been proposed. The purpose is to give voters the opportunity to vote for the candidate they really like—but who has no chance of winning—and not have to make the harder choice between the likely winners, each of whom has flaws. With instant runoff voting, there are a series of computations. Initially, all of the first choices are counted. Any candidate receiving 50 percent or more is declared the winner. If no candidate receives 50 percent of all first choice votes, the candidate with the lowest total is dropped and his or her votes are distributed to the candidates listed as second choices on those ballots. The process continues until one candidate reaches 50 percent. Instant runoff voting has the potential of allowing new candidates with new ideas to emerge; candidates who might otherwise be dismissed as not being mainstream enough. It might also result in moderate candidates being elected. Extremely partisan candidates, if they don't win with first-choice votes, would not likely be the second choice of many other voters.

THE RULES THAT WE HAVE CONSIDERED SO FAR ALL HAVE TO DO IN SOME way with the votes we cast to elect someone to office. Mr. Smith, however, still has to go to Washington, or Springfield, or Madison, where there are legislative rules that have the same purpose as the election rules: influencing the outcome by governing who gets to vote and what gets to be voted on.

In the legislature, there is always a struggle between leaders and members over how broad the participation will be in making decisions, how open the discussion of issues will be, and how much opportunity there will be to present alternatives. In the democratic ideal, legislative decisions are open agreements, publicly arrived at, with every legislator having equal access to information and full opportunity to participate and influence the outcome. Leaders preside over the proceedings, schedule the debate, facilitate the process, and ensure that the procedural rules are followed. Before decisions are made, public participation is solicited at open hearings where anyone with information or an opinion can present a case. At the end of the deliberative process, the final decision is left to the collective vote of all the legislators.

This democratic ideal of shared power has few champions, however. Leaders are elected to lead, to make decisions, to enforce discipline on their members. Power is attractive and addictive. Power is celebrated by the media and in the culture. Success is defined by the ability to get things done, to make decisions and impose one's will by rounding up votes and winning. Leadership has always been measured by what gets accomplished, not by how fair, how open, or how democratic the decision-making process is under the leader. It is a standard with a long history. As a biographer of Cosimo de' Medici, who ruled Florence from 1434 to 1464, noted, "Above all, the welfare of Florence as a whole was so successfully effected, both in home and foreign affairs, that much could be forgiven regarding measures necessary to maintain Cosimo in power." Or more recently, as Piers Morgan suggested during an interview on CNN the night before the 2012 election, after noting President Obama's perceived timidity during his first term, "It is time to knock some heads together and get something done."

In the effort to exercise his or her own best judgment on how to vote, the legislator struggles with two problems: (1) finding out what the bill really does, and (2) dealing with pressure to vote one way or the other. Of the two, it is easier to deal with the pressure. You know it is there. You can feel it. It is individual and personal. You look within yourself, and you either stand up to it or you don't. You make the deal or you don't. Being able to find out what you are voting on, however, is more difficult and depends on how the legislature is run.

Simple things make a difference. Do bills have to be printed, distributed, and made available to members and the public before a vote is taken or a hearing is held? How much time are you given to read—and try to understand—an amendment or a bill before it can be called for a vote? How much time has to elapse between introduction and final passage of any bill? How much advance notice must be given of committee hearings? How much detail must the notice provide? Are there any limitations on what amendments can be offered? Are there limits on when, how, and by whom amendments can be offered? Is the agenda for the day's business made public? When? How? In what detail? Can conference committees appointed to work out differences between the House and Senate versions of a bill add totally new language on totally new issues? Are conference committee meetings public? How much notice must be given? Do conference committee reports have to be printed before they can be voted on? Can the rules governing these procedures be suspended? How many votes does that take?

There is natural power attached to leadership that affects the outcome regardless of how benignly that power is exercised. There is power in control of the agenda. The Speaker can wait until the votes are lined up before a bill is called. There is power in control of the gavel. The Speaker moves things quickly or slowly, giving advantage to one side or the other. (A slow gavel can stretch the debate out while the last vote is being rounded up. A fast gavel can shut debate down and defeat a bill before the last needed votes for passage are rounded up.) The Speaker chooses which members to recognize during debate, and the order confers advantage. The Speaker determines which motions can be voted on and interprets the rules as they apply to a given situation. There is power in appointment. The Speaker determines the outcome of committee votes by choosing the members appointed to that committee. There is power in the control of the flow of legislation. The Speaker can determine whether a bill passes or dies by choosing the committee to which the bill is assigned for consideration.

In every legislative body there is a tradition of how things are done. Are all members who want to speak routinely recognized? Do members have seniority rights in committee and other assignments, or does the leadership have absolute power to appoint? Are parliamentary rulings by the chair even-handed or commonly made to achieve partisan advantage? How many votes are required to overturn a ruling by the chair? How arbitrary is the assignment of bills to committee? How tightly does the leadership control which bills and amendments can be considered? How routinely are the rules that require publication, advance notice, and time for consideration suspended and bypassed?

When I first went to Springfield as a legislative intern, the legislature was run by a powerful few, and there was little pretense that the process was either open or democratic. Committees held hearings, but there was no notice of when or where they were scheduled, or which bills would be considered. There was no staff, and members had no help in finding out what bills and amendments did or meant. There were no offices for members, only their desks on the House floor, a few phone booths at the back of the chamber, and a pool of secretaries to help with correspondence. The public could testify at hearings, but committee members were regularly absent, leaving instructions ahead of time with the chair on how they wanted to vote, thus making testimony meaningless. Amendments were printed only after they were adopted. There was no notice of the order in which bills would be called for debate. There was a tradition, however, that any member who wanted to speak would be recognized. Any member could offer an amendment to any bill from the floor, and it would be called for a vote. Amendments were adopted by a majority of those voting, both in committees and on the floor.

The intern program I participated in was part of a national Ford Foundation project to increase legislative resources, promote public participation, and improve legislative review of proposed laws. As a result, over the next several years the Illinois legislature provided offices and secretaries for members, as well as staff for leaders and committees. Rules were changed to require notice for committee hearings. Absentee voting in committees was eliminated. Amendments had to be printed and distributed to the desks of all members before they could be called for a vote. A regular order of business was established. But, there was no change to the rules that gave a majority of the members the power to adopt any amendment, pass any bill, discharge any committee, take any bill from the table, amend any rule, suspend any rule, and override any ruling by the chair. If you had 89 votes (of 177) in the House you had enough votes to do anything.

Since then, over the years, the rules of the Illinois House have been changed to give the Speaker complete control over what is considered. All committee amendments, all floor amendments, all conference committee reports, all motions to table committee amendments have to be approved by the Rules Committee before they can be considered either by a committee or by the full House. (A bill or amendment can be removed from the jurisdiction of the Rules Committee only by unanimous consent of the full House or by a written motion signed by three-fifths of the members of both parties, all of whom have to be sponsors of the bill in question.) No ruling by the Speaker relating to motions to take bills away from the Rules Committee can be appealed. The rule covering discharge of the Rules Committee cannot be suspended. The Rules Committee has five members, three appointed by the Speaker, two by the minority leader; all can be removed and replaced at any time, unlike members of other committees. Under these rules, taken together, members get to vote only on bills and amendments that have been approved by the Speaker.

The requirements in the Illinois constitution that laws must be passed with identical language by both House and Senate, that bills must be considered a minimum of three days in each body, that sessions must be open to the public, that bills must be printed and publicly available, and that passage must be by recorded vote all serve to slow the process down, make it more deliberative and more open and accountable to the public. The House and Senate rules that require published agendas and advance notice for hearings serve those same goals.

Secrecy and speed, the universal tools used by leaders of every legislative body to manipulate consent from a membership that is not informed, are difficult to maintain when a bill follows all the steps that it is supposed to take. Speed and secrecy are best achieved by having proposals go through as little of the process as possible. Attaching an amendment on the floor avoids the public hearing that would occur if the amendment were considered in committee. Amending a bill on the floor of the second house effectively by-passes public hearings in both houses. If new language is put into a conference committee report, only an hour or two might pass between the time when the language first surfaces and when it is on its way to the governor's desk to be signed into law.

Conference committees with an equal number of senators and representatives are appointed to agree on common language when a bill has passed both the House and the Senate but there are differences in the details. Conference committee reports incorporating the agreed-upon language are sent directly to the full House and Senate for final passage. The reports can be accepted or rejected; they cannot be amended. When the content of the report relates directly to issues that have had public hearings and been fully debated in both bodies, it serves no purpose for the compromise language to go through the whole legislative process again since the requirements for openness and deliberation have already been met. However, if the conference committee strips the bill of its original language and reports new provisions addressing entirely different issues, then all of the steps required by the constitution and the legislative rules to ensure openness and deliberation are effectively bypassed, as conference committees don't have to follow the procedural and notice requirements that apply to other committees.

There is always pressure toward the end of a legislative session to get things done, to get issues wrapped up, and to adjourn on time. There is a natural tendency to move things along, to shorten or waive notice requirements, and to bypass committee hearings. No member wants to be in session any longer than necessary. When agreements are reached on issues that have been discussed for months, sponsors routinely look for a bill, already near final passage, to which the agreement can be attached as an amendment. The original bill becomes a "vehicle" for the late agreement.

Using vehicle bills is addictive, however. What starts as a search for a bill near final passage to which a last-minute compromise can be attached becomes part of the game plan, a conscious, intentional use of speed and secrecy to achieve leadership goals. Noncontroversial bills that do little or nothing are introduced specifically so that they can be used late in the session as vehicles. These vehicle bills are driven empty through all the public checkpoints and then loaded up with freight for final passage in the last hours of a session when activity has already sped up, members are tired from long hours, and judgment is worn down. Vehicle bills become institutionalized, routinely used by leaders to bypass the whole deliberative process. New proposals are presented to the members in the hours just prior to adjournment, giving them little opportunity to review and no opportunity to change the content.

One year, in Illinois, SB 1101 was introduced on February 7 with just a title, an effective date, and a one-line purpose—to make changes in state programs to implement the governor's budget. Nothing else. The bill passed the Senate unanimously on March 20. On May 15, the House amended the bill by deleting the effective date, and on the following day, May 16, passed the bill 117 to 1 and sent it back to the Senate. On May 20 the Senate refused to accept the House amendment and sent the bill back to the House. In four months, both Senate and House had considered the bill. There had been hearings by committees in both houses. The bill had gone through the whole process except for the conference committee. The bill still only had a title, a purpose, and a contrived difference over the effective date. On May 31, the last scheduled day of the legislative session, a conference committee was appointed. In its report, the committee included language that changed or created nineteen statutes that affected twelve state agencies and every school district in the state. Sometime after midnight the report was adopted by both the House and the Senate.

House Bill 1641 was introduced on March 6 to allow the Chicago Metropolitan Reclamation District board of trustees to transfer money among departments after March 1 of a fiscal year rather than after the first half of the fiscal year. The bill passed the House on April 18. On May 15 the bill was amended on the floor of the Senate to add two additional members to the Cook County Sheriff's Merit Board and to change the title of the head of the County's Department of Corrections from executive director to director. The bill passed the Senate on May 16. On May 21, the House refused to accept the Senate amendment. On May 28, a conference committee was appointed. Again, on May 31, the last day of the session, a conference committee report was submitted and adopted by the House and the Senate. The report dropped all of the original language and instead changed or created some forty-four different sections of the statutes to alter the investment practices of public pension funds and the qualification and benefit provisions of eight different public pension systems.

When I served, a multipage conference committee report always appeared on the last day of the session authorizing miscellaneous expenditures of all kinds. Members looked forward to its surfacing, interested (or amused) to see whose pet projects had been included. One year, buried in the middle of about page thirty, a couple of lines appeared, appropriating $1.5 million to the local state university to purchase a small downtown Springfield office building that had been empty for some time and was owned by some of the leading citizens of the city. I was puzzled, since the university was in the process of abandoning its downtown campus. A late-night call at home to a university vice president confirmed that university officials knew nothing of the proposal and had no use for the building. When I questioned the item during floor debate, the report was pulled back and the appropriation was removed. It reappeared again the next year, however—same time, same place, different state agency—and the price had climbed to $2.5 million.

One year, in a nod to "reform," the rules were changed to say that "no subject matter shall be included in any conference committee report on any bill unless that subject matter directly relates to the matters of difference between the House and Senate." The Rules Committee, however, was given the power to authorize the inclusion of any new subject matter that the committee determined was "of an emergency nature, of substantial importance to the operation of government, or in the best interests of Illinois."

Since the rules are adopted by the members at the beginning of each legislative session, it is fair to ask why members acquiesce in the reduction of their own power, turning all-important decisions over to the Speaker. There is no single answer. In part, it makes legislating easier. They don't have to take responsibility for results. They are protected from having to make difficult votes. Nothing controversial makes it to the full body to be voted on. No member has the power or opportunity to force the body to consider and vote on an alternative. Every member can explain a vote by saying, "It was the only solution we had the chance to vote for. It was that or nothing." There is a reluctance to rock the boat. There is always the thought that if one goes along, it will be easier to get appointed to desired committees, get the bills you want passed, get your own projects approved, and get help in the next election.

Most of the complaining comes from members of whichever party happens to be in the minority at the time. A Speaker who is a good leader can make his or her members feel that they are part of the decision-making process by bringing problems to the party caucus for discussion and giving individual members responsibility for getting certain issues resolved. When the rules give you complete power over all parliamentary procedures and the language in every bill and amendment, you can afford to share that power, or appear as though you are sharing it.

Every legislative body has its own rules, customs, and habits. Evolution moves in the direction of concentrating power in the leaders and increasing control over the process. It takes periodic revolution by the members to bring power and control back to the members. The main demands by the renegade Republicans who pushed John Boehner from his post as Speaker of the U.S. House of Representatives in 2015 centered on changing the rules to give members more opportunity to offer amendments and more influence over House procedures. The new Speaker, Paul Ryan, refused to bargain for their support.

DEMOCRACY IS A PROCESS FOR MAKING COLLECTIVE DECISIONS, A WAY OF sharing power based on each person having one vote. We take that vote for granted, thinking that a vote is a vote is a vote. We do not realize that the power we think we have is diminished or taken away in the fine print of the rules that govern voting. Because the vote is the unit of democratic power, it is the most prized object, the center of attention for those who would gather power to themselves and their allies. They, better than the rest of us, realize that if they write the rules for voting, they will make the decisions.

Those rules matter. They give power. They take power away. They define our democracy. They drive the results. They confine and constrict the power of the ballot box. They concentrate power in the hands of the few at the top. If you make the rules, you win the game.

11. YOU ALWAYS KNOW WHEN THE GOVERNOR IS SERIOUS

THE GOVERNOR AND THE MAYOR OF CHICAGO HAD REACHED AGREEMENT on a $2.5 billion transportation package, and a vote in the House was scheduled for the next week. Head counts showed that it was three votes short of passing. On the Thursday before the vote, vice presidents of the two banks I had loans in called me. One opened the conversation with, "There are two things I want to talk to you about, your note and your vote." The next day, an auditor from the Department of Revenue telephoned the restaurant of which I was a general partner and asked the manager to provide to auditors, who would be in the restaurant Monday morning, all of the restaurant's financial records from the day it opened. On that same Monday, two hundred members of construction union locals who had been strong supporters of mine showed up unannounced at the capitol, filled a committee room, and grilled me for ninety minutes on why I wasn't supporting the governor's transportation plan that would provide jobs in the district. On Wednesday, the plan passed with a vote to spare. Four representatives had been persuaded, one way or another.

Politics is a game played for keeps. In this country, we are relatively civil in how we play. Assassinations are not common. Shootings at polling places are rare. It has been 140 years since we fought the Civil War over the issues of slavery and states' rights, and it has been 225 years since our last revolution. Still, in the descriptive words of the legendary Mr. Dooley, fictional bartender and observer of all things political in Chicago, "Politics ain't bean bag." Politics determines who gets what: and when you are in danger of losing what you have or not getting what you want, you get serious.

The legislature is not a debating society. Rhetorical points may get quoted in the media. Good oratory is appreciated and applauded. But the only thing that counted in the Illinois House when I was there was getting to eighty-nine, the number of votes required for passage. The way a legislator voted was not decided by the debate. Eighty-eight was no better than twelve. The last vote, the eighty-ninth, was always the hardest to get.

First-time visitors sitting in the gallery watching the legislature in session were usually dismayed by the sight of members walking around, talking to each other, eating, laughing, telephoning, and apparently paying little attention to the official proceedings. Members were paying attention, however. Not to the debate, because that wasn't important, but to everything else that was going on—the calendar for the day, the next few bills coming up for a vote, who was talking to whom, which leaders were on the floor, the issues the Speaker was talking to members about, who was in the chair, which lobbyists were in the corridors actively working the members, what level of political clout was personally present in the capitol that day, and what the clout was interested in—all clues to what was important.

In the economy, money is what matters: money is power, money allocates resources, money determines outcomes. The more money you have, the more influence you have and the more control you have. In politics, it is the vote that matters. A vote is power, a vote allocates resources, a vote determines outcomes. The more votes you can deliver, the more influence you will have and the more control you will have. Everything in politics is centered on getting the vote, getting enough votes to win.

I had one vote, one of the 177 that could be either *yes* or *no* on each bill, one of the 89 required to make new law. Several thousand times during a legislative session my finger touched one of the voting buttons on the right front corner of my desk, the light next to my name up on the big board that everyone could see went green or red, and the total of *yes* or *no* votes increased by one.

With time, the finger moved almost automatically, the button touched determined by a complex weighing of intuition, personal conviction, experience, reason, prior commitment, obligation, party position, public opinion, constituent pressure, organized support or opposition, media publicity, editorial opinion, personal relationships with supporters and opponents, personal advantage, the potential impact on my political career, and the desire to make friends, build support, and avoid controversy and opposition. All of these things that go into determining which button legislative fingers touch become levers to be pulled by anyone who wants to influence any particular bill. There are no rules on how hard those levers can be pulled. Winning is the only payoff.

Regardless of the rhetoric, legislators always know when the governor is serious. The pressure changes.

It was a winter night. A small private dining room in one of the best restaurants in the city had been reserved. Those present were the governor's top confidants, the small group of men who had planned and run his campaign, and some members of his staff, of which I was one, hired to direct the governor's legislative program. The steak had been the best, the wine excellent, the conversation lively. Over after-dinner drinks and cigars, the main topic for the night was raised. Would the staff put together a file on each legislator that included his political history, his major supporters, the sources of his campaign contributions, his friends, who he hangs around with, who he responds to when they call, how he makes his living, his financial situation and interests, his family, his sexual interests, and who he sleeps with? The evening ended with a discussion of whether a particular senator's closet homosexual proclivities should be used as leverage in getting his vote when needed.

The process of rounding up your vote starts long before any bill is ever scheduled. It begins before you are elected, with the positions you take, the support you seek, and the commitments you make. Everyone on whom you rely for help in getting elected becomes a potential source of influence over you after you are elected. As soon as an election is over and the new members are known, lobbyists begin asking each other and anyone else who might have knowledge, "What do you know about him or her?" Every tidbit is potentially useful. What they want to know is how to get to you. What are your motivations? What are your interests? What kind of person are you? Who influences you? Who do you listen to? Where are your levers? Who can pull them? How hard? Are you susceptible to favors?

The lever is often economic. A friend, a Republican attorney who had bought into the system, who had risen through the party ranks and been rewarded with contracts, position, and responsibility, succinctly described it this way: "The name of the game is control. You control a person by standing on his groceries."

One morning, a respected member who later went on to have a distinguished career in Congress walked into the chamber obviously shaken. It was a showdown vote between the new governor and the old mayor. There was no negotiating, no compromising. It was a straight struggle, power against power. The vote had been delayed three days as the mayor's office, the Speaker, a Republican, and the minority leader, a Democrat, rounded up the last votes necessary to override the governor's veto of a bill the mayor wanted. The member had been one of the most outspoken supporters of the governor's veto, but now he had to publicly vote to override and find an acceptable excuse for changing his mind. The rumor had circulated that his largest client, the one

WHEN THE GOVERNOR IS SERIOUS

who accounted for more than half of his law firm's billings, had telephoned him at four o'clock that morning and told him he was taking his business elsewhere unless he voted to override.

It doesn't take long before the levers that can move you become general knowledge. The game of pulling them begins, with everyone reaching for whatever levers are appropriate for their immediate purpose and to which they have access.

The late-afternoon planning meeting was typical. Five of us, three lobbyists and two legislators, sat at the back table in the nearly empty restaurant with sandwiches and beer. We had a blank roll call and reviewed it member by member, marking down on the basis of our knowledge and collective judgment the *yeses*, the *nos*, the waverers, and the question marks on the bill we were interested in. None of us had any clout or could exert any real pressure, but we had all been around. As the names of the waverers and question marks came up, we discussed what the chances were of getting their votes, how to approach them, and who could make the approach. By the time the meeting broke up three hours later, ten votes had been targeted, ten strategies had been planned, and each participant had his assignments of people to call and things to do. Early the next morning we met for breakfast to report progress, update the vote count, and plan the day's activities.

Pressure on a legislator is always greater if it comes from friends and constituents, particularly ones who were instrumental in the legislator's election or could be helpful in the next election. In the old days when you wanted the vote of a Chicago legislator, you didn't talk to the legislator, you talked to his ward committeeman. The ward committeeman controlled the votes in the ward, and because he controlled the votes, he controlled the legislator. There aren't many ward committeemen in today's politics with that kind of clout, but the principle is the same.

Interests that want your vote in the capitol are always looking for people in your district who helped get you elected to carry their message. When the lobbyist for the teachers' union couldn't persuade Kathleen to change her vote on a bill, yard signs began to show up in front of the homes of teachers in her district. When the trial lawyers in Madison weren't happy with Kathleen, a local trial lawyer who was active in the county party stirred up the local party leaders to go about changing her mind. The vote is the source of power and the lever used most often in applying pressure.

In my one stint as a lobbyist, I was hired to kill an insurance bill introduced by one of the party leaders. The bill would have had a particular impact on restaurants that served liquor. I talked with the sponsor, who told me he was going to let the bill die in committee. I thought my job was done, so I reported to my client and relaxed, but the next week the sponsor scheduled the bill and passed it out of committee before I knew anything had happened. My telephone calls to the sponsor were not returned. It was Wednesday. I went to the public library, found the telephone directories for the hometowns of the sponsor and six of his close legislative friends, and copied the listings in the yellow pages of restaurants that legislators might frequent on a Friday or Saturday night. I sent a flyer to each explaining the bill and its impact on their insurance rates, and suggested that they should have a conversation with their local legislator about it. On Monday, the sponsor called me and said there had been a misunderstanding. The bill would be returned to committee to die.

Pressure is part of the political process. People want things. Different people want different things. They conflict. Politics is the process of resolving conflict in a peaceful way, and you can't be in the middle of that conflict without feeling the pressure. Applying pressure is an essential part of putting together the required number of votes to reach a majority. When there are not enough votes, somebody has to be persuaded to provide one more vote toward reaching the necessary majority.

The pressure you feel comes from two directions: from your constituents who expect you to put together enough votes to deliver on the things they want, and from everyone else who wants you to be one of the votes that delivers on the things they want. So the legislator, with one vote on every issue, goes into the political arena with all the other legislators and all the other political players, each with his or her own agenda, to decide public policy. The only fixed rule is that nothing gets done unless a majority agrees. Balancing all of the demands, keeping one's place in the political system, and parlaying that one vote into achieving your goals comprise the art and skill of politics. There is no single formula for being successful, but in the give-and-take of bargaining, in the continual jockeying for position, the legislator who controls his or her own electoral base and doesn't depend on someone else to be elected has more options from which to choose. As in other endeavors, there are those who are content to be rewarded for going along, and there are those who try to control their own destinies and change what would otherwise be the outcome.

For the legislator, the most immediate and concrete rewards and punishments come from the leadership of one's own party and from the governor. A legislative leader can reward: with good committee assignments, a boost up the political ladder, support for one's pet projects, or access to campaign dollars; but the leader can also punish by withholding all of the above or by actively supporting an opponent. The governor can reward by putting you in the spotlight, entertaining you at the mansion, signing your bills, building bridges in your district, providing political support, and giving jobs or contracts to family members, friends, and supporters. The governor can punish by ignoring you, vetoing your bills, postponing projects in your district, encouraging political opposition, and firing friends and supporters who have jobs. Political leaders from one's home district, the mayor, the ward committeeman, the county chairman, and others can also help or hurt you and your friends, as well as make the next election easy or difficult.

For the most part, political relationships are ones of a shared community of interests, mutual support, and a recognized hierarchy of leadership. One goes along because one is part of a team. If your team wins, you share in the rewards. If your team loses, you work harder in the next election. In a few situations, there is a specific quid pro quo: this reward for this vote; this punishment if you don't vote with us on this issue.

The old patronage system that was based on jobs ensured loyalty, maintained control, and tied together the different levels of the political system. It worked through an interlocking network of sponsorship and obligation. Freelancers were not welcome. In the words of a forgotten Chicago alderman, "Nobody wants nobody that nobody sent." You found a sponsor to attach yourself to, you worked hard, you delivered votes, and your sponsor saw to it you were rewarded. You became part of a team. The system was simple, reflected basic human nature, and served basic human needs.

Bob worked hard in the election, doing everything that was asked of him: putting up signs, running the headquarters, helping with mailings, working the factory gate with me on the late-night and early morning shift changes, knocking on doors, and delivering the vote in his precinct. His heart was in the campaign. When I won, it was as though he had won himself. Ten months later, the factory he worked in closed down and he was on the street. He needed a job and came to me and the county party chairman and asked for help. With the county chairman's blessing I told the governor's patronage person I needed a job for one of my people. A month later, Bob was a highway worker for the Department of Transportation.

Going up the line, Bob and each of his sponsors had demonstrated the necessary ability or clout to get things done. In return, Bob was expected to support the governor, me, and whomever else the chairman told him to in the next election. The chairman was expected to support the governor and me. I was expected to vote for whatever the governor wanted. The job became a string tied to everyone involved. The more important the person you sponsored is to you, the stronger the string is you tied to yourself. The governor's patronage chief liked nothing better than to hear a legislator ask for a job for a brother, daughter, spouse, or bedmate. What had been given could be taken away.

I remember clearly the expressive shrug and the helpless raising of hands by the longtime Italian representative from Chicago—who had many relatives on then-mayor Jane Byrne's payroll—as he explained why he was changing his vote on the Equal Rights Amendment from *no* to *yes*: "The bitch made me do it."

The more you participate as a member of a team, the more support you get from other team members for the votes you want. The more you are included in the team's decision-making, the more incentive there is, and the more pressure you feel, to be a reliable team player and go along with the leader's decisions regardless of your individual feelings or your constituents' desires. The effective leader, however, recognizes that the ties of communal interest are not unbreakable and the strings that attach individual members to the group cannot be pulled all of the time. Strings pulled inappropriately will break. A legislator who is willing to be part of a community of interest may very well rebel and assert independence if she or he feels insulted by a threat or thinks that the exchange isn't equal.

The new governor's chief of patronage envied the control exercised by the mayor of Chicago. He too wanted the power to have *his* legislators switch their votes without question whenever he changed his mind. He wanted the power of Mayor Daley without building the organization that made the power possible. The legislative session scheduled to consider the governor's vetoes was coming up. He fired all the people who had been given jobs at the request of their legislators. He wanted those legislators to come back and ask for the jobs again, to have them beholden to him twice, and to demonstrate that he could punish as well as reward. The typical reaction was, "If that is the way you want to do business, you can kiss my ass." Most of the good will he had gained by giving the jobs in the first place dissipated.

The director of the state fair was called into the governor's office and told to fire a friend of mine who held the public relations and advertising contract for the fair. His sin? He had continued his friendship with me even though I had voted wrong in the Speakership fight and was now an "enemy." My attitude became, "If I am going to be treated like an enemy, I might as well act like an enemy." Their attitude was, "If he is going to act like an enemy, he should be treated like an enemy." That chasm was never bridged.

Most of the old stories about pressuring legislators for votes involve presidents, governors, and mayors twisting arms to get their programs passed and party leaders pushing hard for the party's agenda. The new stories don't get as much publicity, but with the ascendency of money and interests in politics and the demise of the political parties, much of the overt pressure on legislators to vote a certain way, or to change their votes, comes from interest groups on issues involving the private sector.

The process begins subtly enough with the detailed questionnaires that start to arrive in the mail the week after you announce you are running for office. It continues, depending on the importance of the legislation, with organized phone calling, signed petitions, yard signs, direct mail, and radio and television advertising, all presenting the issue to the public in simplistic, black-and-white, terms, urging them to pressure their legislator to vote the "right" way. Sometimes the message is less subtle and more direct, as when the lobbyist for the largest employer in Kathleen's district started a conversation in her office with, "This is about your next election."

The relationship between the legislator and interest groups is always about votes. Most of the political activity of interest groups is designed to demonstrate to the legislator the ability of the group to have an impact on the number of votes the legislator gets in the next election. The group creates a political fund, and it mobilizes its members in a show of numbers for lobbying days at the state capitol. It is the legislator's doctor, the legislator's dentist, the legislator's insurance agent, the legislator's banker, the legislator's newspaper publisher, the president of the legislator's local trades and labor council, the president of the legislator's chamber of commerce, the executive committee of the legislator's local Sierra Club, the superintendent where the legislator's children go to school, and the legislator's friends who are recruited to talk to the legislator about their group's interests. Supportive legislators are invited to address membership meetings and are given laudatory coverage in organization newsletters. Implicit in all of the activity is the message, "We deliver votes, and those votes can be for you or against you." There is reward or punishment for the legislator.

As in all political relationships, the one between the legislator and the interest group depends on the perceived relative strength of each. Potential rewards and punishments run in both directions. A legislator facing a difficult election may fear the opposition of even small groups and work hard for their support. On the other hand, even large groups will not oppose a strong incumbent they disagree with for fear of active retribution the next time the group has a bill up for consideration. The decision to endorse or not to endorse always includes consideration of the candidate's chances of winning.

There is always an element of quid pro quo in the relationship between a legislator and an interest group ("We support only those legislators who support branch banking"). But most of the time there is more to it than that. Often the legislator and the group share the same values and outlook, where support is mutual, friendship and respect exist, and influence goes in both directions. The problem for the observer, and what contributes to cynicism, is that the external characteristics of the relationships between legislators and interest groups are similar regardless of the underlying motivations. It is difficult to determine from a distance the expediency and the genuineness of the relationship. There is always the tendency to attribute the finer motives to the legislators one agrees with and the baser motives to those one disagrees with.

The legislator's vote is not always needed. Not all issues are equally important. Not every vote has the same political impact. Many votes are unanimous. The pressures and influences on the legislator vary from bill to bill. The pressure increases when a lot of money is at stake, when equally strong interests are on each side of the issue, when the two political parties line up on different sides, when the existing political balance of power is threatened, when the vote is close. If all of these conditions converge on a single vote, the pressure on both sides can be great, and the legislator is forced to choose where his or her most basic interests lie.

Votes on these issues in Illinois were always great theater, with members rising to explain their votes or change them, the total teetering at the magic number as party leaders and perhaps the governor walked the aisles to talk to wavering or persuadable members. The air of expectancy in the back hallways and around the railing in the capitol rotunda would heighten all day as members, lobbyists, staff, and legislative hangers-on traded gossip, rumors, and inside information on how the vote count was going, who was making calls, which sick members were leaving hospital beds to be flown in, and who was or was not absent. The House, under care of a stand-in Speaker, would fill time with routine business. The visitor's gallery would begin to fill, and by the time the bill would be called, even if it was midnight or 1:00 A.M., there would be standing room only. The door behind the podium would open. The Speaker would emerge. A hush would fall over the crowd. The Speaker would bang the gavel and call *the bill.*

Pressure is part of the political game, and political officeholders are routinely told, "If you can't stand the heat, stay out of the kitchen." There is truth to that, and if you don't handle pressure well, you should stay out of politics. There are ways of dealing with pressure, however, that reduce the emotional impact and help to preserve your self-identity.

The first is to remember that there is always another vote. No matter how angry the governor or the caucus is with you today for not voting the right way, tomorrow they will be asking for your vote on another issue. They can't afford to be permanently angry with you.

Play today's game today, and worry about tomorrow's game tomorrow. Don't start wondering how a particular vote will affect the rest of your career.

Act like you are in charge; you will be in charge. Pressure and threats feed on insecurity and fear. Most all political threats are empty and not likely to be carried out. It is the fear generated by the threat that creates the pressure.

If you want to avoid pressure on a particular bill, make your position on it public, early and firmly. Pressure is focused on the undecided, increasing as the vote gets closer. If you are on everybody's list as a firm *yes* or *no*, nobody is going to spend much time lobbying you.

You can often deflect pressure by talking specifics. This is particularly true when the pressure is generated by an interest group that has rallied its members to pressure you with phone calls and letters to vote for jobs, the environment, less government, or consumer protection. Sierra Club members who wanted a *yes* for green jobs started questioning their position when they were told that many of the green jobs came from lifting the state moratorium on new nuclear plants. This is also true whenever the person recruited to talk to you is not the one primarily interested in securing your vote. The call I received from the bank's vice president about the governor's transportation package was just the last link in a chain that started with the governor's office and wound through the Asphalt Paving Association, to the largest construction company in the city, to the president of the bank where the construction company held all its assets, to the vice president who handled the loans for the restaurant and who made the call. Other than the fact that he was asking for a *yes* vote, the vice president had no idea of the content of the legislation, was embarrassed to be in the position he was in, and quickly changed the subject when pressed about the particulars of the bill. It was clear that even though the call was intended to apply pressure, it was a threat that was not going to be carried out.

You do learn to be flexible, however. Insisting on doing things your way all the time is not wise. Accommodating and compromising with your enemies and your friends is not evil. Sometimes you have to take an indirect path to achieve a goal. You have to choose your battles. If you try to fight all the alligators in the swamp at once, you will be eaten for lunch.

FROM THE BEGINNING, GOING BACK TO THE MAGNA CARTA IN 1215, THE ROLE of the legislative body in government has been to check executive power. Kings and presidents can't extract taxes from the people or send them to battle without the consent of the legislature. Only citizens elected by their neighbors can pass laws that bind the people. The legislature has always been a hurdle for those who want to wield political or economic power. Instead of being able to wield power personally, governors and others have to persuade a relatively large number of individuals from different communities, who are relatively diverse, and who have independent standing that the power they want is beneficial to the community at large. If the democratic ideal is followed, legislators discuss and debate the request publicly with full knowledge of the details and effects before a vote is taken. It is not surprising, however, that when discussion does not produce the desired approval, those who want a different outcome move to other means of persuasion: rewards, threats, manipulation, coercion.

In terms of numbers, most bills are considered and passed or defeated in a way that reasonably resembles the democratic ideal. Many votes are unanimous. Nobody spends political capital on an issue that is not *important* to *them*, and so there are a lot of free votes; there is no pressure to vote one way or the other.

The legislator is pressured, manipulated, or controlled when someone or some group is not content with leaving the outcome up to each individual legislator and the deliberative process of the legislature as a whole. Pressure comes when the natural outcome is likely to be different from that desired by a person or group that is politically important. It implies a distrust or dissatisfaction with open, deliberative, democratic, collective decisions. Pressure continues because it is successful. Legislators are human, subject to conflicting desires and susceptible to pressure. They desire to avoid difficulty and can be tempted by blandishments.

Pressure has become more common with the increase of contentious issues. It has also become more common as decisions are increasingly made outside of the legislature and those who make the decisions see their task solely as one of rounding up enough votes to have those decisions ratified.

The democratic ideal vanishes when the legislature is treated solely as a barrier, not as a deliberative body. It disappears when the attitude prevails that legislators only vote "right" when they are pressured to do so and that each legislator's vote is to be gained by whatever means necessary.

In recounting how pressure is used, it is easy to forget that it comes with democracy. It is what keeps legislators from straying too far from the desires of constituents. Democracy is built on the idea that if a legislator does not vote the way you would like him or her to vote, you work to replace that legislator in the next election with someone who more closely shares your interests. In most of its forms, pressure is some variation of a promise of support or a threat of opposition in the next election. This political pressure is an integral part of the process. It is when pressure becomes personal rather than political that questions are raised. The distinction between the personal and the political can be maintained theoretically, but where personal goals are pursued through political means, the boundary is often blurred, both for those who exert the pressure and for the legislator who is the object of the pressure.

The legislator always knows when someone is serious about getting his or her vote. The pressure increases.

12. LEAD ME NOT INTO TEMPTATION

MONEY AND POLITICS HAVE ALWAYS HAD AN AFFINITY FOR EACH OTHER. Fifty years ago, Jesse Unruh, the godfather of California politics, put it this way: "Money is the mother's milk of politics." The nourishment continues. Despite all the campaign finance reform laws that have been passed over the years, the flow of cash into politics increases every election cycle.

Does it matter? Is money a corrupting influence? History tells us that the answer is yes. When political bosses ruled, many became personally wealthy from kickbacks from contractors and assessments on the wages of patronage workers. Taxpayers paid for the inflated costs and padded payrolls. Today, money influences policy, and voters live with decisions that benefit only the donors. In both cases money changes the outcome—benefiting those who give at the expense of everyone else. The democratic process based on majority rule and consent of the governed is subverted when the exchange of money alters what would otherwise be decided.

We have grown up believing in the revolutionary principle that "all men are created [politically] equal." When it comes to making final decisions about how we are going to be governed, each one of us has one vote. Rich, poor, owner, employee, farmer, truck driver, professor, or student, it doesn't matter. At the polls on Election Day we all have equal say. But money is not allocated equally. If money is king of the political hill, if money decides who wins the election, if money decides what laws are passed, then we are no longer politically equal. Hence, our discontent. Our promised equality has vanished. Something is basically wrong. The system is not fair.

The thought occurs that we could live with political money if it remained as benign and nurturing as mother's milk. But the money no longer nurtures, it has come to dominate. The sums washing through our political system have become truly astonishing. Money now sets the rules of the political game.

Politicians who don't play by those rules find themselves on the sidelines. Money is the foundation of our political power structure and shapes our political institutions. Money is king.

Where does all the money come from? Who gives it? For what reasons? Some donors just like the game, like being involved, like being active in public affairs. But most have personal, ideological, or economic goals that they can achieve through politics. People want to be close to power. People want influence. People want the world arranged in ways they agree with. People want to increase their own economic well-being. If they can't hold office themselves, then they want their friends to hold office. People want their side to win. People will contribute money to help their side win. Obviously, people who have more will contribute more, particularly if they have greater ambitions, stronger beliefs, or more to gain. As more economic activities—for all sorts of reasons—are pulled into the political sphere, more people have a financial stake in the decisions that are made. They add their dollars to help elect candidates who have beliefs compatible with their own.

Why is all the money needed? To win. It is a lot easier to win with money than it is to win without money. Nobody goes into politics or decides to run for office with the intent of losing. You run to change the world. You run to win. The massive databases that support the targeted messaging that goes out over the "free" internet are not constructed or accessed cheaply. Television advertising has always been expensive. Part of running to win is raising campaign cash, asking people to give you money to pay for the messages that persuade. The motivations of those who have money to give find an echo in the motivations of those who need money to spend. The demand for more political dollars is matched by the increased supply.

The media and the audience—all of us—also pay homage to money and elevate its status. Despite our condemnation of money, money is the primary yardstick used to judge the credibility of a candidate. Candidates who can't raise money are relegated to the "Also running are . . ." paragraph at the end of news stories. When Kathleen had primary opposition in her first race for the state senate, support didn't start rolling in until after the first campaign finance reports showed that she raised three times more money than her opponent did in half the time. Where organizational support used to provide credibility, the dollars in the candidate's campaign account is now the measure.

What can be done? The question is not as easy to answer as it first appears. The most difficult problem is figuring out how to deal with the activities of individuals. In a democratic society it is difficult to justify placing limits on the political activities of any individual, regardless of how rich they might be, when they engage in those activities themselves without any connection to a particular candidate's campaign or a political party. Should we limit the number of ads one person can buy? What if that person owns a newspaper or a television station. Should we limit editorial endorsements? If time is money, should there be a limit on the number of doors a person can knock? (A retired person has a lot more time than the rest of us and can knock on many more doors.) A good word from Oprah has more influence than a good word from Jane.

Although it is difficult to argue that there is a philosophical difference between donating money, knocking on doors, and making an endorsement, the money is what bothers us the most. There are a number of reasons. The disparity between those who are rich enough to have a large effect on election results and the rest of us can be much greater. The other activities are more limited and involve some personal effort. They are also more public. Money can flow anonymously. Then, there is the image. Editorials "persuade"; money "buys." With money, there is a scent of impropriety.

If political parties and candidates were the only players in the game, campaign finance rules would be relatively easy to write and enforce. But in a democracy where everyone has the right to express and advance his or her own views, to work, to contribute, to join others in efforts to achieve political goals, making the rules is more difficult. We all have a vision for our communities. The freedom for every individual to work to make that vision a reality is the essence of democracy. Following that thinking, the courts have ruled that the First Amendment rights of free speech and petitioning the government preclude placing limits on individual political activity. When acting on their own, independently of any candidate or campaign, individuals cannot be constrained.

The laws that have been passed during the last hundred years have tried to address the problem of money in politics by treating parties and candidates differently from everyone else, individuals differently from corporations and labor unions, and contributions differently from expenditures. The courts have agreed that when it comes to political parties and candidates, the government's interest in preventing corruption and the perception of corruption justifies restrictions on their campaign financing. Contributions can be limited; disclosure can be required.

The laws and court decisions have thus brought us to the place where we have two kinds of teams playing by different rules on the same political field. Individuals who act independently have no restrictions. The political teams—the parties and the candidates—are restricted. As a result, resources that used to go to the political teams now flow to the independent players. To keep the process from becoming a shell game, the law requires that there be no "coordination" between the two. But because both share the same goal—electing a particular candidate—the prohibition is about as effective in keeping them apart as the old bundling boards were in separating lovers.

Laws aimed at reducing the influence of money have resulted largely in changing the channels through which the money flows. The new "independent" entities that have been created are far less accessible, less participatory, and less accountable than candidates and political parties. The money still flows in ever-increasing volumes, the messages are still bought and sent, but the channels are murkier.

Campaign finance reform is not a new effort. Laws go back to the Gilded Age of the late 1800s when corporate involvement in presidential campaigns became an issue. Reform has required continual updating to counter the ingenuity of donors and spenders who, in response to new laws, kept devising new ways to bring money and politics together.

The reasons used in court decisions over the years to justify campaign finance laws include "the prevention of corruption and the appearance of corruption," "reducing the effect of aggregated wealth on elections," "ensuring that elections are indeed free and representative," and "preventing the money that is spent on elections from exerting an undue influence on an officeholder's judgment and from creating the appearance of such influence." If elections are subverted, then the legitimacy of democracy itself is called into question. This argument is presented in its starkest form by Justice John Paul Stevens. In his dissent to the Supreme Court's decision in *Citizens United v. Federal Election Commission* that removed almost all restrictions on independent corporate and union political expenditures, he said, "A democracy cannot function effectively when its constituent members believe laws are being bought and sold."

The two separate but related goals of campaign finance laws have been (1) to reduce both actual and perceived corruption—defined as any quid pro quo arrangement that directly connects contributions to specific decisions—and (2) to prevent elections from being dominated, and potentially decided, by large sums of money, particularly corporate money.

Placing limits on contributions that can be given to or received by political parties and candidates was the proposed solution to achieve those goals. In Wisconsin, for example, you can't contribute more than $1,000 to a state assembly candidate, $2,000 to a state senate candidate, or $20,000 to a candidate for governor. The rationale for the limits is, if you can't give very much, you can't buy very much; hence, there is no corruption and no appearance of corruption.

The courts have ruled that because avoiding corruption and the appearance of corruption is a sufficiently important governmental interest, and because direct contributions to candidates and parties are particularly susceptible to corrupting influences (e.g., quid pro quo arrangements), limits on such contributions are constitutional. Expenditures, however, cannot be limited. Candidates and parties are free to spend as much money as they can raise, providing the limits on each contribution are not exceeded. Candidates can spend as much of their own money as they want, since by definition they can't enter into quid pro quo arrangements with themselves.

The same thinking is applied to independent expenditures. Everyone is free to spend as much money as they want on their own activities in political campaigns so long as there is no contact or coordination with candidates or parties. If there is no contact or coordination, there can be no quid pro quo—hence, no corruption or appearance of corruption and no sufficient government interest to justify placing a limit on the political activity. (The requirement that there be no contact or coordination between an independent group and a candidate's campaign is more formal than real. Those who form the independent group are almost always friends, close associates, or former staff members of the candidate. Everyone knows where to send their money.)

Since there can be no limits on individual political activity, efforts to achieve the second goal of preventing large sums of money from dominating elections have focused on forbidding corporate political contributions. States were the first to forbid corporate contributions to candidates and parties. The prohibition became federal law during the Progressive Era of the early 1900s. In 1947 the Taft-Hartley Act extended the federal prohibition to include independent political expenditures from the general funds of corporations and unions. Not only were corporations and unions prevented from contributing to candidates and parties, they were prohibited from independently spending corporate or union dollars on political activity. The Supreme Court upheld Taft-Hartley, citing the "compelling governmental interest in preventing 'the corrosive and distorting effects of immense aggregations of wealth that are accumulated with the help of the corporate form and that have little or no correlation to the public's support for the corporation's political ideas.'" About half the states enacted similar prohibitions on corporate contributions and independent expenditures in state elections.

Over the years, the Supreme Court has given several reasons for treating corporations differently than individuals. Corporations are not part of the electorate. Corporate interests are exclusively economic interests and might not be the same as those of voters. Corporate dollars belong to shareholders, creating a conflict if political contributions from general corporate funds promote goals contrary to those shareholders' interests. Easy access to large sums of money gives corporations excessive advantage in elections, potentially undermining public confidence in those elections. Similar thinking was applied to unions, and using union funds for political purposes was also prohibited. Both corporations and unions, however, could create political action committees (PACs) to collect voluntary donations from their shareholders and members that could then be contributed (within limits) to candidates or used (without limit) for their own independent expenditures.

In upholding the major provisions of the Federal Election Campaign Act of 1972 and the Bipartisan Campaign Reform Act of 2002, the Supreme Court followed the reasoning of those earlier decisions. It wasn't until the 2010 decision in *Citizens United v. Federal Election Commission* that the court changed its thinking and ruled in a five-to-four decision that limits on independent political expenditures by corporations violated the free-speech provisions of the First Amendment and were therefore unconstitutional. The court did not address the constitutionality of the limits on contributions to candidates and parties.

The majority in its opinion made several points. A corporation, in itself, has a right to speak. A corporation speaking through its political action committee is not the corporation speaking. PACs are "burdensome alternatives . . . expensive to administer and subject to extensive regulations," and because a corporation might not have time to form a PAC prior to an election it would lose its right to speak if it could speak only through a PAC. Limits on independent expenditures have a "chilling effect," the court said. Because independent expenditures are designed to persuade voters, it is presupposed that "the people have the ultimate influence over elected officials," which is "inconsistent" with the suggestion that they will become disillusioned and refuse to participate. "The appearance of influence or access . . . will not cause the electorate to lose faith in our democracy." Shareholders who object to corporate political expenditures have adequate recourse through normal corporate processes.

Although recognizing the possibility of corruption and the legitimate interest of Congress to fashion a remedy, the majority in *Citizens United* seemed to treat the problem lightly while leaving little room under the First Amendment to find such a remedy. "If elected officials succumb to improper influences from independent expenditures; if they surrender their best judgment; and if they put expediency before principle, then surely there is cause for concern. We must give weight to attempts by Congress to seek to dispel either the appearance or the reality of these influences. The remedies enacted by law, however, must comply with the First Amendment; and, it is our law and our tradition that more speech, not less, is the governing rule."

The dissenting justices repeated the argument made in previous court decisions: corporations are different from other entities and should be treated differently. There is "distinctive corrupting potential" if companies are allowed to use corporate general treasury dollars in elections. "Corporations, as a class, tend to be more attuned to the complexities of the legislative process and more directly affected by tax and appropriations measures that receive little public scrutiny; they also have vastly more money with which to try to buy access and votes. . . . Corporations, that is, are uniquely equipped to seek laws that favor their owners, not simply because they have a lot of money but because of their legal and organizational structure." The effects from unrestricted corporate election activity may be "far more destructive" than what non-corporations are capable of. In addition, large independent expenditures have become "essentially interchangeable" with direct contributions and have the same "capacity to generate quid pro quo arrangements." Corruption is not limited to explicit quid pro quo arrangements but "operates along a spectrum, and the majority's apparent belief that quid pro quo arrangements can be neatly demarcated from other improper influences does not accord with the theory or reality of politics."

Echoing the "chilling effect on [campaign] speech" argument made by the five members of the majority, the four dissenters argued that unlimited corporate political money might have a chilling effect on "uninhibited, robust, and wide-open" legislative debate. "Corporations with large war chests to deploy on electioneering may find democratically elected bodies becoming much more attuned to their interests. . . . Politicians who fear that a certain corporation can make or break their reelection chances may be cowed into silence."

If barstool discussion is the measuring stick, the dissenters win on both the "perception of corruption" and the "too much money" points. The amount of money spent is offensive. The automatic assumption is that it corrupts.

I have not heard any expressions of faith in our democracy from a person sitting on the stool next to me. What I have heard is, "It doesn't matter who we elect, all politicians are bought." Regardless of what one might think of the legal merit of the majority's reasoning in *Citizens United*, their appraisal of the mood of voters is far off the mark.

It's a fair question, and it should be asked. Is the fight over campaign financing just another example of "make the rules; win the game," with each side clothing political gain in the robes of philosophical principle? The five-to-four vote by the Supreme Court pitted the five "conservative" judges against the four "liberal" judges. Republicans, who in today's world tend to benefit from large contributions, generally oppose limits; Democrats generally support limits. Some have asserted that the campaign finance reform movement is motivated "less from noble ideals of good government than from ignoble motives of partisan gain."

The split along partisan lines on this issue, at least historically, has not always been there. Early laws were supported by Progressives, who were mostly Republicans. President Harry Truman, a Democrat, in his veto (subsequently overridden) of the 1947 law, termed the limitations on corporations and unions a "dangerous intrusion on free speech." And in 1957, Justices William O. Douglas, Earl Warren, and Hugo Black, not noted for being conservatives, wrote in their dissent of the court's decision in *United States v. Automobile Workers* that "[t]he people determine through their votes the destiny of the nation. It is therefore important—vitally important—that all channels of communications be open to them during every election, that no point of view be restrained or barred, and that the people have access to the views of every group in the community." The three concluded that "deeming a particular group 'too powerful' was not a justification for withholding First Amendment rights from any group—labor or corporate."

The Bipartisan Campaign Reform Act of 2002, sponsored by Senators John McCain, R-Arizona, and Russ Feingold, D-Wisconsin, did receive, as its title implies, votes from both parties, even though few Republicans voted for the law and the Republican Senate majority leader challenged the constitutionality of the act in the courts. On more than one occasion, liberal and conservative groups have joined forces to challenge campaign finance laws. Some observers see the dispute over how to deal with political money as one not between different ideological camps but one between incumbents and challengers, between those who have power and those who don't. From their point of view, the Republicans who voted for McCain-Feingold "were, by and large, those most in danger of losing their seats. For them, the incumbent-benefit protections of the law made it irresistible."

There are similarities in the partisan fights over the voting laws and the campaign finance laws, which is not surprising since both have large impacts on who wins elections. With voting procedures, where Democrats want few if any restrictions, Republicans cite the danger of fraud. With campaign contributions, where Republicans want few if any restrictions, Democrats cite the danger of corruption. If one judges by the number of criminal charges and convictions, money presents the larger temptation and corruption the greater danger.

The law is not an adequate tool to ensure good behavior when it comes to campaign financing. The law cannot say, "You shall not engage in corrupt behavior." The law by its nature can apply only to specific behaviors, and there is a lot of space between the specifics. It has been relatively easy for anyone wanting to avoid the specific prohibitions to use their money to fund the political activity they support. If you can't contribute to a candidate to buy advertising, you buy the advertising yourself. If you can't buy the advertising yourself, you create a political action committee to buy the advertising. If you are limited in how much advertising you can pay for with "hard" dollars, you put "soft" dollars into "party-building" activities like voter registration and community organizing. If soft dollars to political parties are cut off, you fund outside groups to do the necessary party-building activities. If you can't specifically urge the election or defeat of a candidate, you run "issue" ads that either praise or damn. Whatever the nature of the transaction, both the donor and the beneficiary understand the intent and the significance.

It is the voter who is left in the dark. Without exception, the independent expenditure groups give themselves positive labels that may or may not reflect their true intentions. Finding out who the individuals are behind these organizations, what their interests are, and where their money comes from is often difficult.

The secrecy could be addressed by law. The courts have not ruled that disclosure requirements are unconstitutional. Most of the existing disclosure requirements apply to political parties and candidates. Few apply to independent expenditures, and the flow of "dark money" is increasing. Attempts to require disclosure of contributors behind independent political activity have generally failed. Pointing to examples of adverse publicity and boycotts, opponents have argued that disclosure would have a chilling effect on the willingness of potential contributors to donate. Incumbents who have benefited from independent expenditures may also be reluctant to reveal the hand that fed them. A recent law passed by popular referendum in Maine, however, requires that all advertising include the names of the three top contributors to the organization paying for the ad. Transparency can be achieved if there is the political will.

When I first ran for the legislature in Illinois, campaigning was quite simple. Limits on contributions were minimal. Donations came from people I knew. There were no outside groups with lots of money poised to elect or defeat me. No PAC asked me to swear allegiance to their issues as a condition of support. The necessity to fund the campaign created few occasions for temptation.

The reality facing a prospective candidate today—particularly in a contested district—is far different. The need for money is much greater. The limits on what you can raise for your own campaign are stricter. Party organizations are weaker. PACs want commitments before they endorse you. People from far away will decide if you are viable. Part of being viable is signing on to what they believe, adopting their rhetoric, spending money on what they recommend, and running the kind of campaign they think you should. In today's campaigns, it is much more common for temptation to sit down beside you and start a conversation. The scene is difficult to navigate, particularly for a candidate new to politics whose experience and contacts are all rooted in the local community.

The emphasis on money starts the day you first think about the possibility of running. Because relatively little comes from people who are interested in you personally as a candidate and so much comes from sources interested in you only as a potential vote for their particular interest, you feel the pressure to conform both on issues and on campaign strategy. Candidates without a political background don't have the necessary experience to say no when appropriate, and they fear the potential response. There is always the implicit, and sometimes explicit, threat that money and support will be pulled from a troublesome race and allocated to another candidate. Political money is always about influence and control. Giving and receiving are parts of the same dance. The goal is to lead. The temptation is to acquiesce and to follow. It starts during the campaign and continues in office.

It is not necessarily a quid pro quo arrangement, but there are similarities when a group with a specific (usually economic) interest makes contributing and helping contingent on the answers a candidate gives to their questions. Voters are entitled to know what candidates think about a wide range of issues as part of making up their minds about whom to support and vote for, but requiring answers to detailed questions on sometimes arcane topics of narrow economic interest as part of an endorsement process comes very close to quid pro quo. The answers may only reflect the candidate's best thinking at the time. The questioners consider the answers to be commitments for future votes.

Politics is a deal. Justice Anthony Kennedy expressed it well in the Supreme Court's decision in *McConnell v. Federal Election Commission*: "Favoritism and influence are not . . . avoidable in representative politics. It is in the nature of an elected representative to favor certain policies, and, by necessary corollary, to favor the voters and contributors who support those policies. It is well understood that a substantial and legitimate reason, if not the only reason, to cast a vote for, or to make a contribution to, one candidate over another is that the candidate will respond by producing those political outcomes the supporter favors. Democracy is premised on responsiveness."

The road from "responsiveness" to quid pro quo, from representing your constituents to selling your soul, however, runs through a valley filled with fog, and temptation sits by the side of that road and offers to take you by the hand and show you the way.

Are there ways we can change the law, cut the influence of money, reduce the temptations, or even the playing field without limiting the ability of people to actively pursue their political interests? The suggestions are numerous. They include removing the limits on contributions to candidates and parties, allowing them to compete on a more equal footing with independent groups; reducing the corrupting influence of money on candidates by setting up a system that would keep candidates from knowing who contributed; full public financing of campaigns; and full disclosure of all sources of funds supporting campaign activities.

Given the fact that the Supreme Court has ruled that the right of free speech includes being able to spend money to spread your message, and given the idea that democracy doesn't readily lend itself to justifying limits on individuals' political activities, it is difficult to visualize solutions that will avoid the appearance of corruption and keep large contributions from unduly influencing the outcome of elections. Even full public financing of campaigns would apply only to what the candidate spends. It wouldn't affect independent expenditures.

One perhaps fruitful approach comes jointly from authors associated with the Campaign Finance Institute, the Brookings Institution and the American

Enterprise Institute. Recognizing that the effort to "restrict money in politics" is "intrinsically limited . . . and in some respects futile," they instead aim "to empower citizens." To counter the influence of the rich and powerful, "you have to find some way to bring more people into the system . . . to equalize by building up instead of by squeezing down. . . . Our primary objective . . . is not to get private money out of campaigns, but to get many more small donors in, if you will, to multiply the power of individual citizens."

Rather than focusing on the "negative goal" of preventing corruption and continuing what have "become rigid and stylized" arguments over contribution and spending limits, the authors seek with their recommendations to further the positive goals of "competition, candidate emergence and citizen participation," making our democracy more robust and reducing the corrupting influence of money (particularly from large single sources).

The authors would retain limits on contributions to candidates and parties but would provide matching grants (at some multiple) from public funds for small contributions to candidates who agree to abide by the more restrictive limits. Small donors with limited income would be eligible for tax credits or rebates. There would be no limit on expenditures, just on contributions. The more small donors a candidate recruits, the more money would be available to spend. Unlimited coordinated spending by political parties in support of their candidates would be allowed, but only with funds collected from small donors.

The authors are particularly concerned about getting the incentives right, so that more individuals are motivated to run for public office, more candidates and parties are motivated to keep seeking out small donors throughout a campaign, and more individual voters are motivated to become involved in politics. To facilitate political participation and transparency, they suggest subsidizing universal and affordable broadband, using the internet to rebuild a "public square," and creating an easily accessible website where all election information relevant to voting would be posted, including all campaign donors, expenditures, and advertising buys.

Their ideas avoid the constitutional questions connected with free speech. They recognize political realities. They work with rather than counter to human nature. They encourage more participation at all levels by more people. They don't try to achieve what can't be achieved. Their suggestions may be doable. What the authors don't do, however, is solve the problem of the billionaire deciding to spend $10 million to elect a couple of friendly legislators.

Some responsibility lies with each of us. We are inclined to think of our opponents as being "bought" by their contributors, while we happily contribute to principled candidates who support what we believe in. We also forget that those are *our* votes being influenced by all the advertising expenditures. It is our choice how we cast them.

The underlying problem that we always have to keep solving is how to achieve a political power structure that is more participatory, more accountable, and more responsive. Just moving in the right direction is a modest goal, but in politics, more so than in most endeavors, trying for the "perfect" often defeats the "good." There is always a political power structure that needs to be kept in check. If money doesn't dominate, some other source of power will. All of the reform efforts directed at removing political bosses and political machines only cleared the way for the ascendency of money. Perhaps the founding fathers had it right: the best way to curb power is to create competing centers of power.

Regardless of what we are able to accomplish, temptation will still sit by the side of the political road offering assistance to all who travel.

13. EVERYBODY WANTS TO GO TO HEAVEN; NOBODY WANTS TO DIE

BUD WAS A RELIABLE VOLUNTEER IN ALL OF MY CAMPAIGNS. A MEMBER OF the United Auto Workers union, he had worked on the heavy machinery assembly line at Fiat Allis for twenty-five years. It was his first job after high school. A natural politician, he always seemed to end up on the winning side of the battles for leadership of the union local. He knew who to see and what to do. He wasn't satisfied with just trying; he kept at it, whatever the task, until he got it done. He had little use for those who pushed to the head of the line when patronage jobs and scholarships were being handed out and then always seemed to have another commitment when volunteers were needed in the days before an election. His laconic comment one day when he was having trouble recruiting people to put up yard signs: "Everybody wants to go to heaven; nobody wants to die."

We all want to win the election; we are not always willing to pay the price and take the necessary steps.

Because politics is serious, because there are winners and losers, because resources, money, and power are taken from some and given to others, because some dreams are fulfilled and others are dashed, the game is played for keeps by professionals who make their living and careers as politicians. As part of our civic heritage, we think that politics is everyone's game; everyone can play, everyone can win. Lured by the excitement and the prospect of making a difference, we abandon the role of spectator and get involved in the action. But in politics, like sports, when part-time amateurs play full-time professionals, the professionals almost always win, and the amateurs lose. If by accident or by fortuitous circumstance the amateurs happen to win one, they almost always lose the rematch.

Good intentions and hard work are rarely enough to defeat those who have spent their lives as politicians, who have worked to establish relationships and credibility, who know the issues that divide people, who are familiar with the motivations that move individuals and groups, who have practiced the skills of communicating, who know the right people to call, and who work at their vocation every day. Some are more skilled than others. Some are naturally talented and have an instinctive feel for the levers of power; they possess a knowledge of what people want and what price they put on themselves. As in other professions, it helps if you grew up in a political family, learning the political skills, with a political name to inherit. The better politicians have a sure sense of the sources of their influence and the actions necessary to preserve and expand that influence. They are hard to beat.

Elections are fundamentally fair, but that doesn't mean that everyone has an equal chance of winning. Those who have power are not reluctant to use it to further their own interests. In politics, neither involvement nor the righteousness of one's cause nor hard work entitles success. Power has to be taken, and the struggle can be long.

Faced with the difficulty of winning, some who would like to reform the political process and change the results never get involved, thinking the fight against the money and power of entrenched interests is "useless"; change will never come. Others who do get involved have the attitude that they should win because they are following the rules and working within the system. When they lose, they lose faith, blame the system, and drop out. A few keep working at winning, and some succeed.

As Saul Alinsky, the "radical" Chicago community organizer during the 1950s and 1960s, told the youth who were deeply disappointed in the 1968 national Democratic convention's support of the Vietnam War, "Go home, organize, build power and at the next convention, *you be the delegates.*" Many did just that.

The path to success is relatively simple: with 51 percent of the vote you can be the one making policy.

The would-be reformer says, "Yes—but . . ."

"But what? Sell the program; get the votes."

"It's hard."

"Yes, it is."

Candidates and campaign workers who have lost elections are often reluctant to acknowledge that perhaps they didn't run a very good campaign, that they could have had a clearer message, that their rhetoric could have been more persuasive, that they could have been more creative, or even simply that the majority of voters just didn't agree with them and that more work needs to be done if minds and votes are going to be changed. Paul Simon, who later served in the U.S. Senate, lost the primary for Illinois governor in a race he should have won. He laid the blame on the voters who weren't "ready" for his message. More recently, a friend, after losing a second race for local office, sent out this message: "I am getting a little tired of fighting for a city that doesn't care enough to pay attention."

We want simple solutions, easy fixes that save us from the hard work of persuading 51 percent of the voters and winning. We prefer symbolic actions to concrete actions because then we don't have to change our own habits. President Ronald Reagan repeatedly called for a constitutional amendment to require balanced budgets and routinely submitted hugely unbalanced budgets to Congress. Voters who want to impose constitutional term limits on elected officials keep reelecting incumbents. Balanced budgets and throwing out incumbents can both be achieved by taking responsibility and just doing it.

With all that is written and spoken about political reform, strategy, power, personalities, and groups, it is easy to forget the one essential fact of democratic majority rule: the individual vote is what matters. From local school board elections to decisions made by Congress, the individual vote is the unit of power. In elections, that power is spread out equally among all of us; each of us has one vote, one unit of power. As we go up the line, from city council, to county board, to state assembly, to Congress, the power becomes more concentrated, but each member of each body still has one vote in that body, one unit of power. The rule for making decisions is simple. If your votes add up to 50 percent plus one, you win. The path to heaven is built on votes. But you have to go out and get them.

Too many think there is a shortcut. David Stockman, former congressman and budget director for President Reagan, is one. Disagreeing strongly with recent policy and seeing no hope for improvement, he proposed to change the political system in a radical way. Assuming that officeholders will do the right thing and make the tough decisions only when they don't have to face the voters in any future election, Stockman argued for the "abolition of incumbency itself." Among the changes he called for in a *New York Times* op-ed piece were limiting the president and all members of Congress to a single six-year term with no possibility of reelection; providing 100 percent public financing of campaigns; shortening campaigns to eight weeks; prohibiting anyone who has ever been on a legislative or an executive payroll from ever lobbying during the rest of their lives; and requiring balanced budgets.

It would be so much easier just to go out, get the votes, win an election, and enact the policies you want than to make all those changes happen with the hope that the changes will get you the candidates who will get you the policies.

Too often, efforts to reform our politics have met with unintended consequences. In particular, term limits and campaign finance laws have reduced the influence of elected officials while increasing the influence of political action committees, lobbyists, agency personnel, think tanks, and other well-funded private organizations that never have to account publicly for their actions. In a democratic system that requires public knowledge and public participation to work well, the relative power balance between the more public political actors and the more private actors makes a great deal of difference. The reforms in recent years have moved us in the wrong direction, shifting power to individuals and organizations that have narrower interests and are less visible, less responsive, and less transparent than elected officials and political parties.

I keep being surprised by how many people tell me that term limits will solve the problems of our politics. Rooted in the public's general disfavor of all politicians, term limits reflect the throw-all-the-bums-out attitude. If, as the thinking goes, limits are placed on the number of terms a person can serve, then we will be free from professional politicians. We will be able to return to the days of the citizen legislator who, with native common sense, goes to the capitol and pursues the common good for a few years, with no thought of personal advancement, before returning home to take up private life again where it had been left.

Knowledge is power, and knowledge doesn't come overnight. A legislator, new to the capitol and new to politics, is much more likely to be influenced, led, fooled, and bamboozled by staff, bureaucrats, leaders, the governor, lobbyists, constituents, supporters, and friends than a legislator who has dealt with the same and similar issues before, knows the various motives of the people involved, understands that nobody tells the whole truth, and has some idea of where the bodies are buried.

In Wisconsin, the state budget runs about fifteen hundred pages; the "plain-language" version runs six hundred pages and comes in four different versions (as it goes through the process) supplemented with agency detail and a lot more pages. Looking back on her first year as senator, Kathleen said several times, "Was that really in the budget? Did I vote for that?" After five budgets she commented, "Every year I go through the budget process, I know more. I better see the trends. I know what to ask. The details are more familiar. I can connect the dots better." Term limits effectively take away from the voter the opportunity of keeping that experience and the influence that comes with it in the legislature.

When I was a reporter in Louisville in the 1960s, Kentucky had a tradition of rotating legislators among the counties that made up a district. One county would nominate a candidate in one election, and another county would nominate the candidate in the next. Effectively, terms were limited. Over the decades leading up to the 1960s, half the representatives and almost three-fourths of the senators served only one term; 90 percent of the representatives served six years or less, and 90 percent of the senators served eight years or less. The legislature, with little cumulative experience, was no match for the governor. The governor's budget was routinely passed by both House and Senate without amendment and sent back to the governor for his signature by the fifth day of the session—the minimum number of days required by the Kentucky constitution. Only once in thirty years had legislators "broken" the budget—allowing amendments to be introduced and considered. Other major bills the governor wanted were treated similarly—passed in five days without amendment.

The inexperienced freshman does not inherit the knowledge, the savvy, or the power of the incumbent who left because of term limits. That power instead flows to the other players, non-officeholders who are not term limited. The powerbrokers will still be the powerbrokers, but with more influence. Just as campaign finance limits on candidates and political parties shifted money and influence to more shadowy and less accountable groups, term limits on elected officials serve to decrease the power of elected politicians and increase the power of nonelected politicians. The power does not flow back to the people.

Not only do term limits shift influence from elected to nonelected centers of power but the thinking behind term limits is profoundly undemocratic. The implication is that voters are a bad influence on officeholders, motivating them to do what is popular rather than to do what is best for the state or the country. That is not what the founders believed. For them, the requirement that officeholders regularly go back to the voters to be reelected was the cornerstone of democratic government. The founders believed that people are capable of governing themselves wisely, and they exercised that power through their votes. The prospect of having to face the voters in the next election was the guarantee that the officeholder would do a good job.

Term limits turn that assumption on its head. Rather than the next election being the incentive for the officeholder to do the right thing, the next election instead motivates the officeholder to follow the most personal of goals—getting reelected. It is only when the politician is freed from checking back in with the voters, that personal ambition will be stilled and the public good will be served. Officeholders who don't have to worry about getting reelected will do what is right instead of what is politically expedient. The unspoken assumption is that doing what the people want in order to get reelected makes for bad government. The argument that decision-makers will make better decisions if they don't have to go back to the voters is more supportive of oligarchy where the rulers rule because they "know better" than the rest of us; in a democracy, the underlying principle is "of the people, by the people and for the people."

In a democracy, it is the voters, with their previous votes and with their anticipated votes, who give legitimacy to officeholders and authority to their decisions. For the term-limited officeholder, that connection to the voter is weakened. Influence and legitimacy are both reduced. The lame duck might be free from the voters, but that freedom is accompanied by a loss of legitimacy and authority. The lame duck really is lame.

The temptation for those who don't get what they want is to blame the system. Advocates of reform—like Stockman—can feel good about themselves and not have to get involved in the messy work of politics. If democracy is the answer, let it work. Let the people decide. If the people don't make good decisions, work at changing their hearts, minds, and attitudes.

Democracy is elegant in its simplicity. The vote is the unit of power. Everyone has one. The elected leader has power because he or she embodies a majority of the votes cast in the last election and can exercise all of the power represented by those votes until the next election. Power and legitimacy come from the direct connection of voters to leaders. Reforms, however well intentioned, that interfere with that connection or make it more complicated serve to diminish the power of the vote, shift power to other sources, and, as a result, weaken democratic structures.

The 1870 Illinois constitution created an elected statewide superintendent of schools. Many of the major education policy and funding decisions originated with the state superintendent, who, because the office was elective, was both political and partisan. One hundred years later, delegates to the 1970 constitutional convention decided that education was too important to be subject to partisan politics and that policy should be set by an appointed state board of education that would in turn appoint the state superintendent. They would take politics out of education by giving authority to a nonelected professional. What happened, however, was quite different. Decisions by the nonelected state superintendent carried no political weight. Funding and policy decisions shifted to the School Problems Commission, made up of elected senators and representatives, and to the governor's office. Important political decisions are always going to be made by elected politicians because our votes give power and legitimacy to those decisions. You can't take politics out of politics.

The fundamental questions for every serious political organizer who wants to win are: Who gets to vote? How many votes does it take to win? How do we get them? Everything else is distraction.

People in a neighboring county who had organized to persuade the county board to place a referendum on the ballot in the next election came to me for advice the night before their request was to be heard by a board committee. I asked: What committee? Who are the members? How many votes are needed? They didn't know. Intent on how best to make the case for their issue, they hadn't given thought to the essential step of getting the necessary votes.

When I was a delegate to the Democratic National Convention, one of our tasks was to elect six people to serve as members of the Democratic National Committee. The vote kept getting postponed as leaders of the various factions in the delegation tried to reach agreement on a consensus slate. In the meantime, one person who wanted the job walked around asking individual delegates, "Will you vote for me?" By adding votes one by one, he won, quite easily, despite not being included later on the "agreed" list.

In Illinois, party precinct leaders are elected in the party primary by the voters who live in the precinct. The county party chair is then elected by the precinct leaders. One year when I was challenging the incumbent for county party chair, there were multiple races for precinct leader, and I was one of those with opposition. I had been around the precinct twice, some of it three times, talking with my neighbors and asking for votes. By election morning I had a stack of three-by-five cards with the names, addresses, and phone numbers of everyone I thought would vote for me—if they got to the polling place. As people voted, I tossed their cards, and as the day wore on, my stack, which was ordered by address, dwindled. At two o'clock I figured the vote was about even. Only half the people who had voted were in my original stack of names. I began asking my supporters as they left the polling place to remind their neighbors who were on my cards that it was Election Day, to tell them that the race was close, and to ask them to come in and vote. Almost without exception, within a half hour of making my request, the neighbor would show up. One woman with a migraine headache came in. If anyone but her neighbor had knocked on the door, she would not have responded; neither would she have responded if I had not talked with her earlier. The margin of victory, a relatively slim seventeen votes, all came in during the last several hours. None of that would have happened without the early conversations at front doors and in living rooms, without knowing the voters, knowing the number needed to win, knowing who would vote for me, and getting their votes cast and counted.

Asked by a staff person of the Wisconsin Counties Association how I was elected chair of the fourteen-member county board in my first term, my answer was somewhat provocative, but simple: "I could count to eight."

The task of the political organizer who wants to win against the odds is to talk with people, give them a vision of what they can accomplish, and show them the connection between voting and the rest of their lives. It is hard work, it takes time, and it requires faith in the intelligence and judgment of the average person. As the revolutionary Frantz Fanon wrote in *Wretched of the Earth* about the struggle against colonialism, "The masses understand perfectly the most complicated problems. . . . [E]verything can be explained to the people, on the single condition that you really want them to understand."

Change will be possible when those who see themselves as victims of the political process—and helpless to accomplish anything—begin to realize that they hold the ultimate power: their vote. The millions spent on campaigns are spent to influence their vote. Their vote is valuable. Their vote counts. They are not helpless. They are not victims. They own a vote.

Political organizers the world over who have gone up against the establishment have done so with confidence in the ability of people to change their thinking, change their lives, and ultimately change their communities. Their common tools have been interacting personally, engaging in dialogue, talking genuinely, treating people with respect, and meeting listeners where they are and moving forward from there. As individuals begin to understand why things are the way they are and how things might be changed, they start to change themselves and become energized to take the necessary actions to make things happen.

The first step is freeing people from the belief that nothing they do will make things better and nothing will ever change. Mahatma Gandhi, who led India to independence, preached incessantly to his countrymen that the first step to freeing themselves from England was to *think* of themselves as being free and to *act* as though they were free. In *The Life of Mahatma Gandhi* by Louis Fischer, Gandhi is quoted as saying, "Man is bound by many chains, and the stoutest are forged in the inner smithy, not by church or state. You are not free because you do not free yourself."

When people see themselves differently, they see the world differently. Omar Cabezas, one of the early Sandinista leaders in Nicaragua, described in *Fire from the Mountain* the transformation of *campesinos*, rural subsistence farmers. "Who can say what the process was, but the thing is they were listening, listening, listening. The ideas would travel from their brains to their eyes, and by the look in their eyes I knew their world was turning upside down . . . and so we recruited more people."

Abraham Lincoln, the consummate American politician, recognized that change didn't come without a personal relationship. In an early speech on temperance to the homefolk in Springfield, he said, "If you would win a man to your cause, first convince him you are his sincere friend." That is the way to his heart, "which when once gained, you will find but little trouble in convincing his judgment of the justice of your cause, if indeed that cause really be a just one." He knew that you can't sell a program to the voters until they are ready and that a leader can't move forward without popular support. In her Pulitzer Prize–winning biography of Lincoln, *Team of Rivals: The Political Genius of Abraham Lincoln*, Doris Kearns Goodwin attributed much of his political success to an "exceptionally sensitive grasp of the limits set by public opinion. . . . [H]e had an intuitive sense of when to hold fast, when to wait, and when to lead."

It is the waiting and the step-by-step-by-step progress that makes us impatient. We have a vision of what can be. We are eager to make things better. We don't understand why not everyone agrees immediately. We are impatient with Alinsky's advice in *Rules for Radicals*, that "it is necessary to begin where the world is if we are going to change it to what we think it should be. That means working in the system. . . . Effective organization is thwarted by the desire for instant and dramatic change. . . . To build a powerful organization takes time. It is tedious, but that's the way the game is played—if you want to play and not just yell, 'Kill the umpire.'"

Vaclav Havel, the dissident playwright who became president of Czechoslovakia after the popular uprising that ended nearly fifty years of Communist rule, started to speak when there was no hope of achieving change. In his essay "The Power of the Powerless," in *Open Letters*, he writes, "For us this waiting was based on the knowledge that it made sense on principle to resist by speaking the truth simply because it was the right thing to do, without speculating whether it would lead somewhere tomorrow, or the day after, or ever. This kind of waiting grew out of the faith that repeating this defiant truth made sense in itself, regardless of whether it was ever appreciated, or victorious, or represented the hundredth time. At the very least, it meant that someone was not supporting the government of lies. It also, of course, grew out of the faith—but this is of secondary importance—that a seed once sown would one day take root and send forth a shoot. No one knew when. But it would happen someday, perhaps for future generations."

Few have the stamina or resolve of Gandhi and Havel who, even without the possibility of using a democratic election to bring change, were able to achieve their goals. Too often in our politics, where participation is easier and elections are relatively civil affairs, those who try once or twice without winning give up and check out, blaming the voters or the system, or they turn their attention away from changing minds and winning elections, where decisions are made, to the largely symbolic act of reforming politics.

The easy part of winning elections is knowing who gets to vote, who is likely to vote, and how many votes it will take to win. The more difficult part is persuading individuals to change their voting habits—from one party to the other, or from not voting at all to casting a vote. Voting habits don't change readily, as any cursory look at ward vote totals over time will attest. People pay attention to "facts" they already agree with and tune out evidence to the contrary. It takes direct experience, or time and personal communication, to change an individual's perceptions, attitudes, and voting habits.

Much of what is described today as political organizing has little to do with dialogue, persuasion, or building consensus from the bottom up. Today's campaigns are not designed to change basic attitudes. They are built around sophisticated databases with individual profiles constructed with information about your personal history, voting habits, purchasing preferences, the magazines you subscribe to, and the internet sites you browse. Few political messages attempt to engage voters in a dialogue. Rather, they follow the basic concepts of commercial advertising, mirroring back to the prospective customer what the customer already thinks and attaching the product to the desires, aspirations, fears and prejudices already in place.

Change will begin to be possible when candidates and officeholders who organize at the neighborhood level and engage voters in conversation are rewarded with votes. Change, if it comes, will come slowly—one step at a time, one campaign at a time—as people who typically vote one way begin to vote another, and as those who typically don't vote begin to do so.

We all want to win the election; we are not always willing to do the necessary work. We want to go to heaven, but we don't want to die.

14. NOT IN MY BACKYARD

CAN WE REGAIN POLITICAL CONTROL OF OUR OWN BACKYARDS? ARE THERE individuals in the community who are willing to commit the necessary time and resources to create locally owned political power? Even so, would that be enough to compete and win?

The conventional wisdom suggests the answer is no. The momentum toward centralization throughout our society is too great. All aspects of our economy—manufacturing, farming, transportation, retailing, banking, financial services, entertainment, information, popular culture—are becoming more centralized. The units are larger. Decisions are made by fewer people, further removed from the results of what they decide. All the stores in the mall are branches of national chains, with local managers who have no roots in the community and will soon be moving on. The bank on Main Street is a branch. The newspaper is part of a national chain. The radio station carries only nationally syndicated programs and no local news. The local department store has been replaced by Target; the local hardware store by Lowe's; the local jewelry store by Kay Jewelers; everything else local by Walmart.

Throughout history, economic and political power have been connected. It is not surprising that as economic power has moved from the local to the center that political power has followed. Where local economic interests and local political power were once centered in the community and worked together for mutual local benefit, centralized economic and political interests now work together to undermine local control. Dollars collected by political and economic interests at the center fund the campaigns of local candidates who are attuned to the interests at the center.

As early as the 1960s, political organizer Saul Alinsky in *Rules for Radicals* recognized that "in a highly mobile, urbanized society the word 'community' means community of interests, *not* physical community." The ties that matter to us are not those we have with our neighbors but the ones we have with those who share our interests, regardless of where they live. Alinsky said there were two exceptions to his observation: ethnic ghettos and political campaigns, where interests and geographical boundaries do coincide. If he were writing today, he would not include political campaigns. Political officeholders are still elected to represent physical communities, but those who play the major roles in electing them represent organized interests from outside the community. The residents of the community are the targets of campaigns, their votes are coveted, but the community is only a battlefield on which interests from outside the community marshal their forces as part of a much larger war to gain control of policy decisions at the state and national levels. Much like the mother country in the old colonial system, organized interests at the center seek to place in power someone out in the "colony" who will be responsive to them.

It is hard to fault the candidates who go to the center looking for support. They are socialized within a system where money is the essential resource for campaigns, and that money is available at the center from organized interests. They may not appreciate all the ties that bind until the strings begin to be pulled once they are in office.

Local political organizing, led by local people concerned with local issues, is now almost always connected with fighting something physical that someone from the outside wants to locate in the community: a landfill, a power plant, a sand mine, a wind turbine, high-voltage transmission lines, a Walmart, or a waste incinerator. "Not in my backyard" is the one motivation that still brings people together to fight for their idea of community. Perhaps it shouldn't be surprising given Alinsky's observation that the issues communities come together over are proposals that would change the physical character of the community, one value we share with our neighbors.

Almost no one shows up at meetings of the Buffalo County Board of Supervisors or at its committee hearings. Turnout at board elections is low. When proposals surfaced to locate sand mines and a railroad loading facility in Buffalo County, however, hearings had to be moved to high school auditoriums to accommodate the numbers who wanted to hear and to be heard. Emotions were high, and the rhetoric was sometimes heated. Overwhelmingly, the people who spoke said they came to Buffalo County because it is a great place to live, and they didn't want that changed. It was the quality of life that had drawn them, the natural beauty, the rural character, the good schools. If they had wanted industrial activity, they would have gone somewhere else. If mining came in, they would move.

Because the connection is not so direct and visible, people tend to forget that most of the policy decisions made at the center by the representatives they elect also change the community and affect the quality of their lives. Banking law dictates what kind of bank, if any, will be on Main Street. School funding formulas affect the number and variety of courses taught at the high school. Access to broadband and other communication networks varies depending on the law. Clean water, workplace safety, transportation, law enforcement, fire protection, and most of the qualities that make a community attractive depend on decisions made by those elected to serve on legislative bodies. Because everything affects the "backyard," the people who live there need to reassert their power on more issues than just those that change the physical environment.

That power exists on Election Day. All of the important decisions that shape the quality of life in a community are made by local voters at the ballot box. That is the time and place to exert local influence. The tools to change election results are there for local people to use. Personal communication is still the most effective way to persuade. Commercial advertisers continually seek new and innovative ways to get their products inserted into social media communications among friends. The "ground game" of campaigns—the phone calls to neighbors, the conversations at front doors, the personal messages that go out over social networks—is credited with making the difference in close elections.

The internet has made person-to-person communication much easier—anyone can freely send out messages. And, although personal communication has often been organized from the center in recent campaigns, it is a tool that is essentially local. Communication between two individuals who know each other is local. Putting a neighbor on front porches is a local activity. Texting a friend is a local activity. All of the resources necessary to make those conversations take place are available in the community. They can be used to build local political power. The pieces missing most often are a vision and leadership.

In part, this is a matter of attitude. Most people are not "politically" inclined. People will work to support an individual candidate they like or a particular issue they feel strongly about, but they are not motivated to get involved in party-building activities—developing a vision for the local community, finding the candidates to support that vision, and gathering the resources to elect those candidates. To effectively make political power local again, some ongoing structures resembling the old political parties that were rooted in their local communities will have to be created. The difficulty of doing that and the reluctance of people to get involved in such an effort cedes power to outside interests and money.

In part also, it is a question of incentive, particularly for individuals thinking about running for office. Every candidate faces a choice of what kind of campaign to run. The prospect of putting together a neighborhood-based political organization and the time and effort that requires can be daunting. It is so much easier to seek the support of the already organized interests at the center who will provide the money and messages to win. The incentive or temptation to tap into the national support networks and gain a financial edge is enormous. There are personal advantages for the candidate in doing so, but the result is an ever-widening disconnect between the local residents who provide the votes and the not-so-local people who provide the money and resources for running campaigns.

WHAT WOULD IT TAKE TO MAKE POLITICS LOCAL AGAIN? WHAT WOULD THAT look like?

First, there has to be an intentional desire on the part of local people to control their own destiny. If we are going to return political power to the local, the impetus, the push, the leadership, the goals for political activity have to originate at the local level. That requires a different mindset. It requires local political organizations that are capable of recruiting, training, funding and electing their own local candidates who reflect local values and respond to local concerns.

To control your own destiny, you have to be self-sufficient. Several times over the last decade the Eau Claire County Democratic Party has come up with plans to organize locally only to go to the state party and ask for funding. Not surprisingly, control accompanied the funds. Staff activities were directed by the state party, not the county party.

A couple of organizing cooperatives have been formed in Wisconsin that do combine local control with local resources. The model is elegant and straightforward. Two hundred or more people form a cooperative and agree to contribute a certain amount of money per month to hire a full-time organizer who works at the direction of the cooperative. Local parties could do the same.

If the intent is there, the second requirement of returning politics to the local level is a shared vision of what that destiny might look like. This doesn't mean that everyone at the local level has to have the same ideas and beliefs, the same vision for the community. It does mean that locals must commit to getting together and working out their differences. They must agree among themselves about what is good for the community.

Over the years we have created all kinds of groups we belong to: professional, occupational, trade, environmental, ideological, promotional, almost all of which are organized on a hierarchical basis. And we have ceded political decision-making to the state and national leaders of those organizations. Local chapters need to take back political power from their state and national committees and make their own endorsements of local candidates. The political dynamic would change if local doctors made the medical society endorsements of local candidates, local farmers the Farm Bureau endorsements, local business owners the chamber of commerce endorsements, local workers the union endorsements, and local environmentalists the Sierra Club endorsements. Power would also move back toward the local if members of these organizations made their political contributions directly to their own local candidates rather than funneling their money through their state or national organizations.

Creating enough local political power to offset the influence of outside individuals and groups seems daunting. It is not a matter of all or nothing, however. The local needs only enough power to provide the margin of victory and determine the winner. If you can do that, everybody will listened to you. During his career, "Lop Ear" Jones was the most sought after precinct committeeman in Springfield. If he was for you, you could count on three hundred votes from his precinct; if he wasn't for you, you could count on three hundred votes going to your opponent. You couldn't beat him. He worked his territory, he knew his people. Statewide candidates knew who he was and sought his support. It matters in which direction power flows. It matters who takes the lead. If you want a say, you have to be able to deliver—deliver votes that is. If you do deliver, others will listen.

The colonial system worked. Officials selected by the mother country served the interests of the mother country, and the mother country favorably rewarded their officials. People in the colonies felt disenfranchised and powerless until they took power and decided for themselves who their leaders would be. So today, if we want to make politics local again, we have to be able to say to the interests at the center, "Not in my backyard." Then we have to make it stick.

The danger we face is that outside individuals and groups are rapidly becoming the only players in our elections, fueling the widespread alienation of voters and their discontent with current politics. It is only as we create organizations at the local level capable of providing a counterforce that voters will begin to feel that they have influence and that elections make a difference.

Power can be taken back once people realize at the gut level that the vote is the unit of power in a democracy and that every vote is a local vote. Money is the only thing that comes from the center, and that money has to persuade local votes before it can win. For voters to have the opportunity to cast their ballots for local interests, however, there has to be a booth with local wares in the political market. Constructing that booth and developing those wares are not easy tasks.

15. SUMMONING THE BETTER ANGELS OF OUR NATURE

THOSE WHO ARE GOVERNED WANT TO KNOW, HOW DO WE MAKE SURE WE are ruled well? It is an old question, but always relevant and urgent and asked in many different ways. It lies behind the complaint expressed more than once by a friend over a beer: "Why can't they just do the right thing?" Aristotle thought the answer was in the way governments are put together. In his many examples of government in *Politics*, he described what was "good and useful" in each one "and what is not." He concluded that none was "entirely satisfactory."

Adlai Stevenson III, after serving a term in the Illinois legislature, wrote that many of our political ills would be cured if more "good people" ran for office. Plato, in his *Republic*, agreed. For him, too, the quality of the leader was more important than the nature of the state. The "best philosophers and the bravest warriors" should be the rulers.

Those who would rule have a different goal: how do we get and keep power? Most still follow Machiavelli's advice in *The Prince*—do what is necessary. "It must be understood that a prince, and especially a new prince, cannot observe all those things which are considered good in men, being often obliged, in order to maintain the state, to act against faith, against charity, against humanity, and against religion."

Can a political leader be both good and successful? Vaclav Havel, in his essay "Thinking about Frantisek K" in *Open Letters*, asked the question this way: "Is it possible in today's complex world for people who are guided by their consciences or the basic ethical categories of the everyday world to take an active part in politics? Or must they always, albeit only within part of themselves, belong also to the world of ideologies, doctrines, political religions, and commonly accepted dogmas and clichés? Is it enough for them to believe in life, in the good, and in their own reason? Or must they also believe in something not quite so pure and simple, such as their own political party?"

It is a difficult question. Can the will to power be made to serve the common good? On all sides there is the drive to win, the demand for advantage, the desire to make others conform. Human nature is not going to change. Can we work with it? Can the better angels of our nature be summoned to our aid?

Perhaps in our political world that is organized around narrow specific interests pursuing their own goals, the question needs to be asked in a slightly different way. Can we achieve the common good by pursuing our individual good, or must we sacrifice our individual good for the common good? Can we pursue our own goals, vote to further our own interests, and still end with what is best for the community?

The economists answered that question by imagining an "invisible hand" that works through the mechanism of a "free market" to magically transform the pursuit of personal gain into the greatest good for the greatest number. Political philosophers, however, have not been as inventive. And so in politics we are left with the problem of how to get there from here. How do we, as we pursue individual political advantage, get to the common good?

What does the common good look like? Will we know it when we see it? If we achieve the common good, will we be ruled well?

The Declaration of Independence is as good a source as any for a description of what the common good might look like to those who are ruled. The rebel authors wrote forcefully that the purpose of any government is to secure the life, liberty, and happiness of the people, and the people have the right to alter or abolish any government that is destructive of those ends. Qianlong, the longest ruling emperor of China who held the throne for sixty-one years from 1735 to 1796, would have added harmony and prosperity to the list. For Aristotle, stability was important. Safety, liberty, happiness, harmony, prosperity, and stability are all things desired by those who are ruled. Each can be enjoyed personally, and all are qualities we want for the communities in which we live.

How do we ensure that power is used to those ends?

The most effective answer to date has been a constitutional democracy that divides power into a lot of small pieces. Each person gets one vote; one piece of power. The power that is delegated to elected leaders to act on behalf of the voters is granted for only a limited time and is divided among executive, legislative, and judicial offices, with each serving as a check on the other two. Decisions are made by majority vote. Placing ultimate power at the local level (with each individual) and separating powers at the center has tended to work. The democratic process is not self-enforcing, however. Those who seek to use power to achieve their own ends start by undermining the process, effectively taking power out of the hands of the voters, controlling elections, and eliminating the separation of powers. Under patronage, the worst offenses occurred in cities where the "boss" controlled everything: the governor, the state legislature, the mayor, the city council, the judges, the prosecutors, even the counting of votes. Every change in the rules, every change in the process that limits participation in any way serves to centralize power and make the common good more difficult to achieve. Spreading power broadly, so that there are checks and not a single source, is essential to achieving the common good.

Exercising power with self-restraint—at all levels, by all participants in the political game—is also essential. One could argue that self-restraint is not a quality likely to lead to political gain, and therefore to propose that politicians exercise self-restraint is idealistic mumbling. But consider again. Self-restraint is essential to successful politics.

The idea that politics makes living together possible goes back at least to Aristotle. As he saw it, the alternative is conflict. The man who has no state, who is not rooted in community is "mad on war . . . a non-cooperator like an isolated piece in a game of draughts." The essential quality that allows man to be political is "reasoned speech." The goal is a community characterized by goodness, rightness, and justice. "It is the sharing of a common view on these matters that makes a household or a city."

For Aristotle, moderation and restraint were both moral virtues and conditions of political stability. "Some people, believing that their own view of goodness is the only right one, push that view to extremes. . . . [States] have been destroyed by means of legislation carried to excess."

Aristotle spent a lot of time discussing various forms of government, particularly oligarchies, in which control lies with the few who are rich and wellborn, and democracies, in which control lies with the majority who are not well off. He described the advantages of each but advised both factions that whichever one ruled at a particular time it should pursue not only its own interests but also take care of the needs of the other if it wanted to maintain its stability and longevity. When neither "sets up a constitution fair and acceptable all round," the result is "constant strife and civil war."

Even Machiavelli saw self-restraint as being necessary for self-preservation. "Wise princes have studied diligently not to drive the nobles to desperation, and to satisfy the populace and keep it contented."

In the beautifully landscaped palace garden, the Emperor Qianlong would meditate and seek wisdom among clusters of small buildings. The names of the buildings give us insight into the emperor's mind and perhaps one of the secrets of his success: the Studio of Self Restraint; the Supreme Chamber of Creating Harmony, and the Pavilion of Prosperity. One can imagine the progression of his thought. Self-restraint on the part of the ruler creates harmony among the people, which leads to prosperity for all.

Self-restraint is not common among the players in today's winner-take-all-regardless-of-what-it-takes politics. There is little desire to accommodate the interest of the opposition. The goal, rather, is to dominate, even if that means subverting democratic processes. The result has been harsher rhetoric, increased animosity, and deeper divisions. Back when I was a member, the Illinois House of Representatives was a cordial body even though the diversity of opinion was very broad. The few times it erupted into angry shouting and near fisticuffs were in response to the Speaker breaking or ignoring the House rules in an attempt to pass something he didn't have the votes for.

The daily demonstrations that brought more than one hundred thousand people to Madison in the spring of 2011 were a response to the governor's attack on public employee rights that they had exercised for fifty years under the administrations of both parties. The governor described the cabinet meeting the night before he announced his plan as "the last hurrah before we dropped the bomb." The mindset behind the choice of those words is one of attacking an enemy. Opponents responded accordingly.

In Illinois and Wisconsin, there was a long history of allowing unions and business interests to work out changes in workers' and unemployment compensation. Whatever they agreed to, the legislature ratified. But there is a downside to simply rubber-stamping agreements between private parties. Not everyone gets to sit at the bargaining table, and the general public's stake in the outcome is too easily overlooked or ignored. On the other hand, if the practice is discontinued and one side or the other decides to go for everything it wants, the result is instability and increasing discord. In my first term when the House, Senate, and governor's office were all controlled by Democrats, the unions exerted huge pressure on members, and pushed through significant changes and large increases—only to see them rolled back several years later when the economics didn't work out. The comity, however, did not return. The same result occurred in Wisconsin when the Republicans, finding themselves in control of the legislature and the governor's office, unilaterally changed the law.

Self-restraint is not behavior we can order; it is behavior we can model. It is a road we can start to walk along. Politics will always be fought hard, and fought to win. Self-restraint would not require us to overlook our differences or to fight less vigorously to achieve our ends. It would require, however, a lowering of our voices, a reduction in the harshness of our rhetoric, a respect for differences in perspective, a sense of self-doubt, a sense that the world is not black and white, an understanding that no answer is perfect, and a belief that we are all in this together.

The inevitable question, of course, is who is going to go first? As long as everybody thinks in terms of war, self-restraint sounds like unilateral disarmament. Even though we might agree that we don't like the direction our politics is heading in, there appears to be no alternative, and we keep going even though we know we are going to end up where we don't want to be.

This is a human problem that shows up in other places, not just in politics. Competition among colleges to attract elite high school athletes has led to programs recruiting younger and younger players, so that now college scholarship commitments are being made to eighth graders. The practice is more common with women's sports (particularly soccer and lacrosse) than men's sports. Coaches and parents are quoted in a *New York Times* story about the damage done: "It is detrimental to the whole development of the sport, and to the girls. . . . It's the single biggest problem in college athletics. . . . It's killing all of us. . . . It's actually rather destructive. . . . It's caused this downward spiral for everybody."

Yet these same coaches fear that "if they don't do it, other coaches will, and will snap up all the best players." And the parents and athletes don't want to take the chance of missing out on scholarship money. "Is it a little bit sick? Yeah. You are a little young to do this, but if you don't, the other kids are going to."

Substitute a few words here and there and it could be political people talking about the political process that forces them to do all the things they don't want to do but have to in order to win.

Self-restraint is most commonly conceived as an altruistic sacrifice of one's own interest. A strong argument can be made, however, following Aristotle's thinking, that self-restraint is recognizing that one's interests are not singular but multiple. Each of one's multiple interests acts as a restraint on the others. No one interest is pursued at the expense of all the others. Self-restraint is hardest for those who pursue only one interest, who are fixated on achieving only one goal, and who elevate that goal above all others as *the* good that must be achieved. For individuals with multiple interests who have found ways to balance those interests within themselves, it is not a big step to also find common ground with others in the community. When we pay less attention to the singular and more to the multiple, we can come closer to achieving our own balance and being able to reach agreement with others on what is mutually acceptable.

Politics, however, is increasingly dominated by narrow, single interests. These are usually economic, connected to a single productive activity (banking, insurance, oil, tech, real estate), or ideological, connected to a particular belief about how the economy should work, how society should be organized, or how individuals should conduct their lives. Everything is seen through the lens of the single interest. The political narrative is one of conflict among interests with winners and losers. We don't recognize that we have multiplicities of interest.

When the political parties were stronger, the contest tended, more so than today, to be between different concepts of the common good. There have always been fundamental differences of opinion about how the community should be organized, most of which have economic roots that reflect the status of the adherents. The parties formed around those differences, and the Democratic and Republican Parties over the years have represented different coalitions of economic interests. Politics and profit have always been connected. But when the parties were strong, it was the party vision that was important, and specific economic interests fit in where they were most comfortable. As party strength diminished, however, the roles reversed, the vision of community dimmed, and the parties and officeholders attached themselves to the specific goals desired by more narrow economic and ideological interests. The political parties became more of a bundle of separate specific interests rather than an embodiment of some version of the common good. Candidates, who once depended on broad-based parties with a strong local presence to get elected, began to depend on centralized organizations with a single interest. Primaries are increasingly becoming contests between narrow interests that want their kind of Republican or their kind of Democrat elected. The various visions of the common good are all narrowing.

In our own communities, where we live, it is relatively easy to recognize that our economic self-interest is bound up with the good of the whole community. When we find ourselves outside of our own community, community interest falls away, leaving only our economic self-interest. As political power moves away from the local to the center, it inevitably becomes attached to the economic self-interests that exist apart from community. The more centralized our politics becomes, the more likely it is to be dominated by individual, narrow, what-we-do economic interests. The more local our politics, the more likely it is to reflect communal and noneconomic interests. Bringing political power back to the community goes a long way toward reconnecting self-interest with the common interest.

One doesn't need to go far to find an example. ExxonMobil, using its considerable centralized political power and pursuing its single economic interest, has promoted numerous fracking projects across the country over the objections of local residents, who see fracking as detrimental to the quality of their neighborhoods. The CEO of ExxonMobil, however, acting as an individual resident of his community, joined the local protest and signed on to a lawsuit seeking to block a fracking-related project, because among other things it would create a noise nuisance and traffic hazards, making his own neighborhood a less enjoyable place to live.

Is our politics doomed, like the adolescent athletes, to be sucked into a system that few want, where power is centralized, interests are narrowly economic, and money is dominant?

Can the better angels of our nature be summoned to our rescue? Can those who play the game be made to see the advantage of acting with some sense of self-restraint, some sense of community, some sense of self-doubt, some understanding of the complexities? Or, like Pogo in the old cartoon strip, will we end by acknowledging, "We have found the enemy and he is us"?

The better angels of our nature will not appear like a deus ex machina to remake our politics. The few at the center will not voluntarily give up the power they now hold. If all we do is hope for change, it will not happen.

The first step is rebuilding local political power structures committed to the welfare of their own communities. The story of organizing against great odds to overthrow established power begins when one person raises a rebel flag and starts talking to neighbors about why things are the way they are and how those things can be made better.

For candidates and officeholders, this means building a direct, ongoing relationship with their own voters (the source of power), thus increasing their control over their own destinies, giving them the ability to be independent of centralized interests and to say no when community interests are not served. Access to the voters is what confers power. Turning over one's campaign to a centralized source of power results in turning over one's legislative vote to that same power.

The contest between the Machiavellians and the better angels of our nature is not so much about tactics or choosing sides on a moral question as it is about choosing the terrain where the battle will be fought. The Machiavellians are most effective working from the center to control the local. They win when local democratic processes are weakened and power is gathered into a few hands at the center. Our better angels win when democratic processes are strong and power lies at the local.

The center and the local are at opposite ends of a continuum. Between them, there will always be a tension. Power never stays static. Its nature is to expand its reach and centralize its authority. Like water flowing downhill, power naturally moves from the local to the center. Periodically power has to be intentionally wrested back to the local. The center dominates now, but the preference of democracy is for the local. The idea of democracy starts with the individual, invests the ultimate source of power in the individual, and only then builds to the center. As power moves farther away from its local source, politics becomes less democratic. The tension is never resolved.

The better angels of our nature are more likely to be present at the local, where every individual participates more directly in the common good, where everyone lives with the results of the decisions they make and desires to be at peace with their neighbors. In your own community, it is more difficult to insist on everything for yourself, more difficult to demonize your opponent, more difficult to pretend you have all the answers, and more difficult to sell a fiction. The Machiavellians are at a disadvantage. Democracy has a preference for the local.

16. THE WORLD IS RUN BY THOSE WHO SHOW UP

WHAT OUR POLITICS (AND THE GOVERNMENT IT PRODUCES) LOOKS LIKE AND feels like at any particular time and place depends on who shows up: who shows up to vote, who shows up at meetings, who shows up to march in the streets, who shows up on their neighbor's porch, who shows up to write checks, who shows up to take a leadership role, who shows up to run for public office. No law or rule requires you to show up. Showing up is purely voluntary. Those who do show up, however, run the world and make the decisions for all of us.

Politics is about as easy a profession as there is to get started in, and advancement can occur relatively quickly. All you have to do is have some interest, show some judgment, and exercise initiative. For those who want to get involved, the door is wide open.

When I returned to Springfield in my late twenties, one of my goals was to be elected to public office. I had been a newspaper reporter, but I decided I would rather make the decisions myself than write about those who did. I started going to the monthly county party meetings. Shortly, I was appointed precinct committeeman and charged with turning out the vote in my neighborhood. Within a year I ran for town office and won by two votes. A year later I was on the ballot for state representative. I lost that election, but ran again four years later and won quite easily.

I remember the first county party meeting that Kathleen and I went to after moving to Buffalo County in Wisconsin. Being used to meetings of 100 to 150 people or more, I found it a dispiriting affair. Fewer than a dozen people sat around a table in the back room of a restaurant. The conversation was not lively. Kathleen, who began to show up regularly, was soon asked to chair the county party, and she began to build activity and enthusiasm. A couple of years later she ran for the state senate, won the democratic primary, and went on to defeat the incumbent Republican. That year, the party vote in the county increased by 39 percent.

Big-city politics is not much different from small-town politics. Phil Rock, reflecting on his early experiences in Chicago's 37th Ward, wrote in his autobiography *No One Calls Just to Say Hello,* "Because of my enthusiasm and work ethic, it wasn't long before I wound up in the ward's inner circle of 10 to 12 people . . . the 'backroom boys.' We would do more than set up and take down chairs. We were in on the political conversation about what was going on in the ward, in Cook County, and in the City of Chicago. . . . I am not sure that I was consulted much, but at least I was in on the conversation." Not many years passed between being "in on the conversation," and becoming president of the Illinois Senate.

In politics, as in every other profession, it helps if a member of the previous generation had started the family enterprise. Name recognition and family connections are nice pluses, but they are not necessary. For most, reaching a position of political influence is achieved by showing up and working at it. Newspaper and magazine profiles of political power brokers tell life stories that follow familiar patterns. They started early. They built relationships. They worked hard. They talked to people. They kept showing up.

Brian Rice, described by the *Minneapolis Star Tribune* as a "vital person" to be seen by those considering a run for office in Minneapolis, started working in campaigns when he was still in elementary school. As a boy he was more interested in reading election results than baseball scores. In the newspaper's profile, Rice was described by a city council member this way: "He's just a whiz at the mathematics of politics. He's seldom wrong and he is sought out by people running." His list of winners is impressive. The mayor added, "Those of us who know how things work certainly see his hand guiding a lot of the hardball politics."

Billy Vassiliadis, called "the kingmaker" by the *Los Vegas Sun* for his success in getting his candidates (regardless of party affiliation) elected in Nevada, has clout "so pervasive and so widely recognized within the state's corridors of power that he has been called Nevada's 'shadow governor.'" He first became politically active in the Young Democrats club at UNLV where he was, as his instructor described him to the *Sun,* brash, bold, energetic and wanting to get involved. A Las Vegas political consultant added, "He is a demon for work. He knows what everybody in town is thinking and doing. He spends so much time amongst them. He is one of the best political networkers that I've ever seen."

The Koch brothers have been credited with making Tea Party conservatism a force within the Republican Party in recent years. Many attribute their success to the money they spend on political campaigns, but it is also built on years of effort, starting with funding the Cato Institute in 1977, the Mercatus Center at George Mason University in the 1980s, Citizens for a Sound Economy in 1984, and the Foundation for Research on Economics and the Environment in 1985. They later joined forces with the Heritage Foundation, the American Enterprise Institute, and the American Legislative Exchange Council, helping to create a network of think tanks that together constructed the intellectual framework that provides the policies and rationale for today's conservatives.

In his obituary in the *New York Times*, Robert Strauss, who was ninety-five when he died, was described as a "backroom power broker" who was "almost invariably included in the tiny, powerful fraternity known as Washington's 'wise men.'" He started working in campaigns as a student at the University of Texas, kept on working in campaigns after graduation, and by the early 1970s was elected chair of the national Democratic Party. He held positions under and was advisor to presidents of both parties. He knew the right people, regardless of their politics, and worked at keeping in touch with them, the *Times* said, repeating one of Strauss's quotes: "If you mention a town to me, I know who the mayor or the sheriff or the commissioner is, and whether he is reliable or unreliable."

Some will read those stories and say, "I should have been born fifty years ago." That is not the point. There are fewer people active in politics today than there were back then. There are fewer people willing to run for office. There are fewer races that are contested. There are more opportunities for those who are motivated. It is still easy to get started. Ten signatures will get you on the ballot for precinct committeeperson in Illinois. Twenty signatures will get you on the ballot for county supervisor in Buffalo County in Wisconsin. Two hundred signatures will get you on the ballot for state Assembly. But you have to want to do it.

How and where to start? There are multiple roles and places for the young person who wants a career in politics or public service: as the activist who works passionately for a single cause; as the campaign volunteer who makes telephone calls, marches, in parades and knocks on doors; as the voter who takes the time to go to the polls; and as the candidate willing to put her or his name on the ballot.

When I first wanted to get involved, the local party headquarters was the place to show up. That is seldom the case now—even when the local party has a headquarters. The parties don't have the clout they used to have; they don't have the members or the resources. Politics is not local anymore. Wealthy individuals, single-issue groups, PACs and super PACs increasingly provide the resources that support political activity. They make the decisions; they wage the battles both within parties and between them over policy and the choosing of candidates.

Today, if you are young and interested in politics and want to get involved, the action and jobs are where the money is: with the super PACs, PACs, various interest groups, consulting firms, advertising agencies, pollsters, and campaigns. There is a lot of money and a lot of jobs in politics; many of them are ideal for those who are young and unattached, free to travel, ready to sleep on floors and subsist on pizza, beer, and coffee. There is a subculture consisting of those who go from interest group to interest group, campaign to campaign, picking up experience and being given more responsibility. The career path is familiar: campaign worker, campaign manager, assistant to the newly elected candidate, policy advisor, consultant, influential figure, power broker.

The downside is that if you do show up in those places, you will be socialized into the money/media political system dominated by the individuals and narrow interests that fund the payrolls. That is what the professional political organizers, consultants, pollsters, managers, and advisors, now in their thirties, forties, and fifties, know. That is what they practice. That is the reality they deal with. They are not interested in changing the system or in hiring those interested in changing the system. The activists and candidates who want to escape the dominance of single-issue groups are at a disadvantage, being limited in the funds they can raise and therefore limited in the talent they can hire. All of the advantage lies with the single-issue groups that are not limited in the money they can raise and spend. For those who are looking for a job and enjoy working in politics, there are few places where you can get paid for working to change the system.

The people who show up to work as volunteers in campaigns, march in demonstrations, attend rallies, sign petitions, organize their neighbors, join a political party, talk to their elected officials, and protest are as important as those who make a living in a political job. Policy doesn't get made in a vacuum. Elected officials make the laws, but laws get made within the context of prevailing public opinion. And it is here where most people first get involved. They find an issue or cause that motivates them to make a difference. Experiencing the connection firsthand between political action and results, they stay involved in shaping the opinions of their neighbors and take their place among those who run the world.

Motivation and interests are as infinitely varied as the personal circumstances in which people find themselves. There are avid followers, occasional participants, and those who have no interest. The most active people are, not surprisingly, those who have the strongest convictions. It takes motivation to leave the rocking chair in front of the fireplace. People with their own jobs, families, and interests often want to be left alone when it comes to politics. That is, until something they don't like affects them personally. When they hurt, they take action to stop the hurt. When things are going well, they become complacent. For many, then, it is one particular thing that gets them involved with politics for the first time. Racial discrimination and injustice led to Rosa Parks's refusal to give up her seat on the bus in Montgomery, the Freedom Marchers in Selma, and the students who sat in at the lunch counter in Greensboro. In Buffalo County, sand mining and zoning issues have filled high school gyms on cold winter nights. School tax referendums, civil rights, gay rights, women's equality, marriage equality, police actions, working conditions, labor organizing, income disparity, and wars have all brought committed people to their neighbors' front porches, into the streets, and into politics. Some have stayed.

In a survey conducted by a local county party of local volunteers who worked in a recent election, about three-fourths were motivated by political concerns. The reasons they gave were almost equally divided: this is my way to help choose future leaders; there was too much at stake to sit this one out; I'm a long-time party member; I liked the candidate. The other quarter presented social reasons: I like connecting with voters; my friends are volunteers; I really like being involved; because someone asked me. Although volunteering can mean a significant commitment of time, it doesn't require an adjustment in one's lifestyle or career. For many it is an enjoyable and meaningful experience.

Like young people looking for political jobs, activists are increasingly associating themselves with single-issue groups and spending their energies supporting a specific cause or a specific candidate rather than working for a political party. Parties are seen as too political, too partisan, and associating one's cause with a particular party is not something that many individuals or groups want to do. The Buffalo County Defenders, who organized themselves to oppose sand mining in the county, stay away from "politics." Even when Democrats overwhelmingly support and Republicans oppose their issues, there is a desire on the part of groups like the unions and the Sierra Club to avoid a partisan appearance. The same is true of the NRA and the Republicans.

For most people, their only active participation in politics is showing up at the polls on Election Day. By showing up and voting, they make the final decisions. But the selection from which they can choose has been determined by all those who showed up much earlier; showed up to be candidates, showed up to provide the resources, showed up to run the campaigns, showed up to knock on doors. What voters want might not be on the ballot. Their power to choose is limited by all of the earlier choices made by individuals to involve themselves as candidates and advocates. What the voter wants has to be embodied in a candidate who is on the ballot for the vote to be meaningful. When there are no candidates on the ballot who embody what voters are looking for, enthusiasm and interest decline. As Jay Leno once quipped, "If God wanted us to vote, he would have given us candidates."

Walter Lippmann, one of the more insightful American political columnists of the twentieth century, put it this way in Preface to Politics: "What the public does is not to express its opinions but to align itself for or against a proposal. If that theory is accepted, we must abandon the notion that democratic government can be the direct expression of the will of the people. We must abandon the notion that the people govern. Instead, we must adopt the theory that, by their occasional mobilizations as a majority, people support or oppose the individuals who actually govern." The individuals who "actually govern" are the ones who showed up much earlier.

Voters and candidates both function within the existing political system and are molded by it. Voter turnout has been trending down for the past fifty years, and in the off-year election of 2014 the percentage of eligible voters who showed up at the polls was the lowest since 1932. That shouldn't be surprising given the increasingly widespread opinion that all politicians are inept and self-serving, that the political system is run by money and special interests, and that political debate has descended to personal attacks, name-calling, and meaningless talking points. Politics today presents significant disincentives to people who might otherwise want to show up and participate—as candidates, as workers, as voters. Democratic self-government, however, depends on people showing up.

The most difficult role to show up for is that of candidate. The decision to become a candidate takes on a different dimension than the decision to get involved in other ways, and few can be persuaded to run even for a part-time local office. When sand mining was a controversial issue in Buffalo County, voters in only half the county board districts had the opportunity to choose sides on the issue. The other districts were uncontested. More recently, it took me three months to find someone willing to fill a vacancy on the county board.

Contemplating a run for the state legislature or Congress is even more daunting. For most, it means an interruption of a career and a significant change in lifestyle. In addition to becoming part of a profession generally held in low repute, you sacrifice your personal life, endure attacks on your integrity, work long hours, and take a cut in pay. It also means a lot of travel and a lot of time away from home. "Why would I do that?" is the most common response to the question, "Will you run for the legislature?" Because there are a lot of personal reasons for the average citizen not to run for public office, the individuals most likely to run are those who want to make a career of politics, those who are strongly motivated by ideology, or those with enough wealth that a "career" and "making a living" have little meaning. If that is the pool from which candidates can be chosen, then the pool is too shallow. But it's increasingly difficult to convince anyone to run who doesn't have a strong personal agenda, particularly as the personal negativity increases, public approval declines, the cost of campaigns skyrockets, and the pay falls further behind comparable jobs in the private sector.

The ideal citizen legislator is largely a myth. Almost no one I have spoken with envisions themselves as political. They don't feel themselves capable of taking part in what they think is a messy and sometimes nasty process, nor do they want to. Convincing people to run for public office, even local offices where there is little controversy, is difficult. They are often curious, fascinated by the details and the stories, but they are emphatic when they say, "I would never be a politician." Recognizing their own lack of experience and unwillingness to do the job, however, does not diminish their belief in the citizen legislator, the amateur politician, who, not beholden to anyone, gets elected, follows common sense, does the right thing, and then returns to private life, letting someone else take up the public responsibility for a time.

The story we tell ourselves doesn't reflect the world we live in. I have never run into anyone who is willing to interrupt a career, submit to a nasty campaign, and spend two to four years in the state capital just because it is their civic duty. The individuals who want to get involved in politics, who do show up, are those who either thoroughly enjoy the process and see it as a career or are committed to achieving some specific goal that requires political involvement.

And your reputation will suffer. People believe that politics is corrupt and that anyone who has been in politics for a while is tainted by the temptation of power. Even as a new candidate, you have to cope with the perception that although you may not be corrupt now, you probably will be soon. When asked for his vote in the county board election, a neighbor of mine, whom I had not previously met, said he was going to vote for me because I was new. He explained: "When people are first elected, they are concerned about what is good for the community, but after they have been in a while they start thinking about what is good for themselves." Even though he expressed hope in my integrity, there was doubt in his voice. It was clear that he would not be surprised if I let him down. I wondered what his reaction would be if I told him I had once been a state legislator in Illinois. I decided it wasn't necessary to tell him.

In addition to the personal disincentives for candidates to show up, there are political ones as well. The constant emphasis on raising money can have a chilling effect. Successive redrawing of district lines has significantly reduced the number of races that are competitive, thereby lowering the opportunity for a challenger to win. The demand by interest groups that candidates agree with them 100 percent on their issues leaves little room for candidates who think for themselves. Potential candidates who are not willing to be wholly owned subsidiaries become increasingly hesitant to show up. There is less and less room on the public stage for a candidate with a strong sense of self and community.

To make showing up easier and more attractive to more people would require changing our politics. But the problem is circular. To change our politics, more people would have to show up. Self-government thrives on participation. The case has been made eloquently numerous times, often by those who have witnessed the results of nonparticipation. With great foresight, Gunnar Myrdal, the Swedish economist and political scientist, writing in 1960, predicted that unless a democratic state is continually vitalized by citizens taking part, it will degenerate into "that rather shallow, bureaucratic, strongly centralized, institutional machinery, manipulated by crafty organizational entrepreneurs and vested interests, which it is doomed to become."

For democracy to work, people have to show up and get involved. There has to be a commitment for the long term, not just for one campaign, as it takes time to build organizations and change public opinion. It is true that amateurs seldom beat professionals. What separates the professional from the amateur is the ability to organize resources across a wide base and build the contacts over time that make organizing possible. One shouldn't underestimate the power of old alliances and connections. At the same time, however, professional politicians of all kinds have created a system over the last thirty to forty years that is thoroughly disliked by 85 percent of the electorate. The essential act of politics is talking to your neighbor, and who better to do that than yourself? There is opportunity for those willing to accept responsibility for demonstrating a different kind of politics, those willing to take chances, those willing to expand the choices presented to voters, and those willing to do the organizing necessary to win.

It is daunting if one contemplates changing politics at the national level, but that is not the place to start. You have to start at the local level, where the barriers to showing up are not as high. From there you have to build, creating an alternative to the centralized, money-dominated, poll-driven campaign model. If you are successful, there will be imitators.

Politics even in its simplest form is a team sport. Success requires that all of the team's players show up: voters, volunteers, candidates, funders, interest groups, policy experts, media people. Keeping all focused and motivated is essential. At the end of the game, however, it is the votes that count. The vote is the unit of power. Those who show up to vote grant authority to those who are elected, giving legitimacy to their actions.

Driving to the Buffalo County courthouse one day, I contemplated with a fresh awareness the democratic idea. The previous spring I had run for county board supervisor in a district made up of three townships. Five volunteers made phone calls to their friends asking them to vote for me. On April 1, Election Day, 231 people showed up to vote. Of those, 155 had been contacted by one or more of my volunteers. I won 127 to 93. Two weeks later, nine county board members voted to elect me county board chair. As a result of those elections and those votes, I was able to make decisions affecting the lives of everyone living in the county. I was the same person that I had been three months earlier, with the same thoughts, but now that I was in office, what I did and what I thought made a difference. All because I had showed up to run, five friends had showed up to make phone calls, and 127 of my neighbors had showed up to vote for me.

We forget, because it is difficult to remember, that elections for governor or president are no more than a collection of votes from individual precincts, wards, and towns. In each precinct, ward, and town, there are multiple ways to show up.

17. REFLECTIONS GOING FORWARD

WHEN I STARTED WRITING *OUR POLITICS* SEVERAL YEARS AGO, I WANTED TO tell what it is like to be a legislator, from campaigning on Main Street to securing the support of the party and othe r organized groups and navigating the various pressures to vote one way or the other on bills. Political science textbooks describe very adequately the formal process that legislation has to go through to become law. I wanted to explore the informal processes of how decisions are made: the forces, motivations, relationships, and traditions that influence how the body works—in short, what candidates and officeholders see, hear, and feel, why they do what they do and how it all fits together.

As I continued to write, however, I was increasingly reminded that the personal experience can't be understood without reference to the underlying social, economic, and technological environment within which politics is practiced. We are all familiar with the consequent elimination of species when the natural environment changes. That principle also holds true in the political environment. Actions that are effective in one environment are ineffective in another. When the political environment changes, the type of politics also changes. Old forms die out. New forms emerge. New power arrangements grow out of new practices, replacing old power arrangements. This is the story of our politics over the past fifty years, and this is what increasingly captured my attention.

The ascendency of new communication technology started the process that has led inexorably to the centralization of political power. As paid media messages replaced precinct workers as the deciding factor in campaigns, dollars became more important than people. Other changes followed. Power gravitated from the local to the center. Broad-based political parties gave way to individuals and groups with singular ideological and economic interests—the source of the dollars. The changes were gradual, but the direction was set when politics became a capital-intensive, rather than labor-intensive, enterprise.

A politics based on labor has to have local roots and appeal to community. Such a politics requires coalition and compromise. Money, however, can have a single source, a single motivation, a single goal. The political operation of the Koch brothers, to mention just one of many, pursues only the interests and goals of the Koch brothers, regardless of which communities and states are targeted for attention. Their money pays not only for media messages but also for many of the activities that used to be carried out by the parties—re-cruiting candidates, campaign planning, precinct organizing, door-knocking, research, and message development. Americans for Prosperity sounds like, looks like, and acts like a political party but is an extension of individual egos rather than a coalition of community interests. With the rise of political ac-tion committees and increased involvement by millionaires, political parties, particularly local political parties, have declined.

Most candidates are now selected by recruiters and committees from out-side their districts; campaigns are planned by those committees; and, once elected, incumbents become extensions of those same committees. Voters, caught in a system they don't like and can't influence, believe they have little say in their own destiny.

Accommodation and compromise have become more difficult. Whereas parties, with their broader community interests, were more willing to compro-mise, PACs and wealthy individual donors motivated by their own economic and ideological interests are less willing. As singular interests gain ascendency, the idea of compromise is set aside. Politics becomes us versus them, a game of winner-take-all. Rhetoric sharpens. Name-calling replaces debate.

A recent appeal by the Wisconsin Farm Bureau asking members to con-tribute to its political action committee illustrates the shift in tone. The mes-sage is confrontational, and the central role of money in politics is accepted as normal. "It seems everyone now has an opinion on how farmers manage their land and raise their livestock. Unscrupulous social media attacks and anti-ag public opinion campaigns, along with laws and regulations that lack a farmer's common sense, are a constant drain on the rural economy and the morale of farmers. . . . It is more critical than ever that ag-friendly candidates are identified, endorsed and financially supported. . . . The reality is that an endorsement needs to be followed up with financial contributions to open up doors and develop political relationships. We are competing against special interest activists who spend millions of dollars each election cycle."

The departure of politics from our neighborhoods, the flood of money into campaigns, the commitment to ideology, the decline of meaningful discussion into empty clichés, and the absence of results that improve lives and communities are all interrelated. In this environment, people are less inclined to get involved in political activity, and fewer are willing to run for public office. Voters become disillusioned and alienated. Confidence in government declines. The political process itself is questioned.

WE THINK OF "GETTING INVOLVED IN POLITICS" AS WORKING TO ACHIEVE A goal. That certainly is part of it; stepping into the public arena and participating, fighting for what you want, achieving your vision of what should be. The art of politics, however, is figuring out how to take all of the competing interests and goals and constructing a solution that works, one that satisfies residents of the community. It is a continuing process.

We can think of the two roles as agitator and conciliator. It takes both to keep politics healthy and invigorated. Without agitators, there is no progress. Without conciliators, there is no community.

We are all, however, becoming advocates all of the time. We all want what we want—now rather than later. Conciliation is for the unprincipled. We have abandoned the messiness and moral uncertainty of "politics" to work for single issues where there is no gray area, we know we are right, and compromise is unnecessary. We have retreated into nonpolitical behavior.

For the candidate, the pressure to remain committed to principle begins with the questionnaires that arrive days within filing for office. It is clear from the questions asked that every group wants a legislator who will fight for their cause and not make accommodations to opponents or competitors. Even when running for reelection, you still have to fill out the questionnaires. It is not enough that you have a record. With a new term, new commitments are required. As one organization leader put it when asked why he was sending a questionnaire to an incumbent who had been an ally, "I like to think of it as renewing our vows once every four years. A series of 'I dos' to remind us why we got married in the first place." And so conciliation is blocked at the beginning. The politician charged with conciliating competing interests is "married" to one side or the other before the election.

Voters are conflicted. Poll after poll suggests that a large majority of the public wants politicians to solve problems and work things out. An increasing percentage of voters in both political parties, however, want the people they elect to support party principles to the very end and not compromise at all. The politician is caught between the pragmatists and the ideologues. The believers have been winning, as they tend to be the funders and volunteer supporters of candidates. They are also the regular voters in primaries where the fights for the soul of the party take place, and they weed out the candidates who would be more political in their approach to governing.

The political system itself is increasingly being challenged. Both liberal and conservative groups have questioned its credibility, arguing that political decisions are made by the establishment for the benefit of the establishment. The interests of the average person are not considered. Money controls the process. The super-rich get richer; everyone else is left behind. It doesn't matter who you vote for, nothing in your circumstances will change. Those feelings were channeled during the 2016 race for president by both Bernie Sanders in his call for a "political revolution" and Donald Trump in his claim that the system is "rigged" and Washington is a "swamp" that needs to be "drained."

Voters responded in large numbers to Sanders and Trump, much to the surprise of the "establishment." There was much more unhappiness in the electorate than the establishment realized. They could have learned from Aristotle and much of subsequent history. "Inequality is generally at the bottom of internal warfare in states . . . exceptional prosperity in one section of the community is to be guarded against." For Aristotle, the primary conflict that politics must resolve is the one between the interests of the few who are rich and the many who are poor. When either has the power and pushes its own interest to the fullest, harming the other, the results are instability, unrest, and revolution. The increasing animosity in this country of the 99 percent at the bottom of the economic pile toward the 1 percent at the top is a reflection of the exceptional prosperity that has accrued to the 1 percent in recent years, while incomes for all the rest have stagnated or declined.

There are political as well as economic reasons for the increasing inequality. Inequality has grown as our politics has become more centralized, more dependent on money, less responsive to community concerns, and more supportive of single interests. Our politics has become the servant of single interests—usually the interests of the 1 percent—rather than the conciliator of competing interests. As tax and economic law and policies have been changed by the newly politically powerful for their own benefit, economic inequality has increased.

In addition to the antipolitical, antiestablishment mood that has taken hold, an antigovernment ideology has been gaining influence, particularly within the Republican Party since the conservatives took control with Barry Goldwater's nomination for president in 1964.

The progression is seen in the changing answer to questions about the proper role of government. Goldwater, still considered by some as the political father of the modern conservative movement, called government "a durable ally of the whole man" when accepting the 1964 Republican presidential nomination. By 1981, in his first inaugural address, President Ronald Reagan expressed the belief that "government is not the solution to our problem, government is the problem." Today, in the words of Grover Norquist, head of Americans for Tax Reform and a current conservative leader, the goal is to "take government down to the size where we can drown it in the bathtub."

Americans for Prosperity, the Heritage Foundation, Tea Party groups, and their Republican legislative allies threatened repeatedly to shut down the federal government if Obamacare, a form of universal health insurance, was not defunded and stopped. In contrast, conservative economist F. A. Hayek, author in 1944 of *The Road to Serfdom* and one of the recognized intellectual founders of modern conservatism, believed that "in the case of sickness and accident . . . where in short we deal with genuinely insurable risks, the case for the state's helping to organize a comprehensive system of social insurance is very strong." He went on to caution that great care needed to be taken in designing such programs to avoid dependence, but he believed that was achievable. Even though he was an advocate of competition, individual initiative, and limited government, Hayek was open to considering the specifics of a problem and the actions government might take to make peoples' lives better. With an unwavering belief that making government smaller will make everything else better, today's modern conservatives rarely ask the pragmatic question about results.

There are also those who intentionally fan the flames of discord. A *Denver Post* article on the increasing rancor in politics quotes Norquist: "We are trying to change the tones in the state capitals—and turn them toward bitter nastiness and partisanship. . . . Bipartisanship is another name for date rape." Norquist has achieved his goal, not only in state capitals but also among the public. A month before the 2016 presidential election, a long-time radio talk show host in Eau Claire walked off the set as his show went into a commercial break, saying, "I'm through doing this show as it is." Interviewed later, he told the *Eau Claire Leader Telegram* that the show had become less of a conversation and more of an exchange of insults. "It started with a lot of Trump and Clinton stuff, but now that same kind of vitriol is starting to permeate our local races and local issues. . . . [Many of the callers] are educated, wonderful people who have become caught up in this hurricane of hate. . . . If I'm an enabler, even inadvertently, to this toxicity through the show, that troubles me. . . . There's got to be a better way to do this. . . . Maybe we can come up with something that's agreeable and turns off this faucet of poison." When the show resumed, politics and current events were forbidden topics.

In discussing his planned retirement at the end of 2016, Charlie Sykes, the leading conservative voice on Milwaukee talk radio, said, "I've long thought the alternative media was a positive development that would counter the mainstream media monopoly. It's only this year you go, 'OK, what have we done here? We've created this monster.' . . . This is the shock of 2016. You look around and you see how much of the conservative media infrastructure buys into the post-factual, post-truth culture. . . . I understand that we are advocates and defenders, but when do you veer off into pure raw propaganda?"

IN HIS WONDERFUL BOOK *IN DEFENSE OF POLITICS*, BERNARD CRICK ARGUES persuasively that politics is the activity of recognizing and reconciling the diverse interests and traditions of different groups living together within a territorial unit under a common rule. "The struggle for power is the struggle for power—it is not politics." Rather, politics "is a way of ruling divided societies without undue violence . . . an attempt to strike a particular harmony. . . . Ideally, politics draws all these groups into each other so that they each and together can make a positive contribution towards the general business of government, the maintaining of order."

For Crick, politics is what holds divided societies together without destroying diversity. The alternatives to politics—tyranny, oligarchy, kingship, dictatorship, despotism, and totalitarianism—hold societies together by force, sacrificing diversity and freedom. Politics rejects force and recognizes the need for restraint. Politics is preferred over the other alternatives because it is "an effective way by which varying interests can discover that level of compromise best suited to their common interest in survival. Politics allows various types of power within a community to find some reasonable level of mutual tolerance and support."

Force takes over "when some group or interest feels it has no common interest in survival with the rest." For Crick, force requires justification, while politics justifies itself. "[It is] hard to respect the morality and wisdom of any who, when politics is possible, refuse to act politically." To renounce politics is to "destroy the very thing . . . which enables us to enjoy variety without suffering either anarchy or the tyranny of single truths."

We have largely forsaken the activity of politics for the pursuit of power. Politics has become combat. Those we elect to public office are expected to continue the fight to victory. They are seen as an extension of the interests that elected them. Those who seek conciliation are rejected by their supporters. Compromise is seen as the abandonment of principle, not as the necessary accommodation of diverse groups and interests that allows us to live with each other in relative harmony.

This decline in politics was lamented by the longtime chief lobbyist of the U.S. Chamber of Commerce R. Bruce Josten in a *New York Times* story marking his retirement. "Washington, he said, has become an 'I win, you lose' town rather than a 'how do we get this done' town. . . . [He is] concerned with the trend toward one party going it alone legislatively, using its power to impose its priorities on the other . . . [an] approach not sustainable in the long run. . . . 'If you want durability and lasting law, the only way to really achieve it is to engage both sides of the aisle. . . .' He sees a current political and legislative climate marked by a certain inflexibility and intransigence that is not conducive to compromise and ends with little being accomplished."

From Aristotle to the U.S. Chamber the message is the same: if there is no politics, there is no community. There is only conflict.

The political mind understands that the foundation of democracy is consent of the governed, recognizes that change comes in small steps, and resists the insistence on all or nothing that makes reaching agreement by a majority impossible. The essential political activity is conversation and dialogue. The political person is a pragmatist intent on solving a problem rather than advancing a chosen philosophy. The political attitude is one of self-restraint. The political goal is stability.

HOW DO WE BRING POLITICS BACK TO FULFILLING ITS ROLE: RECONCILING competing interests and making space for diversity while avoiding anarchy or the tyranny of single truths? What is it about our politics that needs to be changed? What needs to be preserved?

We need politics. We need politicians. The political process with all of its messiness is necessary and should be nurtured and protected. There is no better way to conciliate the competing interests of the diverse groups that make up the community. Politicians are elected to make those decisions, and whatever decisions they make have legitimacy because of the votes that brought them to office. There is no point in trying to initiate reform by taking politics out of politics or political decision-making away from politicians. It doesn't work. Under the 1870 Illinois constitution the state superintendent of education was elected, and the office had major influence over education policy and spending. The writers of the 1970 constitution, however, thought that education was too important to be subject to politics, so they created a state board of education appointed by the governor with the responsibility of choosing the state superintendent. The result was foreseeable. The superintendent's job became primarily administrative. Major policy and budget decisions shifted to the governor's office and the legislative School Problems Commission. The important decisions about education and the allocation of resources—which by their nature are political—continued to be made by elected politicians.

There will always be the few who have more political power than others do. Only occasionally and briefly has power been spread among many. We have said that the unit of power in a democracy is the vote, and each of us has one—we are all equal in that sense. But we are not equal in political power, which is the ability to influence, aggregate, and deliver votes. That power is concentrated. We can work to spread that power out to more and different sources. We can work to make those sources more visible, more responsible, more local, and more accountable, but there will always be a political power structure made up of the few who have more influence than the rest of us.

Politics will also remain a contact sport. Because people have strong opinions, because lives are affected, because communities are changed, because resources are allocated, because one's standard of living can be raised or lowered, and because one's interests can be advanced or not, people who are in politics are in politics to win. For some, the ends they want to accomplish justify whatever means they choose. The old advice is still good advice: if you can't take the heat, stay out.

The field on which politics is played will always be crowded. Lots of people, many with sharp elbows, want a piece of the action. The official politicians—candidates and the elected officials—are only the small, public part of politics. Underneath the surface are party leaders, party members, consultants, pollsters, media organizations, bloggers, reporters, commentators, donors, activists of every persuasion, community leaders, business interests, religious partisans, ideologues, think tanks, policy researchers, interest groups from across the political, social, and economic spectrums, and a host of individuals with opinions. All have their own game plans as they compete to hold a place. All have to be considered by anyone interested in joining the game.

The politics of conciliating competing interests is complicated by the difficulty of knowing what is true and knowing where the public interest lies. Competing groups not only have conflicting interests but they also have different perceptions of reality. Different experts will tell you very different facts. The same facts can fit into very different stories. The different stories reflect competing values. How one balances and decides who to believe is not straightforward. The appropriate political decision is never clear.

Politics will also always be a deal. Those who govern never govern alone. The people, or some part of the people, confer power, because in return they get something they want. When enough people are not getting what they want, they vote officials out, stage a coup, or start a revolution. Those who govern may have plans, but if the people are unhappy, the leaders won't be around long enough to carry them out. As former Speaker of the House John Boehner reflected on his resignation, "A leader who doesn't have anybody following him is just a guy taking a walk."

And politics will remain a free-for-all. There are no barriers for entry, no standards to meet. It is strictly voluntary. Nobody is compelled to participate. Those who do run the world. And so, politics showcases all of our weaknesses and strengths. Those who take part in politics—and most of us do at some level—do so from diverse motivations. For some the motivation is personal gain; for some it's the lure of power, or celebrity, a vision of what is True, or altruism and a desire to serve. But these same motivations exist, more or less, in every occupation, every profession, every way of making a living. The difference in politics is that the stakes are higher, the temptations are greater, and nothing will change that.

We have long outgrown our rural, small-town past when important decisions affecting the community were made at the annual town meeting where everyone who showed up had a vote. (There are still town meetings, but the issues aren't as weighty. Only a few years ago I was the deciding vote in an eleven-to-ten decision to keep the town plowing snow from private driveways. Not as many people showed up to vote the following year, and the practice was discontinued.) We do, however, want to keep a connection to the decision-making even if the decisions are now made by people we elect to represent us at some distant location through a process we don't fully understand.

The connection is what we care about. We want to feel that our vote makes a difference, that what the community wants matters, and that those who have to live with the results are the ones making the decisions. We don't want to have to live with decisions made by outsiders who benefit from those decisions while we bear the costs. Our concern is that we are part of the political process.

We were not as disenchanted with politics when the messiness was more local, closer to where we could participate in a more meaningful way. It is not the political process itself that needs to be changed but the location of political power. Bringing political power back from the center, where it has flowed on a tide of money, to the local is the first step.

WHERE DO WE START? HOW DO WE GO ABOUT WRESTING POLITICAL POWER from the few at the center and distributing it more democratically among the many at the local? How do we create an alternative to the nexus of money and media that funds and disseminates the messages that persuade?

Saying "Just get the money out of politics" is neither a plan nor a solution. Every campaign finance reform law passed in the last thirty years has been followed in the next election cycle with more political dollars. What has changed is that the dollars now flow through murkier channels that are less public and less accountable. Just as the old political boss system came to an end when it was challenged by an alternate source of political power, so the existing power structure will be diminished only when confronted by alternative power. The question is not how to reform our politics, but how to create a new source of political power that is more to our liking and that will challenge what now exists.

There are three main characteristics of the existing power structure: it is centralized, it runs on money, and it pursues singular economic and ideological interests. The three are interrelated. Any activity that increases local influence, motivates personal involvement, and focuses on community goals undermines those characteristics, challenges the existing power, and begins to build an alternative.

Most reform proposals are directed at limiting the activities of those who are perceived to have too much power. They haven't worked very well. It would be more productive to think of ways to proactively bring politics back to the places where we live, create local centers of power, influence voters in ways that don't enhance the centralizing power of money, and deliver messages to our neighbors that are more persuasive than those delivered through the media. These are difficult tasks, requiring the efforts of many individuals and not accomplished in an election cycle. They depend on local initiative, and it's possible to accomplish them without having to pass a law or depend on someone else for enforcement. There is a chance of long-term success.

Reform cannot be imposed from the top. Change will come when countervailing forces are put in place that provide options—options for parties to organize themselves differently, options for candidates to run a different kind of campaign, options for volunteers to be more engaged, options for voters that give them more of what they are looking for.

If we have arrived where we are because money replaced labor as the determining factor in winning elections, political power moved from the local to the center, and singular interests have come to dominate, then any change that slows or reverses those trends—that substitutes human activity for money in campaigns, moves political power toward the local, or elevates community interests over singular interests—is a plus. The goal is to make our politics better; to start the journey, not anticipate or assume the arrival. Change, if it happens, will be gradual—it won't come overnight.

Rebuilding the political parties from the ground up, particularly the local political parties, would be a major first step in changing the power structure. The parties historically have been broad based, rooted in communities, and representative of diverse parts of the electorate. Although supported by allied interest groups, the parties were not dominated by those interests. In recent years, that has all been turned on its head. The parties have become centralized, hierarchical organizations largely dominated by their major donors. The rebuilding of local parties will happen only as local individuals are motivated to make it happen.

Building a local political party requires both a local perspective and a party perspective. So much political activity now is centered on *this* candidate and *this* election. Most volunteers are motivated by the immediate and the personal. The party has to find a way to build on that initial enthusiasm and transfer support of a person to support for a party and program. It has to engage with other community organizations and community projects. Candidates and campaigns then become reflections of what the party has been doing all along rather than just a reflection of whatever candidate happens to be running that year and whatever interests are funding the campaign.

Only as local parties are rebuilt with their own initiative, resources, and goals will local parties regain influence. If power flows back from the center toward the local, it is inevitable that power will also begin to shift away from big-money donors to local decision-makers.

A stronger local party with resources to run a campaign can reduce one of the disincentives that keep individuals from running for office—the demand that they spend enormous amounts of campaign time raising huge amounts of money by calling faraway donors who have specific interests. The candidate who wants to do something different, however, is faced with a dilemma: how does one run a campaign based on community before there are community-based organizational supports strong enough to counter the influence of the organized PACs and leadership committees that dominate the existing system?

The hurdle might not be as big as it appears. The tendency is to think that the center knows better. In the words of gubernatorial candidate Mary Burke quoted earlier in a different context, "I have hired the best consultants, and I am going to listen to them." It may not be the case, however, that they know better. The center, for many reasons, tends to spurn the local knowledge essential to winning. Kathleen, who has run her own campaigns, has continued to win in western Wisconsin when other Democratic candidates who bought into the coordinated campaigns run by the center have lost. The directions from the center sometimes make no sense, and the center tends to persist even when challenged by the local volunteers who are doing the work and see the poor results. The 2016 Wisconsin Democratic coordinated campaign directed by the Clinton presidential organization told college volunteers that they had to start knocking on the dorm rooms of fellow students at 8:30 A.M. on a Saturday. "Walk lists" distributed by the campaign of doors to knock skipped most homes on every street. Local volunteers who broke the rules and knocked on every door or waited until Saturday afternoon to talk with fellow college students reported better results.

Direction from the top in the Republican Party may be just as dysfunctional. Ron Johnson, the Republican U.S. senator from Wisconsin, who unexpectedly won reelection in 2016, attributed his victory to the fact that since he was expected to lose, he didn't get any help from the national committee in Washington and was able to decide on his own message and run his own campaign. He was quoted after the election as saying, "Back here in D.C., I realized how thoroughly I was written off. . . . It definitely was an outside-of-Washington campaign. It was also outside the professional political consultant class. It was breaking away from that and just running a campaign like a businessperson would trying to market a product. . . . We didn't get D.C. help, and in the end that was the winning formula."

Political parties, particularly at the local level, could become stronger if the legal restrictions on their political activities were removed. Court decisions have brought us to the strange situation where there are no constraints on the political activities of individuals and private groups because that would limit their constitutional rights of free speech and assembly. But political parties can be restricted—in fundraising, expenditures, and coordinating with candidates—because those activities, if carried out by them, could lead to corruption or the perception of corruption. With the same freedom that others have to promote programs and support candidates, parties with their broader interests would be stronger, potentially reducing the influence now held by other organizations with their more narrow interests.

ULTIMATELY, WHAT THE VOTERS REWARD WILL GET DONE. THE VOTERS HAVE the final say on what our politics will be, the final say on what campaigns will look like, the final say on how politicians act. They can reward conflict or conciliation, ideology or pragmatism, aggression or restraint, reason or prejudice, a singular interest or the community interest. Whether they vote, how they vote, and why they vote will shape the choices presented to them by candidates in the next election.

The voter, however, can choose only among the options presented. There is a reciprocal relationship. If what the voters want is not embodied in a candidate, then what the voters want won't be among the choices they can make. If the disconnect between what the voters want and what they are given lasts too long, the political structure becomes unstable. Voters become disillusioned, they lose faith in the process, they believe the system is rigged against them, they become likely prey for those who promise to tear everything down and make everything new: "It can only get better." Both community stability and long-term political success require sensitivity to the underlying desires of voters and giving them the opportunity to choose what they want.

Presenting new choices, running a different kind of campaign with a fresh vision and message, is difficult for any candidate. Leaders, consultants, incumbents, and challengers are all socialized into the same system: raise money, go negative, don't say anything substantive or controversial, smile, shake hands, throw candy in parades. If you want to do something different, you are dismissed as naive and not a team player. The recruiters begin to look for someone more responsible and more reasonable to get behind. So the voters keep getting the same array of choices despite all of the evidence that they have become increasingly unhappy with those choices.

The world is run by those who show up. Those who show up, however, tend to be people who are willing to fit in with the existing way of doing things. To break our politics out of its downward cycle, it is necessary for those who want a different kind of politics to show up, to act on the belief that we are not locked into the accepted way of doing things, that we can move against the stream, that we can change the rules.

There is tremendous incentive, however, for everyone to act powerless and just go along.

We have seen a parade of candidates and officeholders over the years who say that they despise the role that money plays in campaigns, but because "that's the way the game is played," they are going to play that way. They have to be realistic. They are not going to tie their own hands. In their 2016 U.S. Senate campaigns both John McCain and Russ Feingold, cosponsors of the Bipartisan Campaign Reform Act of 2002, enlisted the aid of super PACs with their "dark money." The *Washington Post* reported that neither was particularly happy about it, but they were not apologizing. The *Post* quoted McCain as saying, "You've gotta play the game by the rules." So the sums escalate, and the perception that money is essential to winning is solidified. Political power continues to concentrate in the few who can afford to contribute.

What is missing is a different play, a different script, in which the lead actor acts out a different vision that resonates with the audience and leads to a different ending.

Vaclav Havel, in his 1978 essay "The Power of the Powerless," which he wrote to the Czech people then living under a communist system that had controlled all public life for three decades, made the point that they were not only victims of the system but also its instruments. "By accepting the given rules of the game . . . [you] become a player in the game, thus making it possible for the game to go on, for it to exist in the first place." By conforming, "individuals confirm the system, fulfill the system, make the system, *are* the system." The power of the powerless comes from refusing to accept the rules, regaining "one's own sense of responsibility," and working to "rekindle civic self-awareness and confidence."

Havel acknowledged that this was not easy and success was not assured. It is only for someone who is "unwilling to sacrifice his own human identity to politics, or rather, who does not believe in a politics that requires such a sacrifice."

Against all odds, enough of the Czech people decided in the following decade that they would not keep playing by the rules, thus ending the old game. The communist system collapsed, and Havel, who refused to play by the accepted rules, was elected president.

As long as we continue to follow existing political rules, those rules will continue to control our politics. Money will dominate. People and organizations at the center that control the money and create the media messages will make the decisions and determine the results. To beat big money and the centralization of power that comes with it, big money has to be defeated. If my large donors beat your large donors, large donors still win. The messages delivered freely by individuals have to be more persuasive than the messages bought with dollars. When we figure out how to do that and are willing to do the hard and necessary work in our own communities, we will bring politics back toward the local, diminish the power of the ideologues and single interests, and regain some influence over our own destinies. Wishful thinking is not a strategy for success. There are no easy answers. We may have to adopt Sisyphus as our role model and keep pushing the rock up the hill. We can't turn back the clock. The power won't all come back, but it may be possible to bring some of it back.

OUR POLITICS WILL BE CHANGED, NOT BY THINKING UP REFORM SCHEMES to change the system, but by candidates and parties acting out a different approach, giving voters something different to respond to, something different to vote for. The commitment has to be for the long run. It can't be a one-and-done deal. I tried. It didn't work. No revolution has been won with a single battle.

The time may be right. The voters are ready—polls say that 85 percent are fed up with our politics—even if the professionals are not. The communication tools are available to make local organizing easier. Every voter lives in the local community. The most persuasive medium for changing votes is personal communication. A vision, personal effort, and a commitment to organize are all required. Our politics is big and complex, with many interrelated interests and individuals. If it evolves in a way that brings power back to the community and reduces the influence of money and singular interests, it will be because residents decided to act in the neighborhoods where they live, one community at a time.

BIBLIOGRAPHIC ESSAY
INDEX

BIBLIOGRAPHIC ESSAY

THE QUESTIONS ABOUT HOW WE ORGANIZE OURSELVES IN COMMUNITY HAVE been with us throughout human history. Who will make decisions? How will the decision-makers be chosen? What powers should they have? What is the goal? What does the community we want look like? The debate, the struggle, the conflict over those questions and the practical application of the answers are the stuff of politics.

There have been as many philosophers as there have been practitioners. Over time, words have been as powerful as swords in shaping answers. My own understanding has been informed and enriched by the thoughts and writings of many. I include a few here, not to be comprehensive but to represent different ways of understanding power and community, different ways of weighing the tradeoffs of benefits and costs, strengths and weaknesses, of varying political arrangements.

THE PHILOSOPHERS

THE IDEA OF DEMOCRACY AS AN ANSWER TO HOW WE ORGANIZE OURSELVES in community had its beginnings in the city-states of ancient Greece. The questions of how that democracy should be structured were discussed and debated by the philosophers; questions that were not resolved back then are still being debated and are still not resolved.

Plato, in the *Republic*, argued for an aristocracy of merit and intelligence. He believed that some were natural leaders by birth. They trained in philosophy or succeeded as generals in the city's wars. The rest are "not born to be philosophers and are meant to be followers and not leaders." His ideas underlie the thinking of all those fearful of the masses, of democracy being carried too far.

Edmund Burke, the English conservative politician, reacting to the excesses of the French Revolution, embraced Plato's thought (see *Burke's Politics, Selected Writings and Speeches*, edited by Ross Hoffman and Paul Levack). He argues for the benefits of an aristocracy and for a polity that upholds a moral order rooted in natural law that comes to us from outside the temporal.

Aristotle, in *Politics*, is much less prescriptive than Plato, focusing instead on the structure of constitutional arrangements rather than the qualities of the leader. He discusses the strengths and weakness of different constitutions. He pays particular attention to the division of power, both political and economic, between the few and the many, the wealthy aristocracy and the poorer masses. He argues that long-term stability depends on the extent to which the ruling group, elected or otherwise and from whichever camp, takes care of the needs of the other.

Niccolo Machiavelli, in *The Prince* and *The Discourses*, has no interest in constitutional arrangements. He gives practical advice to the ruler—any ruler—on how to maintain power. More than anyone else, he is identified with the ideas that "the end justifies the means" and that one should "do whatever it takes to stay in power." Machiavelli understands that the ruler can't rule alone but can stay in power by buying support, dividing adversaries, and manipulating the populace.

In *Quotations from Chairman Mao Tse-tung*, Mao, the leader of the communist revolution in China, recognized and approved the use of force to achieve political ends. His aphorism "Political power grows out of the barrel of a gun" is the phrase he is most remembered by.

Arguing the other side, from both philosophical and practical considerations, Albert Camus, in *The Rebel*, makes the case that the lure of utopia does not justify killing. Using force today in the service of creating a heaven on earth tomorrow never ends well.

In *Resistance, Rebellion and Death*, a collection of essays, Camus, who was part of the French resistance to Nazi occupation during World War II, reflects on when the use of force is justified in resisting and throwing off tyranny.

In the years after the war when the Communist Party was active and relatively strong in France, Jean Paul Sartre and Camus engaged in a public and sometimes rancorous debate over whether the social and economic goals pursued by the Soviets in Russia justified the repressive tactics that were then becoming common knowledge in the West. Sartre defended the Soviet tactics as necessary for the ends they wanted to achieve. Their still relevant arguments are collected in *Sartre and Camus: A Historic Confrontation*, edited and translated by David A Sprintzen and Adrian van den Hoven.

Vaclav Havel, poet and playwright, one of the leaders in the successful effort to free Czechoslovakia from Communist rule and later its president, argues for an entirely different kind of politics in *The Art of the Impossible* and in *Open Letters: Selected Writings, 1965–1990*. The people are not pawns to be used or manipulated. The goal is not to gain and keep power by whatever means necessary. The goal is achieving the common good. The means is a conscious appeal to, and a level of trust in, the better nature in all of us.

"Politics must do far more than reflect the interests of particular groups and lobbies. After all, politics is a matter of serving the community, which means it is morality in practice. . . . I don't believe a politician who sets out on this risky path inevitably jeopardizes a political future. . . . It is a wrongheaded notion that . . . assumes that the citizen is a fool and political success depends on playing to this folly. This is not the way it is. A conscience slumbers in every human being, something divine. And that is what we have to put our trust in."

THE INDIVIDUAL AGAINST THE STATE

OTHER WRITERS, APPROACHING POLITICS FROM THE VIEWPOINT OF THE individual rather than the state, emphasized that individual rights and autonomy must be protected and that state power over the individual must be limited. The Declaration of Independence argues strongly that when state power is exercised arbitrarily and infringes on individual freedoms, it is appropriate to throw off that authority and reconstitute the state. Ultimate power resides with the people, not the state.

In his relatively short essay *On Liberty*, John Stuart Mill makes the classic case for limited government power, describing the "limits of the power which can be legitimately exercised by society over the individual." He recognizes the propensity on the part of all of us to use the state "to impose personal inclinations as rule of conduct on others," but that desire must be restrained by making sure the power of the state is limited. The personal inclination to control the activity of others must not be harnessed to the authority of the state.

Henry David Thoreau, in *Walden and Other Writings*, edited by Brooks Atkinson, argues that individual conscience must be followed regardless of the law.

On Liberty: Man v. the State by Milton Mayer and *Man and the State* by Jacques Maritain discuss the same issues in more recent contexts.

F. A. Hayek, in *The Road to Serfdom*, deals with the same subject, the relationship between individuals and the state, but starts from a very different place. He argues that socialism, government creation of social programs to benefit and support individuals, inevitably leads to centralization of power, government control, fascism, and Nazism. The Helping Hand turns into a Fist.

The Conservative Mind from Burke to Eliot by Russell Kirk traces the development of conservative political thought about the proper role of government and its relationship to its citizens. There are two themes. One is a distrust of the masses who will always want more. The second is that values are given to us, they come from somewhere outside our temporal human sphere. It is our task, and the task of government, to conform to those values. If we abandon them, we are doomed. Values cannot be based on communal discussion and agreement. The argument is summed up succinctly by the character Ivan in Fyodor Dostoevsky's *The Brothers Karamazov*: if there is no god, then everything is permitted. Conservative thought values traditional roles and traditional economic relationships. The elite are the natural leaders. Self-reliance and self-responsibility on the part of the masses will result in their greatest good.

Tony Judt makes the opposite argument in *Ill Fares the Land*. What binds people together are the activities they undertake as a community, the things they do collectively to make their lives and society better. If we are individuals on our own, competing with each other and not connected together in a common purpose, life is "solitary, poor and a little nasty," and society is reduced to the "thin membrane of interaction between private individuals." In that setting the state has all the power. "If there is nothing that binds us together as a community or society, then we are utterly dependent on the state . . . the loss of social purpose articulated through public services actually increases the unrestrained powers of the over-mighty state." That, Judt argues, is the result if we follow the libertarians, free marketers, Jacobins, Bolsheviks, or Nazis. Without the Helping Hand, there is only the Fist.

ORGANIZING FOR CHANGE

IF YOU ARE ON THE BOTTOM AND DON'T LIKE WHAT THE GOVERNMENT IS doing to you, how do you go about changing policies, programs, and those in charge? How do you achieve change? Authors advocate different tactics, but they share a common belief in the masses and their capacity to achieve a better future.

Franz Fanon, who was active in the movement to free Africa from European colonial rule, is best known for *The Wretched of the Earth*, in which he justifies "absolute violence" as the only way to throw off foreign rule imposed by and supported by violence. What is often missed is his faith in and reliance on the masses to build a better, more responsive politics. Leadership must come from the masses who can be taught, organized, and empowered. "To educate the masses politically does not mean, cannot mean, making a political speech. What it means is to try, relentlessly and passionately, to teach the masses that everything depends on them."

Omar Cabezas, in *Fire from the Mountain: The Making of a Sandinista*, makes no philosophical or theoretical point, but in the day-by-day account of his activities, discussions, and connections with people in the villages, he models what organizing from the bottom looks like.

Saul Alinsky, the community organizer from Chicago, gives hope to people whose interests are ignored by those holding political office. In his books *Rules for Radicals: A Pragmatic Primer for Realistic Radicals* and *Reveille for Radicals*, he describes methods and rationale for neighborhood organizing and collective action to achieve the changes that people want for themselves and their communities.

Fanon, Cabezas, and Alinsky celebrate and seek to empower the people that Burke fears.

THE PURPOSE AND PRACTICE OF POLITICS

IN HIS EXTRAORDINARY AND UNUSUAL BOOK *IN DEFENSE OF POLITICS*, BERnard Crick, following Aristotle's thought that stability is the chief goal of politics, describes and defends the practical steps that must be taken if democracy is to stay viable. Again following Aristotle, he argues that competing interests must be recognized and accommodated, that compromise is necessary, that the pursuit of absolutes is dangerous, and that creativity in finding solutions is essential.

He writes, "So much of politics is the ability of turning impossible demands into possible substitutes. . . . The man who treats everything as a matter of principle cannot be happy with politics, dooming himself to frustration or pledging himself to authoritarianism. . . . Conciliation is better than violence. . . . The two great enemies of politics are indifference to human suffering and the passionate quest for certainty in matters which are essentially political. . . . To renounce or destroy politics is to destroy the very thing which enables us to enjoy variety without suffering either anarchy or the tyranny of single truths. . . . Politics is the practical reconciliation of interests; not a set of fixed principles to be realized. . . . In politics is found the creative dialectic of opposites. . . . Politics is the attempt to find particular and workable solutions to the perpetual and shifty problem of conciliation."

Walter Lippmann, in *Preface to Politics*, makes a similar argument. "The important thing about social movement is not its stated platform but the source from which it flows. The task of politics is to understand those deeper demands and find civilized satisfactions for them."

Austin Ranney, in *The Doctrine of Responsible Party Government*, describes the role of political parties in translating the popular will into governmental action.

Franz Fanon, in *The Wretched of the Earth*, also writes that for political parties to be effective, they must be participatory and built from the bottom. "The party should be decentralized to the extreme. . . . [It is] the only way to bring life to regions that are dead." What he saw and what he argued against was a party in name only, with a leader in the central city and no followers, and a party used for the personal advancement of the leader.

Liu Shaoqi, in *Three Essays on Party-Building*, describes the Communist Party's perspective: subordination of the part to the whole; subordination of the immediate to the long range.

COMMUNICATION

COMMUNICATION IS AN ESSENTIAL PART OF POLITICS AND GOVERNING. COMmunication technology shapes political power structures and the means used to achieve political influence and control over subjects.

Harold Innis, in *Empire and Communications* and *The Bias of Communication*, and Marshall McLuhan, in *Understanding Media* and *The Medium Is the Message: An Inventory of Effects*, both describe the historical connections between communication technology and political and governmental power.

Murray Edelman, in *The Symbolic Uses of Politics*, explores the meanings "of the acts and gestures of leaders, of the settings in which political acts occur, of the language styles and phrases that permeate political discussion and action."

Joe Trippi, in *The Revolution Will Not Be Televised: Democracy, the Internet, and the Overthrow of Everything*, predicts that the internet will change politics, campaigning, and governing.

THE NOVELS

IN MANY WAYS, THE BEST POLITICAL NOVELS PROVIDE A PRACTICAL UNDER-standing of politics, adding insight, immediacy, and concreteness to the works of philosophers, thinkers, and even practitioners.

Robert Penn Warren, *All the King's Men*, a story of Louisiana politics.
William Kennedy, *Roscoe*, Albany, New York, politics.
Edwin O'Connor, *The Last Hurrah*, Boston, Massachusetts, politics.
Billy Lee Brammer, *The Gay Place*, Texas politics.
Graham Greene, *The Quiet American*, American politics in Vietnam.
C. P. Snow, *Corridors of Power*, British Parliament politics.

INDEX

Illinois Medical Society, 28, 100, 107–8
Illinois Nurses Association, 99–100
Illinois State Capitol, 96–97
incumbents, 5, 7, 28, 30, 135, 203; control of campaigns lost, 56–57; disclosure of money sources and, 164–65; McCain-Feingold and, 163–64; outside influence on, 87, 204; party goals and, 93; term limits and, 171–74
In Defense of Politics (Crick), 207–8, 223–24
independent expenditure groups, 34–36, 50, 160–68
independents, 69, 91, 94; rules for getting on ballot, 132–33
individuals, 14–16; lack of power, 126; lack of restrictions on, 158–59; local, 38–39; state and, 221–22
inequality, 76, 205
Innis, Harold, 225
instant runoff voting, 136
Institute for Wisconsin's Future, 110
interest groups, 9, 21–23, 93, 202–4; control of issues, 83–84; executive branch and, 89–90; legislation as ratification of private sector agreements, 98–99; legislative leaders and, 80; local candidates not supported by, 61; multiple objectives, 84; origination of legislation in, 115, 123; outsider, 34–38, 87, 154–55, 180, 183–84; outsider, mistakes made by, 34–35, 213; pressure by, 151–55; producer interests, 24–25; replace patronage, 22–23; single-issue groups, 196–98
internet, 43–45, 112, 181; centralization and, 45–49; as educational tool, 48–49; local politics and, 45–46; subsidizing, 167
issue development, 77–78
issues, 21; ideology and, 7, 61–62, 83–84

Johnson, Lyndon, 5, 92
Johnson, Ron, 213
Jones, "Lop Ear," 183
Josten, R. Bruce, 208
Judt, Tony, 222

Kennedy, Anthony, 166
Kennedy, John F., 14
Kennedy, Ted, 68
Kentucky constitution, 173
Kerry, John, 68
Kirk, Russell, 222
knowledge, 105–13; academic, 109–10; assessment of colleagues, 111–12; competing claims, 109; experts, role of, 105; public discussion, 112; talking points and, 107–8, 111; think tanks and, 110; values and, 108–9
Koch brothers, 35, 36, 48, 54, 62, 93, 195, 203

labels, 83, 107
labor unions, 35, 117–18, 169; PACs, 161
lame duck, 174
language, poll-tested, 58–59, 72
The Last Hurrah (O'Connor), 52–53, 70
laws: allocation of resources for, 124–25; basic assumptions, 115; "get the government off our backs," 114; limits imposed by, 115–16; origination of in interest groups, 115, 123; as symbolic, 124–25. *See also* legislation, proposed (bills)
lead actor, candidate as, 67–79; audience, 70–72, 78; genuineness, 68; issue development, 77–78; meaning and, 75–76; opposition's story, 77–78; polls and, 73–74; scripts that don't fit, 67–69; strengths and weaknesses, 78–79. *See also* campaigns; candidates

DOUGLAS KANE served as the director of staff for the Democratic leadership of the Illinois House of Representatives from 1969 to 1973, staff assistant to the governor of Illinois from 1973 to 1974, and Illinois state representative from 1974 to 1983. Prior to his public service, he was a reporter with the *Courier Journal* in Louisville, Kentucky. He is an economist and for twenty years was president of Program Analysis, Inc., a consulting firm that specialized in economic and public policy issues. He served two terms as the chair of the Buffalo County (Wisconsin) Board of Supervisors and currently serves as a member of the local school board. He resides in Alma, Wisconsin, with his wife, Kathleen Vinehout, who served three terms in the Wisconsin State Senate.